Cities of Hope
Solving the Homelessness

Jobs + Housing = Hope

By
HUSEYIN BURAK ERTEN

Contents

Introduction

Homelessness is a deeply rooted issue that has persisted in the United States for decades, affecting every layer of society. It's a crisis that extends beyond the visible suffering we often see on the streets; it's a complex dilemma deeply entwined with economic inconsistencies and social disparities.

This book endeavors to offer practical solutions to homelessness by exploring various perspectives and innovative approaches. My goal is not merely to provide temporary relief but to <u>develop sustainable communities that reintegrate the homeless into society</u>, <u>thereby stimulating economic growth and national well-being.</u> This multi-faceted issue demands a concerted effort from all sectors of society, guided by comprehensive strategies and collaborative involvement.

In 2011, I began spending time in Washington, DC, working with Crowell & Moring law firm on a World Bank arbitration case representing my company. One day, while out for lunch with a few attorneys, I saw a homeless person with a broken arm. Concerned, I went outside and asked him what had happened. He told me he had been attacked at night, explaining that such attacks on people experiencing homelessness were becoming common, a cruel sport for some. Even today, I remember the fury I felt, unable to digest the fact that people could do this to others. Homeless people are our people; they are Americans. I hugged him and reassured him that God would care for him as He does for all Americans. When I turned around, I noticed the looks of surprise from the people around me, questioning how a suited-up man could be hugging a homeless person in the heart of Georgetown.

That night, I woke up around 3 am, worrying about the folks outside. I went out and walked the streets of Georgetown, close to the US Treasury, at the heart of DC. After about 10 minutes, I found a group of homeless individuals sleeping, around 8-9 of them. I stayed nearby without disturbing them for close to two hours. I was prepared to defend them, if necessary, even if it meant ending up in the hospital. Sometimes, protecting the innocent outweighs the consequences. This belief is a fundamental pillar of being a true American, a conviction that has guided me in my 30 years of geopolitical work, being an American by heart myself.

This routine continued for 10-12 days, becoming increasingly challenging. Working with the legal team during the day and patrolling the streets at night left me with little sleep. During this period, the idea of finding a solution began to take root. Over the years, whenever I was in the US, I engaged with homeless individuals, gaining valuable insights into their needs and how we can help them.

Some of my proposals you will read may seem odd or massive, but I am inspired by the great work of the US Army Corps of Engineers and the remarkable structures they have built. The US Military, ranked 19th globally in 1939, became Number 1 in just six years. I firmly believe in the American Dream and its ability to create miracles when pushed to the brink. This belief has allowed the world to enjoy peace and prosperity for nearly 80 years.

My proposal to introduce over 50,000 foreign workers into these cities of hope is not just about meeting immediate labor needs. It is a strategic move aimed at creating a sustainable pipeline of skilled labor. By attracting qualified individuals from around the world, we can significantly enhance the inclusiveness of our workforce and lay the foundation for long-term socio-economic resilience. This emphasis on sustainability is a key aspect of the initiative.

Additionally, I am driven by the understanding that these foreign workers are motivated by a profound desire for a better life—a new beginning in America. The comprehensive package is designed to be globally competitive, ensuring that it appeals to a wide range of talent. I am confident that these individuals, in their quest for a brighter future, will demonstrate extraordinary commitment and adaptability, particularly during these towns' challenging initial stabilization phase. Their resilience will aid their integration and cultivate a culture of empathy and understanding towards our homeless population.

This initiative presents a unique opportunity for both sides: the foreign workers gain a fresh start and the chance to pursue the American Dream, while our homeless citizens are given the chance to reintegrate into society and reclaim their lives. This vision of mutual benefit is central to the broader narrative I aim to convey in this book.

My advocacy for establishing 100 Cities of Hope across the United States is not a random suggestion but a carefully planned initiative driven by a set of strategic objectives:

1. **Eradicate homelessness** by providing stable housing, employment, and community integration.

2. **Create vibrant towns across the U.S.** to spur economic growth and prosperity.

3. **Achieve inclusivity for homeless citizens** by reintegrating them into the economy with dignity, transforming the approach from charity to a mutually beneficial partnership where the benefits extend beyond initial support.

4. **Attract qualified foreign workers** through a novel visa program that co-finances the initiative and tackles stabilization challenges while these workers earn their new lives in America.

5. **Generate global goodwill** through the visa program, creating a positive perception of the U.S. and building a valuable database of skilled individuals eager to contribute to the nation's growth, particularly in the manufacturing sector.

6. **Accelerate the growth of U.S. manufacturing industries** by creating new jobs and fostering a self-sustaining economy that can thrive independently if needed.

7. **Expand and strengthen American cities** by transforming the Cities of Hope into thriving hubs that alleviate pressure on overcrowded urban centers, spreading opportunity across the nation.

8. **Foster national unity** by transcending political differences, with Cities of Hope symbolizing a united effort to embrace each other and work towards a shared future—whether Democrat or Republican, we are all part of the same nation.

These objectives form the backbone of my proposal, which aims to turn untapped potential into thriving communities while simultaneously addressing one of our time's most pressing social issues.

One of the inherent challenges in founding new towns or cities is the classic dilemma of attracting both population and business activity. The absence of job opportunities deters people from relocating, while the lack of population discourages businesses from investing—creating a Catch-22 situation. However, this challenge is addressed head-on with the model I am proposing. By focusing on our homeless population—individuals in search of stability and a fresh start—, we can offer them an opportunity to relocate to these new towns, which will provide quality of life, healthcare, job opportunities, and more. These towns will present a compelling alternative for those seeking a renewed sense of purpose and belonging.

Moreover, this concept simultaneously brings job opportunities to these areas. <u>Combined with my proposed financial architecture, it creates a robust framework for establishing and growing new cities and towns.</u> Over time, these towns will naturally evolve into thriving ecosystems as the growth of supply chain requirements and other economic factors will inevitably drive their expansion. This approach will lead to the flourishing of new cities and towns across the United States, enhancing interconnectivity, stimulating economic growth, and contributing to the long-term sustainability of the nation's demographic landscape.

Furthermore, the surge in homelessness can be traced back to the de-industrialization that began in the 1970s. Reversing this trend by reindustrializing may well prove to be the most effective solution to this pressing issue.

I am proposing the establishment of basic industries within these towns, ranging from textile production to electronic assembly. The economic framework of these towns will be further diversified by incorporating call centers, greenhouses, waste-to-energy and waste recycling projects, and food processing and frozen food manufacturing.

In addition to the industrial focus, I have carefully considered the social dimensions of these towns. For instance, they could provide catering services to local businesses and government offices, which could potentially evolve into a program for offering free lunches to students in nearby schools. This initiative could be developed in collaboration with federal and state governments, NGOs, and private enterprises, creating a comprehensive model that integrates both economic and social sustainability.

In essence, while the initial perception of these homelessness transformation towns may be that they are primarily designed to assist and support our homeless population, I am confident that the long-term benefits they will bring to the United States as a whole will far exceed the immediate advantages to the homeless community. **This proposal should not be seen merely as an act of charity towards our**

homeless population; instead, it is about giving them a second chance—an opportunity for them to contribute significantly to our nation.

These individuals will play a crucial role in revitalizing our country by fostering the development of vibrant new towns in currently underutilized areas, attracting qualified talent to the U.S., and generating substantial economic value through their efforts. Furthermore, their involvement in social initiatives, such as free lunch programs for school children and other community-driven projects, will offer additional societal benefits.

This approach not only dignifies the concept but also resonates deeply with American values. I am confident that our homeless citizens will embrace this opportunity and, in doing so, help drive the positive transformation of our society.

In the ensuing chapters, I will examine historical trends and current data to understand the scope of the country's homelessness. I will dissect the economic, social, and personal root causes—factors like mental health, addiction, and domestic violence—that push individuals into homelessness. By evaluating federal, state, and local policy responses and analyzing past solutions, I aim to outline a comprehensive strategy that addresses both immediate needs and long-term objectives.

A crucial part of my proposed plan involves creating self-sustaining communities, particularly through the innovative concept of industrial parks. By combining stable housing and employment opportunities, we can offer hope and a pathway to a better life for homeless individuals. Additional chapters will delve into the practicalities of planning, infrastructure, job training, housing strategies, and integrating community services, all designed to foster a supportive environment that uplifts its residents.

By leveraging policy recommendations, technological innovations, and collaborative efforts with existing programs, I seek to propose a transformative change if it is applicable in practice (I firmly believe so). I will emphasize measurement and accountability, utilizing key performance indicators and data collection methods to ensure our solutions are effective and adaptable.

Ultimately, this book isn't just about addressing homelessness; it's about creating a society where everyone can thrive. We can turn the page to a new chapter of inclusivity, economic vitality, and societal well-being.

My overall goal is to contribute humbly to the issue of homelessness, recognizing the immense efforts already made by tens of thousands of dedicated individuals. I seek to assist in the broader problem-solving process that engages Americans at the federal, state, and NGO levels. Many organizations are tirelessly addressing this challenge and achieving remarkable results. **I have no doubt these great patriots will solve this issue.** <u>There is no limit to what Americans can achieve; this is my unwavering belief, rooted in firsthand observations.</u>

I firmly believe in the American Miracle and the boundless potential of what Americans can achieve, as has been demonstrated for centuries for the betterment of humanity. Americans have reached this level of progress and prosperity through blood, sweat, and tears, with nothing coming easily, all while internalizing the challenges of other nations and striving to help in every possible way. As one example, out of thousands, during the Second World War, Luxembourg lost 5,700 heroes, while Americans lost

5470 in Luxembourg—almost the same number of people. This is a great nation because Americans are good people, and God always rewards the good ones. Homeless citizens are a vital part of this great nation; they are Americans, and no solution should be considered too challenging or difficult to pursue if we believe it will help them and address the issue effectively.

Although my proposed Cities of Hope concept may seem bold or massive, I firmly believe that this great nation can eradicate this chronic problem with the right approach and methods. The establishment of the US Interagency Council on Homelessness is extremely encouraging and gives me firm hope that this problem will be eradicated soon. **I just hope to add my small contribution to these efforts to support the collective mission**.

Lastly, I would like to express my deepest gratitude to **Timothy Keegan**, The President of the COH Foundation, for his unwavering support and inspiration throughout this journey. A special thank you goes to **Wells Hall** for his continuous support and encouragement and to my brother, **Clinton G. Bryan,** for the honor of writing the foreword for this book. My heartfelt thanks go to my sister, **Ayse Berna Erten**, for her invaluable editorial and research assistance and to my mother, **Birten Erten**, whose thoughtful conversations and constant encouragement have been the driving force behind my commitment to search for a solution to this critical issue.

H. Burak Erten
info@burakerten.us

United We Stand:
A Vision for National Unity
Through the Cities of Hope

Introduction

In a nation as diverse as the United States, unity is not just an ideal but a necessity. The motto "**United we stand**" has long served as a guiding principle for America, reminding everyone that strength lies in the ability to come together despite our differences. This principle is particularly relevant as we confront one of the most pressing challenges of our time: homelessness. The Cities of Hope initiative embodies this spirit of unity, offering a transformative approach to addressing homelessness while fostering a renewed sense of national cohesion.

Bridging Political Divides

Homelessness does not discriminate between political affiliations. Whether one identifies as a Republican or a Democrat, the issue of homelessness impacts all communities, transcending party lines. The Cities of Hope are designed to unite people from all walks of life, united by the shared goal of providing opportunities and support to those who need it most. This initiative represents a rare opportunity to transcend the political divides that have often hindered progress, demonstrating that we are all on the same side when it comes to fundamental human dignity.

By actively involving citizens from across the political spectrum, the Cities of Hope can serve as a powerful example of how bipartisan collaboration can lead to meaningful change. These towns will be living embodiments of the belief that, although we may have different perspectives, we are ultimately united in our desire to build a better future for all Americans.

A Symbol of American Resilience

The Cities of Hope are more than just a solution to homelessness; they are a testament to the resilience and ingenuity that define the American spirit. **Throughout history, America has risen to meet its most significant challenges by coming together and embracing the values that have made this nation strong: compassion, hard work, and a commitment to justice**. The creation of these towns will demonstrate that, even in the face of seemingly insurmountable challenges, we can forge a path forward that benefits everyone.

In these communities, homeless citizens will not be seen as burdens but as valuable members of society eager to contribute to the growth and prosperity of the nation. Their involvement in building and sustaining these towns will instill a deep sense of pride and accomplishment, reinforcing the idea that everyone deserves a second chance. This approach will not only help eradicate homelessness but will also strengthen the social fabric of our nation, creating a more inclusive and compassionate society.

The Role of Citizenship and Participation

One of the most powerful aspects of the Cities of Hope is their potential to foster a renewed sense of citizenship and participation among all Americans. In these towns, every resident, whether formerly homeless or not, will have the opportunity to contribute to the community's success. This shared responsibility will create a strong sense of ownership and belonging, encouraging residents to take pride in their town and in their country.

This initiative will also provide a platform for Americans to come together and engage in meaningful dialogue about the values that unite us. Through community meetings, public forums, and collaborative projects, residents of the Cities of Hope will have the chance to actively participate in shaping the future of their towns. This emphasis on civic engagement will help rebuild trust in our democratic institutions and remind us of collective action's power.

Fostering Unity Beyond the Cities

The impact of the Cities of Hope will extend far beyond the boundaries of these new towns. As these communities thrive and grow, they will serve as models of what can be achieved when we work together. The lessons learned and the successes achieved in these towns can be replicated across the country, fostering a renewed sense of unity and purpose nationwide.

Moreover, the Cities of Hope will demonstrate that the American dream is still within reach for everyone. By providing homeless citizens with the tools they need to succeed, these towns will show that you can achieve greatness with hard work, support, and determination no matter where you start in life. This message of hope and possibility will resonate across the nation, inspiring others to come together and work towards a brighter future for all.

Conclusion

"**United we stand**" is more than just a motto—**it is a Call to Action.** The Cities of Hope initiative embodies this call, offering a bold vision for a united and prosperous America. By bringing together people from all walks of life, these towns will demonstrate the power of unity in overcoming one of our nation's most pressing challenges. Through collaboration, compassion, and a shared commitment to the common good, we can build a future where everyone has the opportunity to thrive. **The Cities of Hope are not just about eradicating homelessness—they are about reinforcing the foundation of our nation's greatness: unity, resilience, and unwavering belief in the American dream.**

This initiative invites every American to be a part of this mission, to contribute to the creation of a society where everyone is valued and where the strength of our nation is reflected in the unity of its people. Together, we can turn the page to a new chapter of American history, one where unity is not just an ideal but a lived reality in communities across the nation.

Dedication

In Loving Memory of My Father, Ali Cengiz Erten / 1940-1995

This book is dedicated to the loving memory of my father, Ali Cengiz Erten. A man of immense character and boundless generosity. He served his military service at JUSMMAT, where he had the privilege of working alongside American soldiers, whom he affectionately considered his brothers. His time at JUSMMAT Office of Defense Cooperation Turkey - Wikipedia nurtured a profound love for America, a country whose values and ideals he held in the highest regard.

It was my father who instilled in me a deep admiration for the United States and its principles. He constantly encouraged me to build my life on the foundation of American values and to strive for what this great nation stands for—freedom, bravery, continuous progress, and the pursuit of happiness.

His greatest dream was to establish a chain of food banks, reflecting his unwavering commitment to helping those in need. My father was always the person who would go the extra mile to assist anyone in distress, offering whatever help he could. The outpouring of love and respect at his funeral was a true testament to the countless lives he touched with his kindness and generosity.

This book is a tribute to his memory, his dreams, and the values he cherished. I am forever grateful for the love, guidance, and inspiration he provided, which continue to influence me every day.

Foreword

Homelessness, a persistent and complex challenge, is reaching a critical point as urbanization accelerates and economic disparities widen. This urgent issue demands more than temporary solutions; it requires an innovative, scalable, and sustainable approach that can fundamentally alter the socio-economic landscape. In Solving Homelessness, Burak Erten presents a transformative vision that is as bold in its ambition as it is detailed in its execution, offering a beacon of hope for a better future.

At the core of Burak's strategy is the concept of Homelessness Transformation Towns—a revolutionary model that integrates housing, employment, healthcare, and community development into self-sustaining urban ecosystems. These towns are meticulously designed to address the multifaceted nature of homelessness, providing not just shelter but also a pathway to dignity, self-sufficiency, and long-term stability. For government leaders, this model offers a comprehensive framework that aligns with national goals of economic growth, social equity, and sustainable development, providing reassurance of its effectiveness.

Each town, as envisioned by Burak, is a microcosm of potential—a fully integrated community that houses 5,000 individuals and is equipped with essential services, educational facilities, healthcare, and employment opportunities. The model's strength lies in its holistic approach: modular housing solutions, scalable infrastructure, and robust public services are all intertwined with economic engines such as industrial facilities, call centers, and urban farming projects. This integration ensures that residents are not merely recipients of aid but are active contributors to the economic and social fabric of their communities.

The economic implications of this model are profound. Burak outlines an innovative financing strategy that leverages federal bonds and a novel visa program to generate the necessary capital for these ambitious projects. By combining public investment with private sector engagement, this model ensures financial sustainability while also creating significant economic opportunities. Introducing special economic zones (SEZs) within these towns further incentivizes business investment, stimulates local economies, and reduces the burden on government resources.

For government officials and policymakers, Burak's blueprint offers a pragmatic and actionable solution to one of society's most pressing issues. The proposed model is not just about providing immediate relief; it is about creating a long-term, systemic change that addresses the root causes of homelessness. By integrating job creation with housing solutions and by embedding these initiatives within broader economic and social policies, Burak presents a model that is scalable, replicable, and adaptable to various regions and contexts.

The potential for replication and scalability is particularly compelling. With the right support, these Homelessness Transformation Towns could be established nationwide; each adapted to local conditions and needs yet grounded in a proven framework. This approach not only addresses the immediate needs of the homeless population but also contributes to broader national objectives, including economic revitalization, social cohesion, and public health improvements.

Moreover, the involvement of celebrities, corporations, and other key stakeholders underscores the model's viability and broad appeal. Their participation not only brings additional resources and attention to the issue but also helps to shift public perception and galvanize collective action. This multi-stakeholder approach ensures that the model is not only funded but also championed by influential voices, making it more likely to succeed in the long term.

Solving Homelessness is a critical read for anyone involved in policymaking, urban planning, or social services. It provides a detailed roadmap for transforming how we address homelessness—moving from reactive, short-term interventions to proactive, sustainable solutions. Burak Erten's work challenges us to think bigger, act bolder, and commit to a future where homelessness is managed and eradicated.

This book is more than a policy proposal; it is a visionary plan that combines economic innovation with social responsibility. As governments worldwide grapple with the complexities of homelessness, *Solving Homelessness* offers a beacon of hope, providing a clear, actionable path toward a more just and equitable society. It is a call to action for leaders at all levels to embrace this innovative approach, harness its potential, and work together to create a future where every individual has the opportunity to thrive.

Keep up the amazing work, my Dear Brother!

Clinton Bryan

About Clinton G. Bryan -

Clinton Bryan is a U.S. Navy Seabee Combat Military Veteran and serial entrepreneur. His military experience in the U.S. Navy, combined with his formal education in business and travels, has refined Clinton into the philanthropic individual he is today.

His love for family, friends, people, and travel has set him on the journey to paying it forward through his writing as a legacy to help others envision the life they deserve—a life of intrinsic love, fulfillment, and happiness.

Clinton has authored seven books

https://www.amazon.com/stores/author/B01JJO7A9G/about

The First Truly Holistic Solution for the Problem – Turn of Events

May 18, 2023

FACT SHEET: Biden-Harris Administration Announces New Initiative to Tackle Unsheltered Homelessness

1. Home

2. <u>Briefing Room</u>

3. <u>Statements and Releases</u>

Today, the Biden-Harris administration will announce the launch of ALL INside, a first-of-its-kind initiative to address unsheltered homelessness across the country. ALL INside is a key part of All In: The Federal Strategic Plan to Prevent and End Homelessness, which set a bold goal to reduce homelessness 25 percent by 2025 and ultimately build a country where every person has a safe and affordable home.

Through the ALL INside initiative, the U.S. Interagency Council on Homelessness (USICH) and its 19 federal member agencies will partner with state and local governments to strengthen and accelerate local efforts to get unsheltered people into homes in six places: Chicago, Dallas, Los Angeles, Phoenix Metro, Seattle, and the State of California.

To accelerate ongoing efforts by local leaders, the Biden-Harris Administration will offer innovative and tailored support to participating communities for up to two years, including by:

- Embedding a dedicated federal official in each community to accelerate locally-driven strategies and enact system-level changes to reduce unsheltered homelessness;

- Deploying dedicated teams across the federal government to identify opportunities for regulatory relief and flexibilities, navigate federal funding streams, and facilitate a peer learning network across the communities; and

- Convening philanthropy, the private sector, and other communities to identify opportunities for follow-on support and collaboration.

In addition, the Administration will launch new efforts to address major barriers to housing, health care, and other support for people experiencing unsheltered homelessness. They include:

- The U.S. Department of Health and Human Services (HHS) will provide technical assistance to help communities leverage federal programs like Medicaid to cover and provide housing-related supportive services and behavioral health care.

- The U.S. Department of Housing and Urban Development (HUD), the U.S. Department of Veterans Affairs, the Social Security Administration (SSA), and HHS will collaborate to address barriers that people may encounter when obtaining various forms of government-issued identification and other critical documents.

- The SSA will work with the communities and the federal *ALL INside* team to leverage data-sharing and regulatory flexibilities that can help facilitate access to support services like housing vouchers or Medicaid.

- The U.S. Department of Labor will connect the communities with local workforce boards and Job Corps sites to fully leverage local and state government employment opportunities for unsheltered youth.

- The Federal Emergency Management Agency will provide technical assistance to the communities to facilitate greater operational coordination in response to disasters, which often increase homelessness.

- HUD will help communities troubleshoot barriers to connecting people to rental assistance or housing programs, as well as assist communities to use regulatory flexibilities to speed up the processes enabling residents to move into properties and transition into permanent housing.

Additional USICH member agencies, including AmeriCorps, Department of Agriculture, Department of Justice, Department of Energy, Department of Transportation, the General Services Administration, as well as the Department of the Treasury, have also made commitments to support the ALL INside communities.

Today's announcement builds on historic support by the Biden-Harris Administration to help states and cities battle homelessness. President Biden's American Rescue Plan (ARP)—which represents the largest single-year investment in ending homelessness in U.S. history—helped prevent a surge of homelessness. Through the Treasury Department's State and Local Fiscal Recovery Fund, for instance, the six ALL INside sites have invested more than $2.5 billion in projects focused on reducing and preventing homelessness. The ARP provided $5 billion for 70,000 Emergency Housing Vouchers—the first HUD voucher specifically for people experiencing homelessness beyond veterans. The ARP also delivered over $21 billion in emergency rental assistance, standing up a first-of-its-kind national eviction prevention infrastructure that has helped 8 million struggling households make rent and pay utilities bills, and kept eviction filings below pre-pandemic levels in the 1.5 years after the end of the eviction moratorium. Through the House America initiative, HUD and USICH worked with more than 100 communities to make the most of the American Rescue Plan; and in just over a year, they helped more than 100,000 people experiencing homelessness move into permanent homes.

Earlier this year, HUD released a first-of-its-kind package of grants totaling $486 million and approximately 3,300 housing vouchers to help 62 communities address unsheltered homelessness and homeless encampments, including $60 million to Chicago, $22 million to Dallas, $60 million to Los Angeles, and $36 million to other communities across the state of California.

The President's Fiscal Year '24 Budget proposes unprecedented investments not only to urgently address homelessness but also to <u>prevent homelessness,</u> including through additional housing vouchers; emergency rental assistance; increasing the supply of affordable housing; and establishing a guarantee of rental assistance for extremely low-income veterans and youth aging out of foster care—two groups disproportionately at risk of and experiencing homelessness.

> *"My plan offers a roadmap for not only getting people into housing but also ensuring that they have access to the support, services, and income that allow them to thrive."*
>
> *Joseph R. Biden Jr*

46th President of the United States of America

> *"The people of the United States have a right to economic and social security and to decent housing, and it is the responsibility of the government to see that those rights are respected."*
>
> *Dwight D. Eisenhower*

34th President of the United States of America

The Scope of Homelessness in the US

Understanding the scope of homelessness in the United States is crucial for formulating effective strategies to address this persistent issue. Homelessness is not new; it has evolved over decades, shaped by economic shifts, social transformations, and policy decisions. This chapter aims to provide a comprehensive overview of historical trends and current statistics, offering insights into the magnitude and dynamics of homelessness in the US today.

Historical Trends Over the Last 50 Years

The landscape of homelessness in the United States has undergone significant changes over the past five decades. During the 1970s, the issue became more visible due to **deindustrialization** and the decline in affordable housing. These economic transformations led to job losses in manufacturing sectors and created a growing population of individuals experiencing homelessness.

In the 1980s, policy shifts, including reductions in social welfare programs and mental health deinstitutionalization, exacerbated the situation. The closure of state mental institutions without adequate community-based support systems left many individuals without care, often resulting in homelessness. This decade marked a critical point as homelessness began to be recognized as a national crisis.

In the 1990s, efforts to address homelessness increased through federal initiatives such as the McKinney-Vento Homeless Assistance Act. However, the problem persisted due to persistent economic inequality and rising housing costs. Efforts continued into the 2000s and 2010s with varying degrees of success as federal, state, and local policymakers implemented preventive and reactive measures.

Current Statistics and Data

As of the most recent data available, the United States continues to grapple with significant levels of homelessness. According to the U.S. Department of Housing and Urban Development's (HUD) 2022 Annual Homeless Assessment Report, approximately 580,000 individuals were experiencing homelessness on a single night in January 2021. This marked a slight increase from the previous year, highlighting the ongoing challenges of adequately addressing the problem.

Homelessness affects various demographics differently. For instance, African Americans and Native Americans are disproportionately represented among the homeless population compared to their percentage of the general population (HUD, 2022). Furthermore, significant subsets include veterans, families with children, and unaccompanied youth, each facing unique challenges and requiring tailored interventions.

Geographically, homelessness is concentrated in urban areas, with states like California and New York reporting the highest numbers. However, rural homelessness presents its own set of challenges, often exacerbated by limited access to services and support networks.

The COVID-19 pandemic has added a new layer of complexity. Economic disruptions, job losses, and health vulnerabilities have amplified the risk of homelessness for many Americans. Programs such as temporary eviction moratoriums and rental assistance were implemented to mitigate these effects, but their long-term impact remains to be seen.

In conclusion, understanding the scope of homelessness in the US is foundational for anyone looking to contribute to solving this challenging issue. By examining historical trends and current statistics, we can better grasp the multifaceted nature of homelessness and tailor solutions to meet the diverse needs of this vulnerable population.

Historical Trends Over the Last 50 Years

The landscape of homelessness in the United States has undergone significant changes over the past half-century. By understanding these historical trends, we can gain insights into the underlying causes and effective strategies for addressing homelessness today.

In the early 1970s, homelessness was often seen as a temporary issue affecting a relatively small segment of the population. Economic factors, such as the post-industrial economic transition and the decline of affordable housing, started to create more widespread vulnerability. The deinstitutionalization of psychiatric hospitals also played a significant role, releasing many individuals with mental health issues into communities without adequate support systems. The compounding effect of these factors began to visibly increase homelessness in urban areas.

The 1980s saw a dramatic rise in homelessness, particularly in cities. The economic recession, along with cuts to social service programs and affordable housing, exacerbated the problem. During this decade, homelessness started to become a recognized social crisis. Efforts to address the issue included the enactment of the McKinney-Vento Homeless Assistance Act in 1987, which aimed to provide federal support for shelter and other essential services. However, systemic solutions remained elusive, and the number of homeless individuals continued to climb.

The 1990s and early 2000s witnessed a shift towards more structured approaches, including the development of various programs aimed at prevention and rapid rehousing. Despite these efforts, the issue persisted due to a combination of rising housing costs, stagnant wages, and inadequate social safety nets. Programs like the "Housing First" initiative gained traction, emphasizing the importance of providing stable housing before addressing other issues such as employment and health.

More recently, the Great Recession of 2008 had a profound impact, leading to an increase in homelessness due to widespread job losses and housing foreclosures. Although the economy has recovered, the cost of living has continued to rise, outpacing wage growth and contributing to sustained levels of homelessness.

Throughout these decades, one persistent trend has been the demographic shift within the homeless population. Originally seen as predominantly affecting older single men, homelessness has increasingly impacted families, women, and young people, revealing the multifaceted nature of the crisis.

Understanding these historical trends is crucial as we move forward. They highlight the need for comprehensive, multifaceted solutions that address not only the immediate need for housing but also the broader socio-economic factors contributing to homelessness. By learning from the past, we can better inform the policies and programs that aim to create self-sustaining communities and reintegrate homeless individuals into society, ultimately benefiting the U.S. economy.

Current Statistics and Data

Homelessness in the United States has reached a critical juncture, as indicated by the most recent data available. According to the U.S. Department of Housing and Urban Development (HUD), on a single night in January 2022, the nationwide point-in-time (PIT) count identified approximately 580,000 individuals experiencing homelessness (HUD, 2022). This figure encompasses both sheltered and unsheltered populations, providing a snapshot that underscores the urgency of addressing this complex issue.

Breaking down the statistics further, it's evident that certain demographics are disproportionately affected. For example, families with children represent about 30% of the homeless population, a staggering number that demands targeted intervention (HUD, 2022). **Veterans who have served the nation with honor** account for around 7% of the homeless population, a figure that highlights gaps in the existing support systems.

Racial disparities also persist within the homeless community. African Americans, who comprise roughly 13% of the U.S. population, represent nearly 40% of those experiencing homelessness (HUD, 2022). Similarly, Native Americans and Alaskan Natives are overrepresented relative to their percentage of the general population. This data underscores the need for equity-focused policies and solutions that address the unique challenges faced by these groups.

The geography of homelessness reveals significant variations across states and cities. California, for example, accounts for nearly a quarter of the country's homeless population, with major urban centers like Los Angeles and San Francisco showing particularly high numbers (HUD, 2022). Conversely, states with smaller populations and rural areas tend to have lower overall numbers but face unique challenges related to service provision and access to resources.

Chronic homelessness remains a significant concern, accounting for around 25% of the homeless population. These individuals have been homeless for extended periods, often due to disabling conditions such as mental health issues or substance abuse. Addressing chronic homelessness requires a nuanced approach that integrates both housing and comprehensive supportive services.

Troublingly, the impact of the COVID-19 pandemic has exacerbated the issue. While some short-term measures, such as moratoriums on evictions and enhanced unemployment benefits, provided temporary relief, the long-term economic fallout has pushed many more individuals and families to the brink of homelessness. Preliminary studies indicate a potential rise in homelessness as these temporary measures are lifted.

Understanding these statistics reveals that homelessness in the U.S. is not a monolithic issue but a multifaceted crisis that demands a coordinated, multi-pronged response. Addressing the root causes, implementing effective policy responses, and leveraging data-driven strategies will be essential in crafting sustainable solutions that can restore dignity and hope to those affected.

Root Causes of Homelessness

Understanding the root causes of homelessness is essential to developing effective and sustainable solutions. While homelessness may appear to be a simple issue of a lack of housing, it is, in fact, a complex problem with multifaceted causes. This chapter delves into the primary root causes, categorized into economic factors, social and personal issues, including mental health and addiction, and domestic violence.

Economic Factors

Economic instability is one of the most significant contributors to homelessness. The lack of <u>affordable housing</u> and <u>stagnating wages</u> play pivotal roles. Over the last few decades, the cost of rent has skyrocketed in many urban areas while wages have not kept pace. <u>Compounding this is the scarcity of affordable housing partly due to policies that favor investors and developers, leading to the gentrification of low-income neighborhoods.</u>

Job loss or underemployment also exacerbates homelessness. Despite a robust economy in some periods, many people live paycheck to paycheck without sufficient savings to cover emergencies. A sudden financial setback, like the loss of a job or unexpected medical bills, can push individuals and families into homelessness. According to the National Alliance to End Homelessness (2020), nearly half of all people experiencing homelessness have incomes at or below the federal poverty level, highlighting the fragile economic situations many face.

Social and Personal Issues

Beyond economics, social and personal issues significantly contribute to homelessness. These factors often intertwine with economic conditions, creating a cycle that's difficult to break. Let's explore some of the most prevalent issues.

Mental Health and Addiction

Mental health disorders are both a cause and consequence of homelessness. Approximately one-third of individuals experiencing homelessness in the U.S. suffer from severe mental illness, such as schizophrenia, bipolar disorder, or major depression (National Institute of Mental Health, 2019). These conditions can hinder one's ability to maintain employment and stable relationships, leading to housing instability. Furthermore, the lack of access to mental health services only intensifies the issue.

Addiction is another major factor. Substance abuse often precipitates homelessness and is worsened by it. For many, addiction problems arise from attempting to self-medicate untreated mental health issues or as a way to cope with the trauma of living on the streets. Treatment services are frequently inaccessible or insufficient, leaving many unable to break the cycle of homelessness and addiction.

Domestic Violence

Domestic violence is a leading cause of homelessness for women and children. Many victims are forced to choose between staying in an abusive environment or facing homelessness. Shelters for victims of domestic violence cannot often accommodate all those in need, pushing many into homelessness. According to the National Network to End Domestic Violence (2021), approximately 38% of domestic violence victims become homeless at some point in their lives.

Furthermore, the trauma inflicted by domestic violence has long-term psychological effects, making it challenging for survivors to regain stability. The intersection of domestic violence with economic dependence on the abuser makes escaping the situation exceedingly difficult, leading many to cycle between unsafe environments and homelessness.

In understanding the root causes of homelessness, it's evident that this issue is not only pervasive but also profoundly intricate. **Economic instability, mental health disorders, addiction, and domestic violence are just a few of the critical factors that contribute to the situation.** Addressing these root causes requires coordinated, multifaceted approaches that go beyond providing temporary shelter. It demands comprehensive strategies that focus on prevention, intervention, and sustainable solutions to help individuals regain stability and reintegrate into society, ultimately benefiting the U.S. economy.

Economic Factors

Understanding the economic factors contributing to homelessness is crucial for developing comprehensive solutions. Economic stagnation, rising housing costs, unemployment, and underemployment are substantial contributors to homelessness.

First, **housing affordability** remains a persistent issue. As wages have stagnated over the past decades, housing costs have skyrocketed. This disparity burdens low-income households, who are often just an economic shock away from losing their homes. For instance, a study by the U.S. Department of Housing and Urban Development found that over half a million Americans experience homelessness on a given night, with high housing costs cited as a significant driver (HUD, 2021).

Unemployment and underemployment further compound the issue. When individuals lose their jobs or cannot find adequate employment to meet basic needs, they struggle to afford rent or mortgage payments. This lack of financial stability creates a precarious living situation where individuals and families are at constant risk of homelessness. A 2020 study highlights that unemployment rates are closely correlated with increases in homelessness, particularly in urban centers where the cost of living is higher (U.S. Bureau of Labor Statistics, 2021).

Additionally, the erosion of social safety nets, such as the reduction in affordable housing programs and cuts to social services, exacerbates the problem. Many people rely on government assistance for housing, food, and healthcare, and any cuts to these programs can abruptly push them into homelessness. **Research by the National Alliance to End Homelessness indicates that investment in affordable**

housing is essential in mitigating homelessness, as it provides a stable foundation that allows individuals to seek and maintain employment (NAEH, 2019).

Addressing these economic factors requires multi-faceted approaches. Policy initiatives must focus on increasing affordable housing, expanding social safety nets, and creating job opportunities that offer living wages. Doing so can create a more stable and equitable economic environment, reducing the risk of homelessness for vulnerable populations.

Social and Personal Issues

Homelessness is a multifaceted issue influenced by economic factors as well as a range of social and personal factors. Addressing these underlying factors is essential for crafting effective, long-term solutions. These issues often intersect in complex ways, making it crucial to understand them in depth.

One of the primary social factors contributing to homelessness is the breakdown of family and community structures. The erosion of supportive family networks often leaves individuals without a safety net during times of crisis. Problems such as divorce, family estrangement, and the death of a loved one can push people, particularly the vulnerable, into homelessness. Social isolation can exacerbate the situation by reducing access to resources and emotional support, leading to a vicious cycle that is hard to break.

Issues of mental health and substance abuse also play a significant role. Mental health disorders like depression, anxiety, and schizophrenia can severely impair an individual's ability to secure and maintain stable housing. Often, these individuals struggle to access mental health services due to a myriad of reasons, including stigma, financial constraints, or lack of availability, which further deteriorates their situation. Substance abuse issues, including addiction to drugs and alcohol, compound these challenges. Addiction often drains financial resources and deteriorates health, making it increasingly difficult for individuals to escape the cycle of homelessness.

Domestic violence is another critical factor contributing to homelessness, especially among women and children. Escaping from an abusive household often leaves individuals with no choice but to seek refuge in shelters or on the streets, especially when they lack financial independence and social support. These victims often face additional challenges, such as trauma and legal issues, which complicate their path to stability.

Additionally, experiences of discrimination and social stigma can hinder access to housing and employment opportunities for many homeless individuals. Those who belong to marginalized groups, such as racial minorities or LGBTQ+ individuals, often face additional barriers and biases, making it even more challenging to find a way out of homelessness.

To effectively combat homelessness, addressing these social and personal issues is imperative. Solutions must go beyond providing temporary shelter and involve creating robust support systems that include mental health services, addiction treatment programs, social reintegration efforts, and protection for victims of domestic violence. Tackling these issues with a multifaceted approach will offer paths to stability and self-sufficiency for those affected.

Mental Health and Addiction are significant factors contributing to homelessness. Mental health disorders and substance abuse issues often intersect, creating a web of challenges that make it difficult for individuals to maintain stable housing.

It's essential to recognize that mental health challenges do not simply predispose individuals to homelessness; they exacerbate the difficulties of life on the streets. Mental health disorders like depression, bipolar disorder, schizophrenia, and post-traumatic stress disorder (PTSD) are prevalent among the homeless population. When untreated, these conditions can impair a person's judgment, making it hard to hold a job, manage finances, and navigate social services, further entrenching them in homelessness.

Substance abuse, often intertwined with mental health issues, adds another layer of complexity. Addiction can lead to job loss, strained relationships, and financial ruin, all of which increase the risk of becoming homeless. Conversely, the stresses and dangers of homelessness can exacerbate substance dependencies, creating a vicious cycle that's hard to break. Streets and shelters are not conducive environments for recovery; they may even foster relapse due to easy access to drugs and alcohol, as well as the absence of sustainable support systems.

The interaction between mental health, addiction, and homelessness demands an integrated approach to intervention. Traditional siloed services often fail to address the interconnected nature of these issues. Instead, approaches like "Housing First," which prioritize stable housing as a basic need before tackling mental health and addiction issues, have shown promise. Individuals are better positioned to utilize supportive services such as therapy and rehabilitation programs by providing a stable home. The "Housing First" model has been successful in various cities, offering not only hope but practical results in reducing homelessness among those with severe mental health and addiction problems.

However, a comprehensive solution demands more than housing. It requires coordinated care involving mental health professionals, addiction counselors, social workers, and community organizations. The implementation of multidisciplinary teams that offer wrap-around support is essential. These teams work together to create individualized care plans that address each person's unique needs, ensuring continuous and consistent care.

In summary, addressing mental health and addiction is a critical component of any effective strategy to combat homelessness. By offering stable housing coupled with integrated support services, we can begin to break the cycle that traps so many in a precarious existence, ultimately aiming to reintegrate them into society and the economy in a meaningful and sustainable way.

Domestic Violence is a critical factor contributing to homelessness, often underscored by the complexity of personal and social issues facing victims. The intersection of domestic violence and homelessness creates a cycle that is devastating and challenging to break. Women and children are disproportionately affected; many flee their homes to escape violence, only to find themselves without a safe place to go. When domestic violence pushes individuals into homelessness, they face a slew of additional issues, including exposure to further violence, health problems, and severe economic instability.

Recent statistics indicate a worrying trend: <u>approximately one-third of all women who experience homelessness cite domestic violence as the primary cause</u> (National Network to End Domestic Violence, 2020). Understanding this connection requires acknowledging that the effects of domestic violence extend beyond physical harm. Emotional and psychological abuse can erode an individual's self-efficacy and financial control, making it nearly impossible to remain in the home environment safely. For many, leaving is the only option, regardless of the uncertainty that lies ahead.

Addressing the impact of domestic violence on homelessness requires multi-faceted solutions. Shelters and transitional housing must be equipped to offer immediate safety and comprehensive support services such as counseling, legal assistance, and job training. Programs focused on financial empowerment and legal protection for victims are essential to enable survivors to rebuild their lives and achieve long-term stability. It's also critical to enhance partnerships between homeless services and domestic violence organizations to ensure that victims don't fall through the cracks.

Successful interventions hinge on a coordinated approach. Policymakers and community leaders must focus on expanding safe housing options tailored for domestic violence survivors. This includes providing sufficient funding for emergency shelters and ensuring that transitional housing and supportive services are available. Additionally, prevention efforts aimed at reducing domestic violence through education, community outreach, and stricter enforcement of protective laws can mitigate the risk factors that lead to homelessness in the first place.

A considerable challenge lies in ensuring that these services are accessible across different geographic regions, particularly in rural areas where resources may be scant. Innovative solutions like mobile counseling units and virtual support groups can help bridge this gap. Employing a holistic, trauma-informed approach in these interventions is crucial. Understanding the psychological toll of domestic violence and offering tailored mental health support can significantly improve outcomes for survivors.

In summary, the nexus between domestic violence and homelessness is an area of urgent need that demands immediate and sustained action. By implementing robust, supportive, and preventive measures, we can break the dual cycles of violence and homelessness, paving the way for safer futures for countless individuals.

Policy Responses to Homelessness

Addressing homelessness requires more than mere compassion; it mandates structured policy responses that span federal, state, and local levels. This chapter aims to dissect these policy responses, exploring what has worked and what has not in the intricate fabric of American governance.

Federal Initiatives

Significant policies have been initiated at the federal level to combat homelessness. Historically, the McKinney-Vento Homeless Assistance Act, enacted in 1987, serves as a cornerstone federal legislative framework to alleviate homelessness. The act provides federal funds for shelter, food, and healthcare services, targeting immediate relief and longer-term stability.

In recent years, programs like the Housing First initiative have shifted policy paradigms from providing temporary shelters to prioritizing stable, long-term housing solutions. Housing First posits that securing housing is a fundamental step to addressing other determinants of homelessness, such as mental health or addiction issues. Evidence suggests that Housing First models achieve higher rates of housing stability than traditional models.

Another federal effort is the Continuum of Care Program (CoC), which promotes community-wide commitment to ending homelessness. Managed by the U.S. Department of Housing and Urban Development (HUD), CoC provides funding for nonprofit providers and state and local governments to quickly rehouse homeless individuals and families while minimizing the trauma and dislocation caused by homelessness (HUD, 2023).

Additionally, the United States Interagency Council on Homelessness (USICH) is critical in coordinating the federal response to homelessness. The USICH brings together 19 federal agencies to create a national strategic plan, ensuring that efforts across departments are aligned and effective. The council's strategic plan, "Home, Together," outlines a comprehensive approach that includes increasing affordable housing, creating economic opportunity, and providing robust health and social services.

The collaborative nature of USICH's work exemplifies the federal government's commitment to a unified, multifaceted strategy to end homelessness.

State and Local Efforts

State and local governments have added unique flavors to the battle against homelessness, given that one-size-fits-all approaches are often ineffective. In California, the *Homeless Emergency Aid Program (HEAP)* provides block grants to cities and counties to support innovative solutions tailored to local needs. This approach grants greater flexibility at the ground level, enabling quicker, more responsive action.

The state of Utah, for example, has garnered national attention for its success with the Housing First model. By focusing on providing housing before addressing other issues, Utah significantly reduced its chronic homelessness rate by over 90% between 2005 and 2015.

Local collaborations, such as the partnership between San Antonio City and Haven for Hope, encapsulate how municipal governments can work with non-profits to offer comprehensive services, including job training, medical services, and mental health support. This model has significantly reduced San Antonio's unsheltered homeless population.

Yet, not all local efforts are uniformly successful. New York City's shelter-centric approach has faced criticism for perpetuating a cycle of dependency rather than fostering self-sufficiency. While the city spends billions annually on homelessness services, the lack of affordable housing means many remain stuck in shelters.

In conclusion, the fight against homelessness is multifaceted and requires coordinated efforts across all levels of government. Federal initiatives provide essential funding and framework, while state and local governments tailor solutions to meet specific community needs. By learning from the successes and pitfalls of various policy responses, we can develop more effective strategies to create a future where homelessness is a rare, brief, and non-recurring experience.

Federal Initiatives

The federal government has long played a crucial role in addressing homelessness in the United States. Over the decades, various programs and policies have been initiated to mitigate this complex issue. Recent federal initiatives have emphasized more comprehensive approaches, integrating housing, healthcare, and employment services to create sustainable solutions.

One of the landmark federal responses to homelessness is the McKinney-Vento Homeless Assistance Act of 1987. This act represented the first major federal legislative effort to address homelessness and has since been amended multiple times to refine its scope and effectiveness (National Coalition for the Homeless, 2019). The McKinney-Vento Act focuses on providing emergency shelter, transitional housing, job training, primary healthcare, and education for homeless children and youth.

Another pivotal initiative is the establishment of the Interagency Council on Homelessness (USICH), which coordinates the federal response across 19 agencies. The USICH's "Opening Doors" strategy, the first federal strategic plan to prevent and end homelessness, has laid out detailed goals for reducing homelessness among various population groups, including veterans, families, and the chronically homeless.

In recent years, the U.S. Departments of Housing and Urban Development (HUD), Veterans Affairs (VA), and Health and Human Services (HHS) have partnered in implementing the HUD-VASH (Veterans Affairs Supportive Housing) program. The program combines rental assistance from HUD with case management and clinical services provided by the VA, targeting homeless veterans for permanent housing (HUD, 2020). This initiative not only provides a stable living environment but also addresses the broader needs of veterans, an often marginalized population in the homelessness crisis.

Other significant federal initiatives include the Continuum of Care (CoC) program, which promotes community-wide planning and strategic use of resources to address homelessness. Funded by HUD, the CoC aims to quickly rehouse homeless individuals and families while minimizing the trauma and dislocation caused by homelessness. The program encourages local organizations to partner and design comprehensive plans tailored to their specific community needs, fostering a more dynamic and responsive approach to homelessness at the local level.

Furthermore, the Emergency Solutions Grants (ESG) program funds state, local governments, and nonprofit organizations for emergency shelter, street outreach, homelessness prevention, and rapid re-housing. Administered by HUD, ESG addresses both immediate needs and long-term solutions, emphasizing the importance of a quick and efficient response to housing crises.

One of the current administration's commitments is the American Rescue Plan Act, which addresses the economic fallout from the COVID-19 pandemic and includes substantial allocations for homelessness initiatives. The Act has provided millions in grants for emergency housing vouchers and homelessness prevention services, revealing the federal government's adaptive strategies in crisis periods.

While several federal initiatives have made noticeable impacts, challenges remain in service coordination, funding allocations, and meeting the diverse needs of the homeless population. Continuous evaluation and adaptation of these programs are essential to their success. Collaboration at all levels—federal, state, and local—is necessary to craft holistic approaches that yield sustainable outcomes in the fight against homelessness.

Efforts by the federal government highlight a multifaceted strategy, focusing on immediate relief and long-term solutions. As policies evolve, it is critical to base them on empirical evidence and best practices to effectively tackle this persistent and complex social issue.

State and Local Efforts

Addressing homelessness effectively requires a multi-faceted approach, incorporating policy responses not just from the federal level but critically from state and local governments. These efforts are vital, given that the impacts of homelessness are felt most acutely at the community level. State and local initiatives tend to be more adaptable and responsive to their populations' specific needs and conditions, making them crucial components of a comprehensive strategy to combat homelessness.

Across the United States, states and municipalities have developed various measures to address homelessness tailored to their unique challenges. Successful state and local efforts often involve collaboration between government agencies, non-profit organizations, private sector partners, and the affected communities. This collaboration is essential for creating sustainable solutions that provide immediate relief and work toward long-term stability for homeless individuals.

Many cities and states have implemented initiatives focusing on providing affordable housing. For instance, California, which has one of the highest homelessness rates in the nation, has allocated significant state funding toward the construction and maintenance of affordable housing units. The "Housing First" approach adopted by cities like Los Angeles and San Francisco prioritizes providing permanent housing to homeless individuals without preconditions such as sobriety or employment, which is effective in reducing chronic homelessness.

Several states have invested in comprehensive support services beyond housing. For example, New York State's Empire State Supportive Housing Initiative (ESSHI) provides funding for the development and operation of supportive housing for individuals who are homeless or at risk of homelessness. These supportive housing models combine affordable housing with critical services such as mental health and addiction treatment, job training, and case management.

Local governments also recognize the importance of preventative measures. Programs for rent assistance, eviction prevention, and rapid rehousing services are increasingly common. In Washington State, the Eviction Rent Assistance Program (ERAP) assists households that are behind on rent and facing potential eviction, helping stabilize families before they become homeless.

Community-based solutions are another essential element of state and local efforts. For instance, the Community Homelessness Assessment, Local Education and Networking Groups (CHALENG) for Veterans initiative, supported by the U.S. Department of Veterans Affairs, is a partnership between local communities and VA medical centers to address homelessness among veterans. This collaborative approach has facilitated sharing resources and information, strengthening local capacity to address homelessness.

In summary, state and local efforts are indispensable in the fight against homelessness. By leveraging community resources, tailoring solutions to local conditions, and fostering partnerships among various stakeholders, these efforts create a cohesive and dynamic framework for addressing and ultimately ending homelessness. The success of these initiatives highlights the importance of localized strategies that complement broader federal efforts.

Multi–Level Response

Agencies and Associations are working Tirelessly on the Issue.

1. **U.S. Department of Housing and Urban Development (HUD)**

   - Programs: Continuum of Care (CoC) Program, Emergency Solutions Grants (ESG) Program

   - Website: <u>HUD</u>

2. **California Interagency Council on Homelessness**

   - Program: Homeless Emergency Aid Program (HEAP)

   - Website: California Interagency Council on Homelessness

3. **National League of Cities**

   - Focus: Local government partnerships for innovative housing solutions

- Website: <u>National League of Cities</u>

4. **Downtown Emergency Service Center (DESC)**

   - Focus: Integrated care combining housing with healthcare services

   - Website: <u>DESC</u>

5. **Community Solutions**

   - Campaign: Built for Zero

   - Website: <u>Community Solutions</u>

6. **National Alliance to End Homelessness**

   - Focus: Research papers, policy analyses, advocacy

   - Website: <u>National Alliance to End Homelessness</u>

7. **National Coalition for the Homeless**

   - Focus: Advocacy, awareness, volunteer opportunities

   - Website: <u>National Coalition for the Homeless</u>

8. **Homeless Management Information Systems (HMIS)**

   - Focus: Data collection on homeless individuals and services

   - Website: HMIS

9. **U.S. Interagency Council on Homelessness (USICH)**

   - Strategy: "Opening Doors" federal strategic plan to prevent and end homelessness

   - Website: <u>USICH</u>

10. **HUD-VASH (Veterans Affairs Supportive Housing)**

    - Program: Rental assistance and clinical services for homeless veterans

    - Website: HUD-VASH

11. **Empire State Supportive Housing Initiative (ESSHI)**

    - Focus: Supportive housing for homeless or at-risk individuals in New York State

    - Website: ESSHI

12. **White House Initiatives**

    - Program: American Rescue Plan Act

    - Website: <u>White House</u>

These agencies and programs are critical in addressing homelessness, from providing immediate shelter and long-term housing solutions to supportive services and advocacy efforts.

Analyzing Previous Solutions

Assessing past attempts to combat homelessness is critical to understanding what has worked and what hasn't and how we can move forward more effectively. This chapter delves into the strengths and weaknesses of previous solutions, offering a comprehensive analysis to guide future initiatives.

Strengths and Weaknesses

Various strategies have been implemented to address homelessness, each with distinct advantages and limitations. Evaluating these methods helps identify effective practices and potential pitfalls.

Strengths:

- *Comprehensive Support Services:* Many programs have successfully integrated support services such as mental health counseling, addiction treatment, and job training with housing assistance. This approach recognizes the multifaceted nature of homelessness and addresses underlying issues.

- *Housing First Approach:* The Housing First model prioritizes providing permanent housing before addressing other needs and has shown high success rates in reducing chronic homelessness. Participants often experience improved stability and well-being, allowing them to tackle personal challenges more effectively.

- *Collaborative Efforts:* Partnerships between federal, state, and local governments, non-profits, and community organizations have amplified resources and broadened the scope of outreach efforts. **These collaborations maximize the impact of limited resources.**

Weaknesses:

- *Insufficient Funding:* Many programs struggle with inconsistent or inadequate funding, hindering their ability to provide continuous and comprehensive support. Budget constraints often result in limited housing options and reduced support services.

- *Lack of Affordable Housing:* While support services are critical, the fundamental issue often remains a shortage of affordable housing options. Without increasing the availability of low-cost housing, many programs can only offer temporary relief.

- *Fragmented Services:* In some cases, services are not well-coordinated, resulting in fragmented support that can be confusing and inefficient for the homeless population. A lack of integration can mean individuals fall through the cracks and miss out on crucial services.

Case Studies

Analyzing specific case studies offers valuable insights into the practical application of homeless intervention strategies. The following examples highlight different approaches, illustrating both successes and the inherent challenges.

New York City's Homeless Outreach Population Estimate (HOPE):

New York City's HOPE program involves annual surveys to count the homeless population and connect them to services. This initiative has improved data accuracy and resource allocation. However, despite these efforts, the city's affordable housing crisis persists, exacerbating homelessness.

Utah's Housing First Initiative:

Utah adopted the Housing First model in 2005, drastically reducing chronic homelessness by 91% over a decade. This success is attributed to the state's commitment to providing permanent housing without preconditions, coupled with supportive services. However, scaling the program to address acute homelessness has proven more challenging.

Learning from these examples can help design future solutions to address homelessness more effectively. A nuanced understanding of what has worked in various contexts informs the development of innovative and sustainable strategies.

As we continue exploring potential solutions, it is crucial to keep the focus on creating integrated, well-funded, and scalable programs. Only through a comprehensive and coordinated effort can we hope to make lasting progress in resolving homelessness.

Strengths and Weaknesses

In examining previous solutions to homelessness, it's crucial to assess both their strengths and weaknesses. Understanding what has worked and what hasn't allows us to build more effective strategies moving forward. This section will delve into key insights from past efforts, shedding light on both their positive impacts and limitations.

Strengths

One of the strengths of prior solutions is that they are close to the holistic approach that many programs have tried to adopt. Comprehensive strategies that address not only housing but also factors like mental health, addiction, and employment have shown promising results. For instance, programs such as Housing First, which prioritizes stable housing without preconditions, have been particularly effective. This model has successfully significantly reduced chronic homelessness by providing immediate access to housing while concurrently offering supportive services.

Moreover, the emphasis on collaborative efforts between federal, state, and local governments has led to more coordinated and structured responses. Cities that have integrated their homeless services with other social services have seen improved outcomes in terms of individual stability and cost-effectiveness.

Weaknesses

Nevertheless, previous solutions are not without their weaknesses. A significant limitation has been the inconsistent funding and resource allocation. Many programs start with substantial support but lack long-term sustainability, leading to their eventual decline once initial funding is depleted.

Another notable weakness is the limited scalability of successful models. While approaches like Housing First have been effective in urban centers, their implementation in rural areas has faced unique challenges, including a lack of infrastructure and services (National Alliance to End Homelessness, 2020). Additionally, policies that focus predominantly on emergency shelters rather than permanent solutions tend to keep individuals in a cycle of temporary stability without addressing underlying issues.

Lastly, there's a data collection and analysis gap, which undermines the ability to track long-term outcomes and the effectiveness of different interventions. Standardized metrics and robust data systems are essential for evaluating which strategies provide sustained benefits over time.

Successful Cases

Housing First Model in Utah

The state of Utah implemented the Housing First model with remarkable success. This approach provides immediate housing to individuals experiencing homelessness without preconditions such as employment or sobriety. The rationale behind this program is to stabilize individuals by meeting their basic need for shelter, thereby enabling them to focus on other issues like employment and mental health.

Between 2005 and 2015, Utah reduced its chronic homelessness rate by 91%. One key strength of this model is its emphasis on housing as a fundamental human right. However, some critics argue that it can be resource-intensive and may not comprehensively address underlying issues such as addiction and mental health.

Community Land Trusts in Burlington, Vermont

Burlington, Vermont, has utilized community land trusts (CLTs) to create affordable housing and prevent homelessness. CLTs are nonprofit organizations that acquire and hold land for the benefit of a community, ensuring long-term housing affordability. The Champlain Housing Trust, for example, has become the largest CLT in the United States, serving over 2,000 families.

One of the strengths of this model is its ability to provide permanent, affordable housing solutions while preserving the value of community assets. However, the scalability of this solution can be challenging, as it requires substantial initial capital and ongoing community engagement and support.

The Beacon Centre in Houston, Texas

The Beacon Centre in Houston offers a comprehensive service model to address homelessness through a combination of emergency services, transition programs, and long-term solutions. It provides meals, showers, laundry, health services, and case management to guide individuals toward self-sufficiency.

A 2019 evaluation revealed that access to multiple services under one roof significantly improved clients' outcomes, including better health and increased employment rates (Houston Coalition for the Homeless, 2019). However, critics note that the program's reliance on donations and grants makes it vulnerable to funding fluctuations, which could limit its long-term sustainability.

Effective solutions often combine immediate housing with supportive services tailored to individual needs. Financial sustainability and community involvement are critical factors that can drive success or pose significant challenges. Understanding and integrating these lessons will be essential as we develop and implement new strategies to create self-sustaining communities for the homeless.

Now Let Us Talk About the Industrial Parks Concept
Overview of the Cities of Hope Concept

The concept of Cities of Hope is a multifaceted approach aimed at addressing one of the most pressing issues in the United States: homelessness. Beyond just providing shelter, these towns are envisioned as self-sustaining communities where employment, education, healthcare, and other essential services are readily available. This holistic approach ensures that every resident has access to the resources they need to lead a stable, productive life.

Introduction to Cities of Hope

An industrial town isn't just a cluster of factories near residential areas. It's a well-planned community where industrial parks coexist with residential, recreational, and commercial spaces. The idea is to integrate everything a person might need within a functioning town. The goal of offering job opportunities, skill development programs, and community services within the same geographical area is to create an ecosystem that promotes well-being and economic independence.

Historical Context and Modern Need

The concept isn't entirely new. Historically, company towns were established during the Industrial Revolution to house workers near factories or mines. These towns provided basic amenities but were often criticized for their poor living conditions and exploitative labor practices. **I am proposing a modernized, humane, and economically viable model that reflects contemporary labor laws, environmental considerations, and community-centric planning.**

In today's context, and in my humble opinion, there is a need for my proposed industrial town solution. With the rise in homelessness and the scarcity of affordable housing, it's become clear that we need additional perspectives in approaching this matter. A strategic approach that provides housing and focuses on creating employment opportunities and community well-being can offer a sustainable solution. Moreover, this model can offset some social costs associated with homelessness, such as healthcare and law enforcement expenses.

We can harness collective economic benefits by integrating various industries like manufacturing, call centers, green energy production, recycling, and other basic sectors within the benefits. Employment opportunities will cater to the low-skilled workforce and open avenues for skilled labor, attracting a more diverse population. The economic upliftment of such towns can have multiplier effects, leading to the region's overall prosperity.

The industrial town concept is not merely about constructing living spaces near workplaces. It aims to create thriving communities where residents are empowered through job opportunities, access to essential services, and a sense of dignity and purpose. As we delve deeper into the specifics in the subsequent chapters, it will become evident that this approach is feasible and imperative for addressing modern-day social issues.

The primary catalyst for the rise in homelessness was the deindustrialization of the United States. Reversing this process through innovative concepts may offer the ultimate solution to ending this chronic issue.

Introduction to Cities of Hope

Cities of Hope is a novel solution aiming to merge social responsibility with economic potential. At their core, these towns are designed to provide safe, stable, and affordable living conditions while simultaneously fostering a robust local economy through various industries. This concept hinges on the synergy between housing, employment, and community services — creating an environment where residents can personally and professionally thrive.

The genesis of Cities of Hope lies in the need to address homelessness and unemployment, two pervasive issues with significant socioeconomic ramifications. Cities of Hope can offer a self-sustaining model that reduces the dependency on external welfare programs by integrating housing and employment within a single, well-structured locale.

Typically, the design of an industrial town includes dedicated zones for residential areas, industrial parks, communal services, and green spaces. The industrial parks serve as the economic backbone, generating job opportunities right within the community. This ensures that residents have easy access to employment, significantly reducing commuting times and related expenses.

A key feature of Cities of Hope is their adaptability and scalability. They can be tailored to various geographic and demographic needs, making them viable in both urban and rural settings. Additionally, these towns aim to incorporate sustainable practices, such as green energy production and waste management, making them environmentally friendly.

Moreover, Cities of Hope are not just about economic development but also about building a cohesive community. Access to healthcare, education, and recreational facilities creates a supportive environment where residents can lead balanced and fulfilling lives. This holistic approach is essential to breaking the cycles of poverty and homelessness, ultimately fostering a stronger, more resilient society.

The vision for Cities of Hope extends beyond mere housing and employment; it's about creating ecosystems that nurture human potential. In this sense, they represent a transformative approach to urban planning and social welfare, offering a blueprint for future development projects to eradicate homelessness and generate economic growth.

Historical Context and Modern Need

The concept of Industrial Towns is not new; its roots can be traced back to the early days of the Industrial Revolution. During the 18th and 19th centuries, Industrial Towns emerged as manufacturing and trade hubs, fundamentally transforming the social and economic landscape. Towns like Manchester in the United Kingdom and Lowell in the United States became synonymous with industrial growth. These towns were meticulously planned to house workers near factories, reducing commuting time and increasing productivity. This model showcased an early understanding of integrated community planning, emphasizing a close relationship between living spaces and employment opportunities.

Fast forward to the contemporary era, the need for a similar model is glaringly evident, given the multifaceted crises we face today. One of the most pressing issues in the United States is homelessness. Traditional solutions have often fallen short due to a lack of sustainable employment opportunities and affordable housing. In this context, revisiting and modernizing the industrial town concept offers a viable solution to these interconnected problems.

Modern industrial towns could serve as multi-functional spaces designed to address economic, social, and environmental needs. By fostering industries such as green energy production, Call Centers, recycling, and manufacturing, these towns can provide sustainable job opportunities for displaced and homeless individuals. Additionally, they can be designed to offer affordable housing, healthcare, education, and other essential services, thus creating a self-sustaining ecosystem.

The vision is straightforward yet transformative: integrate housing and employment in a manner that leverages modern technological advancements, regulatory frameworks, and community-driven governance.

> **This approach doesn't just aim to eradicate homelessness but also seeks to create profitable towns that contribute positively to the broader economy. Doing so can turn a persistent societal issue into an opportunity for economic revitalization and community building. Adopting industrial towns revived and tailored for the 21st century can thus be a linchpin in transforming both lives and landscapes in the United States.**

Understanding the historical success of Industrial Towns and adapting these lessons to address modern-day challenges is crucial. It involves a seamless blend of historical insights and innovative practices, making the industrial town concept a nostalgic reflection and a practical blueprint for the future. By mobilizing government action, private investment, and public enthusiasm, the transition from idea to reality becomes feasible and imperative.

The Vision for Cities of Hope

The concept of Cities of Hope involves creating self-sustained communities with a primary focus on industrial activities. This chapter will explore what this vision entails and how it can transform the socio-economic landscape, particularly for the homeless population.

Design and Layout of the Towns

The design of an industrial town is central to its success. At its core, the town should be organized into zones that serve different purposes but work collectively to create a thriving community.

Residential Zones: These areas would be dedicated to housing, featuring affordable and diverse housing models to accommodate different family sizes and individual needs. Proximity to industrial areas would minimize commute times, making day-to-day life more convenient.

Industrial Parks: Large areas would be designated for industrial activities. This should include manufacturing plants, textile mills, call centers, recycling centers, and other basic industries. The design would need to consider environmental regulations and ensure that industrial activities do not negatively impact residential zones.

Amenities and Community Services: To build a holistic community, the town would also include healthcare facilities, educational institutions, and recreational centers. These services are crucial for maintaining the well-being and morale of the residents.

Green Spaces: Parks and open areas would contribute to the quality of life and provide residents with spaces for relaxation and recreation, promoting mental and physical health.

The Role of Industrial Parks

Industrial parks are the backbone of these towns. They serve multiple purposes, from providing employment opportunities to driving economic growth. Here's how:

- **Job Creation:** By concentrating various industries in one area, the town can offer numerous job opportunities, ranging from skilled labor to entry-level positions. This variety ensures that residents can find suitable employment irrespective of their skill levels or previous work experience.

- **Training and Development:** Industrial parks can collaborate with local trade schools and community colleges to offer on-site training and skilling programs. This will not only benefit the industries by supplying a skilled workforce but also improve the employability of the residents.

- **Economic Synergy:** When multiple industries operate in close proximity, it can lead to economic synergies. For instance, waste materials from one industry could serve as raw materials for another, thereby minimizing waste and reducing costs.

- **Environmental Considerations:** Modern industrial parks would incorporate green technologies and sustainable practices to reduce their environmental footprint. This includes using renewable energy sources, waste recycling, and efficient water management systems.

Overall, the vision for Cities of Hope is to create a self-sustaining model where economic activities are seamlessly integrated with community living. By doing so, we can address the pressing issues of homelessness and unemployment while fostering an environment that promotes growth, sustainability, and well-being.

Design and Layout of the Towns

The design and layout of the proposed Cities of Hope are central to their success and functionality. These towns are envisioned as vibrant, self-sustaining communities that seamlessly integrate residential, industrial, and commercial spaces. The ultimate goal is to create environments where individuals work, live, and thrive.

First and foremost, the spatial arrangement of these towns prioritizes accessibility and convenience. Residential areas are strategically located within reasonable proximity to industrial and commercial zones to minimize commute times and enhance the overall quality of life. The placement of essential services, such as healthcare facilities, educational institutions, and recreational centers, is also carefully considered to ensure that all residents' needs are met within a short distance.

Street design plays a vital role in the layout of these towns. Streets are laid out in a grid pattern to improve navigation and optimize space usage. This design facilitates easier movement for vehicles and pedestrians and creates a logical flow throughout the town. The integration of green spaces and pedestrian pathways not only promotes physical activity but also contributes to a sense of community and well-being.

Planning the town's industrial zones requires special attention to both efficiency and environmental impact. Industrial parks are situated at the periphery to reduce potential noise or pollution-related issues while being conveniently accessible. These parks are designed with modular layouts that allow for flexible use and expansion, accommodating the changing needs of industries over time.

Central to the town's design is the incorporation of sustainable practices. Utilizing green building techniques and renewable energy sources, such as solar and wind power, significantly reduces the carbon footprint. Waste management systems are also integrated into the town's infrastructure to ensure recycling and proper disposal, showcasing the commitment to environmental stewardship.

To foster a sense of community and social cohesion, public spaces like parks, retail boulevards, plazas, and community centers are scattered throughout the town. These areas serve as hubs for social interaction, cultural activities, and community events, reinforcing the town's sense of identity and belonging.

The layout also includes robust infrastructure for both digital and physical connectivity. High-speed internet and smart technologies are embedded into the fabric of the town, enabling continuous improvement and efficient management. Public transportation systems, including buses and bicycle-sharing programs, are planned to ensure that all parts of the town are well-connected, reducing dependence on personal vehicles.

By carefully considering the various elements that make up the design and layout of these Cities of Hope, we can create spaces that are functional and foster community and sustainability. Thoughtful planning ensures that these towns can address the homeless issue effectively while offering a profitable, sustainable solution that benefits all stakeholders.

The role of industrial parks

Industrial parks are critical to realizing the vision for Cities of Hope. Their primary function is to provide a designated area where businesses, especially those in manufacturing and related industries, can cluster together. This clustering effect enhances operational efficiency and drives innovation through collaboration and shared resources.

We can address several socio-economic issues by strategically placing industrial parks within the Cities of Hope. These parks serve as hubs of economic activity, creating a concentration of job opportunities that are accessible to residents. This proximity to employment helps alleviate transportation barriers, making it easier for individuals, particularly those facing economic hardships, to secure stable employment.

Furthermore, industrial parks contribute significantly to the local economy. The businesses operating within these parks generate revenue, which flows back into the community through local spending. This economic stimulus helps fund public services, enhancing town residents' overall quality of life.

From a business perspective, industrial parks offer a wealth of advantages. Companies benefit from shared infrastructure, including roads, utilities, and communication networks, which reduces individual overhead costs. Additionally, the close proximity to other businesses fosters a competitive yet collaborative environment, driving industrial efficiency and innovation.

These industrial parks could be exempt from all taxation and structured as partnerships between the towns and the businesses that will co-own and operate them. This partnership would provide cities with sustainable revenue streams to finance communal services, while businesses would benefit from lower costs and competitive provision of goods and services. This arrangement would ensure profitability for both the towns and the American companies involved in co-owning and running these enterprises.

In essence, these towns can be structured as 'Tax Exempt Designated Economic Zones '.

Moreover, the concentrated presence of businesses in industrial parks can attract further investment. As these parks become established, they draw in suppliers, service providers, and additional companies looking to capitalize on the synergistic benefits. **This ripple effect can lead to the town's business ecosystem's organic growth, creating a self-sustaining economic development cycle.**

It's also worth noting that industrial parks can play a pivotal role in advancing sustainable practices. Towns can minimize their environmental footprint by implementing green technologies and promoting eco-friendly industrial processes within the parks. This helps meet regulatory requirements and positions the town as a forward-thinking, responsible community that values economic and environmental health.

In closing, the role of industrial parks in Cities of Hope cannot be overstated. They are engines of economic growth, centers of innovation, and crucial components in the effort to create sustainable, self-reliant communities. Their successful development and management are essential steps toward achieving the broader vision of Cities of Hope, both economically viable and socially inclusive.

Basic Industries for Employment

One key component to making Cities of Hope a viable solution for tackling homelessness and creating economically sustainable communities is clearly identifying and leveraging basic industries for employment. By focusing on fundamental sectors such as manufacturing, agriculture, Call Centers, textile production, basic industries, recycling and waste management, and green energy production, these towns can offer numerous job opportunities for residents. This chapter outlines how each of these sectors can be developed and integrated within the framework of Cities of Hope, presenting practical pathways for employment and economic stability.

Manufacturing

Manufacturing has long been the backbone of economic development, offering a wide array of jobs requiring various skill levels. Establishing manufacturing plants within the Cities of Hope can employ many people, from assembly line workers to skilled technicians and engineers. These facilities can range from producing consumer goods to essential industrial components.

To ensure sustainability and local acceptance, manufacturing initiatives should prioritize eco-friendly practices and local community needs. Partnerships with existing companies can also facilitate technology transfer and provide training programs, preparing residents to take on these roles efficiently. Furthermore, Manufacturing could be particularly impactful as it can offer stable, well-paying jobs that significantly improve residents' quality of life.

Agriculture

Agriculture provides another foundational industry that can be seamlessly integrated into Cities of Hope. By dedicating land for farming and related activities, we can generate employment opportunities in various capacities—from fieldworkers to agronomists and technicians specializing in modern farming techniques.

Urban agriculture, vertical farming, and greenhouse management are innovative approaches that can maximize productivity in limited spaces. These methods ensure food security for the town and create avenues for export, generating additional revenue streams. Training programs can help residents acquire the necessary skills, turning agriculture into a sustainable employment sector.

Textile Production

Historically, textile production has been one of the leading industries in providing mass employment. Setting up textile mills and garment factories in Cities of Hope can tap into this potential. Jobs in textile production range from manual labor such as sewing and weaving to more specialized roles like machine maintenance and quality control.

A focus on ethical practices, fair wages, and safe working conditions will be crucial in making textile production a respectable and sought-after employment avenue. Collaborating with fashion brands and local designers can also open up new opportunities, adding diversity to the types of jobs available.

Recycling and Waste Management

In today's world, sustainable waste management is both necessary and an opportunity. Establishing robust recycling and waste management systems can create numerous jobs while addressing environmental challenges. Tasks can range from collection and sorting to more technical roles in material processing and quality assurance.

By incorporating advanced technologies like automated sorting systems and waste-to-energy plants, these Cities of Hope can manage their waste efficiently and use it as a resource for generating energy and other products. **These towns can also function as recycling centers for other cities, creating additional revenue streams**. Education and training programs in waste recycling management can further enhance the employability of residents, preparing them for these vital roles.

Green Energy Production

Green energy production stands out as a futuristic and essential industry for employment. Setting up solar farms, wind turbines, and biomass plants can supply sustainable energy to the town while creating various job roles—from field technicians and engineers to administrative and maintenance staff.

Advancing into this sector offers dual benefits: it contributes to national and global sustainability goals while providing residents with well-paying and future-proof jobs. Programs focusing on renewable energy education can help residents gain the necessary skills, ensuring that the town remains at the forefront of green innovations.

By strategically developing these basic industries, Cities of Hope can provide employment to their residents and improve economic resilience and sustainability. These efforts contribute to creating vibrant, self-sufficient communities that address homelessness while generating economic opportunities for all.

Call Centers

Call Centers are an ideal industry for Cities of Hope focused on addressing homelessness, as they require relatively low startup costs, minimal infrastructure, and can be implemented quickly. **These centers provide immediate employment opportunities with short training periods, making them accessible to individuals with varying skill levels.** Call Centers can employ a diverse workforce by offering customer service representatives and technical support roles while delivering essential services to businesses nationwide. The rapid setup and ease of operation make Call Centers a practical and effective solution for creating jobs and economic stability in these towns.

Food Processing

Food processing is a critical industry within Cities of Hope, converting agricultural products into packaged goods like canned fruits, frozen vegetables, and dairy items. This sector creates a wide range of employment opportunities, from manual labor in sorting and packaging to technical roles in quality control and food safety. By adding value to raw agricultural materials, the food processing industry supports the local economy, enhances food security, and generates additional revenue streams through the sale of finished products.

Manufacturing of Animal Food

The cat and dog food manufacturing is a strategic addition to the industrial town's economy, tapping into the growing demand for high-quality pet food. This industry creates jobs across the production spectrum, from sourcing ingredients to packaging finished goods. Utilizing local agricultural products as ingredients supports the town's farming sector, while innovation in product formulations, such as organic and grain-free options, caters to market trends. This industry provides stable employment and positions the town as a key player in the lucrative pet food market.

Catering Services

Catering services within Cities of Hope offer a dynamic business opportunity, providing meals to businesses, federal offices, schools, and other institutions in neighboring areas. This sector creates diverse job roles, from chefs and kitchen staff to delivery drivers and administrators. The catering service ensures high-quality, sustainable meal options by leveraging local food processing capabilities. The service can operate on a flexible basis, catering to various clients and events, thereby supporting local economies and fostering community ties.

Free Lunch Program

The Free Lunch Program is a social initiative that provides nutritious meals to schoolchildren in adjacent towns and cities. Managed by the town's catering services, this program addresses child hunger and promotes healthy eating. The program is financed through a combination of the town's revenue, government support, NGO contributions, and corporate sponsorships. By ensuring that every child has access to daily meals, the program not only enhances student well-being but also strengthens community support and involvement.

Manufacturing

Manufacturing forms a cornerstone of economic activity in the Cities of Hope. Historically, manufacturing has driven job creation and economic growth, making it a vital industry in our effort to build sustainable, productive towns. This sector will offer a wide range of employment opportunities and contribute to the larger goal of eradicating homelessness by integrating individuals into a stable work environment.

One of the main advantages of focusing on manufacturing is its ability to provide jobs for a variety of skill levels. From entry-level positions to highly specialized roles, manufacturing can accommodate a broad workforce demographic. This inclusivity is crucial when considering the diverse backgrounds of individuals experiencing homelessness. By offering training and skill development opportunities, we can ensure that residents are equipped to take on these roles and advance within the industry.

Suppose specific jobs require specialized skills that are not present in the homeless population. In that case, other Americans and immigrants (through the novel visa program that will be explained in the following chapters) can fill these positions. This approach addresses the skill gap, creates additional employment opportunities, and stimulates economic growth. Integrating these specialized workers will contribute to job creation and provide an economic boost, benefiting the local community and the broader economy.

In addition to job creation, the presence of manufacturing facilities can also stimulate subsidiary industries and services. Suppliers, logistic firms, and maintenance services are all integral to a functioning manufacturing hub. This creates a ripple effect, boosting economic activity and generating further employment opportunities within the town.

Moreover, manufacturing can be aligned with environmentally sustainable practices. By incorporating green technologies and waste-reduction initiatives, we protect the environment and reduce operational costs in the long run. Eco-friendly manufacturing can serve as a model for other industries within the town, fostering a culture of sustainability.

It's important to note that successful manufacturing operations depend on robust infrastructure. Adequate transportation systems, utility networks, and digital infrastructure must be in place to ensure efficient operations. Coordination between local governments, private companies, and community stakeholders will be essential to address these needs effectively.

In conclusion, manufacturing is more than just an industry; it is a catalyst for comprehensive community development. As we move forward with the industrial town concept, focusing on manufacturing will help provide employment, stimulate local economies, and contribute to the broader vision of building resilient, self-sufficient communities that can thrive for generations.

Basic Industries for Employment: Agriculture

Agriculture is not merely a traditional cornerstone of American industry but also a vital component in our proposed Cities of Hope framework. It has the potential to provide immediate employment opportunities while addressing food security and sustainability needs. Given its versatility, agriculture offers a broad range of job roles, from manual labor to advanced scientific research, making it accessible to a diverse workforce.

Modern agricultural practices are deeply intertwined with technological advancements. Precision farming, biotechnology, and sustainable practices can be integrated into our town's agricultural sectors, thereby enhancing productivity and reducing environmental impact. By adopting these methods, we can cultivate a workforce skilled in both traditional and innovative farming techniques.

One specific approach to agricultural integration is the development of urban farming initiatives and vertical farming structures within the town. This can significantly reduce the dependency on external food supplies and serve as a model for self-sufficiency. Urban farming also has the added benefit of utilizing otherwise underutilized spaces, thus maximizing land use efficiency. Participation in community-based urban farms can instill a sense of ownership and responsibility among residents, creating a cooperative community spirit.

Moreover, agriculture can serve as a conduit for education and training programs. Partnerships with local schools, colleges, and universities can facilitate agricultural research and offer new opportunities for student involvement through internships and co-op programs. Offering training programs that focus on sustainable practices and organic farming can prepare residents for future trends in the agricultural industry.

Economic incentives can further bolster the agricultural sector. Grants, subsidies, and low-interest loans can support startups and existing businesses, encouraging innovation and expansion. Residents can also be encouraged to participate in co-operatives, where profits are shared among members, ensuring economic stability and viability.

In conclusion, agriculture stands as a multifaceted industry capable of providing numerous benefits, from employment generation to food security and environmental sustainability. By incorporating advanced farming techniques and promoting educational partnerships, our proposed Cities of Hope can turn agriculture into a thriving, sustainable industry that enriches the community and boosts economic resilience.

Textile Production

Textile production is one of the critical pillars of the strategy to develop cities of hope. This sector has historical significance and holds modern-day relevance in terms of job creation and economic stimulation. The intent behind incorporating textile production into these towns is multi-faceted: to provide stable employment opportunities, support ancillary industries, and contribute to the community's overall economic health.

The textile industry encompasses a broad range of activities, from spinning and weaving to dyeing and finishing. Each stage offers varied employment opportunities, catering to different skill sets and educational backgrounds. For instance, spinning and weaving are labor-intensive processes that can absorb a large workforce, including unskilled and semi-skilled labor. On the other hand, the dyeing and finishing stages often require more specialized skills, thus opening doors for vocational training and advanced job positions.

Moreover, the textile sector has the potential to invigorate other local industries. The demand for raw materials like cotton and wool can stimulate the agricultural sector, creating a symbiotic relationship between the two. Additionally, the need for machinery and equipment can boost the local manufacturing and metalworking industries. <u>In essence, textile production acts as a catalyst for a broader industrial ecosystem.</u>

Government and community involvement are essential to ensure the success of textile production in Cities of Hope. Public-private partnerships can incorporate sustainable practices. These collaborations can also foster innovation, making the industry more resilient and competitive on a global scale.

On the sustainability front, adopting eco-friendly practices within the textile industry is a moral obligation and an economic opportunity. Green technologies in production processes can reduce waste and lower operational costs. From water-saving dye processes to using recycled fibers, sustainable practices can make textile production more attractive to environmentally conscious consumers and investors.

The economic benefits are clear, but what about the social impact? Textile production can significantly contribute to community building by providing reliable income and a sense of purpose to many. Moreover, job training programs tailored to the textile industry can offer pathways for upward mobility, enabling workers to increase their skills and improve their livelihoods over time.

In conclusion, textile production integrates seamlessly into the vision for Cities of Hope. It offers diverse job opportunities, supports other local industries, and can be a model for sustainable and ethical business practices. Therefore, its inclusion is an economic strategy and a comprehensive plan to build more resilient and vibrant communities.

Recycling and Waste Management

Recycling and waste management are critical components in the framework of creating sustainable Cities of Hope. These practices contribute to environmental sustainability and significantly generate employment, thereby addressing the homeless crisis through job creation and economic opportunities.

Integrating recycling and waste management into Cities of Hope ensures that waste is handled efficiently, reducing the environmental footprint and fostering a cleaner, healthier living environment. Advanced waste management systems can be established to achieve comprehensive waste reduction, reuse, and recycling measures.

One of the practical strategies involves setting up recycling centers within these towns. These centers can process various materials such as plastics, metals, paper, and organic waste. These centers can create a circular economy by converting waste into valuable resources, reducing the need for raw materials, and lowering overall production costs. Moreover, these facilities can offer a range of job opportunities for residents, from manual labor to technical positions in managing and operating recycling technologies.

Waste management systems can also incorporate cutting-edge technologies such as automated sorting machines, waste-to-energy plants, and composting units. These technologies make waste processing more efficient and open up skilled job positions for technicians and engineers. For instance, waste-to-energy plants can convert organic waste into electricity, contributing to the town's energy needs while providing specialized employment in operating and maintaining the plant.

Educational programs aimed at teaching residents about the importance of recycling and proper waste disposal can foster a culture of responsibility and environmental stewardship. Partnerships with schools, community organizations, and non-profits can amplify these efforts, ensuring that waste management becomes a community-driven initiative.

Furthermore, the towns can explore public-private partnerships to co-fund and manage recycling and waste management systems. Collaboration with private companies can bring investment and expertise, ensuring that these systems are financially viable and technologically advanced.

In conclusion, embedding robust recycling and waste management systems in Cities of Hope addresses environmental concerns and creates many job opportunities. This multifaceted approach underscores the feasibility and sustainability of the industrial town concept, aligning with the broader goal of eradicating homelessness and developing profitable, viable communities.

Green Energy Production

Green energy production is a cornerstone for both Cities of Hope's sustainability and economic viability. It's not just a buzzword; it's a practical pathway that can drive job creation, reduce environmental impact, and cut energy costs significantly. Green energy isn't merely an add-on for a concept aiming to eradicate homelessness and build profitable towns; it's integral to the overall strategy.

First, green energy production can provide a multitude of employment opportunities in various sectors, from solar panel manufacturing to wind turbine maintenance. These aren't just temporary jobs but roles that require training and offer long-term career prospects. In doing so, we can tap into unemployed or underemployed sections of the population, offering them a chance to learn new skills and stabilize their lives.

Moreover, the transition to green energy presents a lucrative business case. Cities of Hope adopting renewable energy sources can massively cut down on energy expenses in the long run. Solar farms, wind turbines, and even bioenergy solutions can offset the initial capital investment through substantial savings on utility bills. This reduction in operational costs can, in turn, attract more industries, creating a virtuous circle of economic growth and sustainability.

The environmental benefits are equally significant. Reduced dependency on fossil fuels lowers greenhouse gas emissions, helping these towns become models of eco-friendly living. This isn't just about attracting green-conscious industries or residents; it's about ensuring a healthier environment for everyone in the community. Cleaner air, less pollution, and a conscientious approach to resource management contribute to the overall well-being of the inhabitants.

Implementing green energy solutions also aligns seamlessly with Cities of Hope's broader goals. For instance, these towns can utilize advanced technologies like smart grids to manage their energy needs efficiently. Integration with other sectors, such as recycling and waste management, can further enhance sustainability. Organic waste could be converted into bioenergy, thus creating a closed-loop system that minimizes waste and maximizes resource utilization.

Collaboration and funding are crucial in making green energy production a reality. Government grants, subsidies, and public-private partnerships can lower the financial barriers for initial setup. **The overall financing model will be explained in the following chapters and will not require any of these aids; however, as these towns have the potential to grow, additional businesses might benefit from these funding programs.** Moreover, policies encouraging renewable energy use could spur greater investment from both private and public sectors. A concerted effort involving multiple stakeholders is key to overcoming the often-prohibitive initial costs and ensuring long-term feasibility.

Let's not forget public acceptance and involvement. Educating the community about the benefits of green energy can foster a culture of sustainability. Residents can also partake in small-scale initiatives like rooftop solar panels or community gardens that produce bioenergy. These community-driven projects supplement larger-scale industrial efforts and democratize the benefits, creating a sense of ownership and shared responsibility among residents.

In summary, green energy production isn't just feasible—it's a strategic imperative for the success of Cities of Hope. **Focusing on renewable energy addresses the town's goals: job creation, financial viability, environmental sustainability, and community well-being.** It's high time to harness the full potential of green energy, transforming it from a lofty ideal into a tangible reality that can redefine how we live, work, and build our future.

Call Centers

Introduction to Call Centers in Cities of Hope

Call Centers present a highly viable and practical industry for Cities of Hope dedicated to addressing homelessness. Their ease of implementation, low infrastructure requirements, and relatively short training periods make them an excellent fit for communities that need to create jobs and stabilize their local economy quickly. By establishing Call Centers, Cities of Hope can provide immediate employment opportunities for residents, particularly those transitioning from homelessness, while meeting the growing demand for customer service, technical support, and telemarketing services nationwide.

Ease of Implementation and Rapid Deployment

One of the primary advantages of Call Centers is their relatively simple setup process. Unlike industries that require extensive physical infrastructure or specialized facilities, Call Centers can operate in modest office spaces equipped with basic telecommunications technology. This low barrier to entry means that Cities of Hope can establish these centers quickly, providing almost immediate job opportunities for residents.

Additionally, Call Centers typically require minimal capital investment compared to other industries. Basic equipment such as computers, headsets, and internet connectivity is sufficient to get a center up and running. This cost-effectiveness makes call centers particularly attractive to towns looking to maximize the impact of limited resources.

Short Training Periods and Workforce Accessibility

Another key benefit of Call Centers is the short training periods required for most roles. Customer service positions, for example, often involve basic communication skills and familiarity with company protocols, both of which can be taught in a matter of weeks. This quick turnaround allows residents to start earning income sooner, which is crucial for individuals transitioning out of homelessness.

The relatively low skill threshold for entry-level positions also makes Call Centers accessible to a broad range of individuals, including those who may not have extensive work experience or advanced education. For many, these jobs serve as an entry point into the workforce, providing essential job experience and company advancement opportunities.

Furthermore, training programs can be tailored to the specific needs of the Call Center, focusing on the particular industries or services they support. This targeted training ensures that employees are well-prepared to deliver high-quality service, which enhances the center's reputation and attracts more business.

Operational Efficiency and Scalability

Call Centers are not only easy to establish but also highly scalable. As the town's workforce grows and gains experience, these centers can expand their operations to take on more clients and offer a wider range of services. This scalability allows the industry to grow in tandem with the town, creating a dynamic and adaptable economic environment.

Advanced telecommunications and data management technologies further enhance operational efficiency. By integrating systems like customer relationship management (CRM) software and automated call distribution (ACD), Call Centers can handle large volumes of calls with minimal delay, ensuring high levels of customer satisfaction. These technologies also enable remote work options, which can be particularly beneficial in expanding the workforce without requiring additional physical space.

Economic and Community Impact

The establishment of Call Centers within Cities of Hope provides immediate economic benefits. As residents gain stable employment, their increased income contributes to the local economy, supporting other businesses and services in the community. This economic activity helps to create a self-sustaining environment where the success of one industry feeds into the growth of others.

Moreover, the relatively low environmental impact of Call Centers makes them a sustainable option for job creation. Unlike manufacturing or agriculture, which require significant physical resources, Call Centers primarily rely on human capital and technology, aligning with the town's broader sustainability and environmental stewardship goals.

Strategic Partnerships and Client Acquisition

To ensure the long-term success of Call Centers, it is essential to establish strategic partnerships with businesses across various sectors. These partnerships can provide steady contracts, ensuring consistent work and income for the town's residents. Marketing efforts should focus on the cost-effectiveness and reliability of the town's Call Centers, highlighting their ability to deliver high-quality service with a dedicated workforce.

Call centers can develop niche expertise that sets them apart from competitors by specializing in particular industries—such as healthcare, finance, or technology. This specialization attracts higher-value contracts and fosters long-term relationships with clients, providing economic stability and growth for the town.

Conclusion

Call centers are a highly practical and effective industry for Cities of Hope that aims to combat homelessness. Their ease of implementation, short training periods, and scalability make them an ideal choice for creating jobs and fostering economic stability quickly. By leveraging modern technology and building strategic partnerships, these centers can deliver essential services to businesses while providing stable employment for residents, ultimately contributing to the broader goal of creating self-sustaining, vibrant communities.

Food Processing Industry

Introduction to Food Processing in Cities of Hope

Food processing is a critical industry that fits seamlessly into the broader economic and social strategy of the Cities of Hope proposed in your book. As a cornerstone of these towns, food processing offers multiple benefits: it creates a wide array of jobs, adds value to agricultural products, and strengthens food security within the community and beyond. By integrating food processing facilities into the industrial town model, we can create a self-sustaining ecosystem that supports the local economy and enhances the quality of life for residents.

Economic and Employment Opportunities

Food processing facilities can be established to process a variety of agricultural products produced within the industrial town's agricultural zones. This could include fruits, vegetables, grains, and dairy products. Processing these raw materials into packaged goods such as canned fruits, frozen vegetables, bread, dairy products, and snacks adds value and creates a robust supply chain within the town.

The industry can employ residents in diverse roles, ranging from manual labor in sorting and packaging to more technical positions in quality control, machinery maintenance, and food safety management. Training programs can be developed in partnership with local educational institutions to ensure a steady stream of skilled workers. Furthermore, by focusing on modern and efficient processing techniques, the industry can remain competitive, meeting both domestic and international market demands.

Sustainability and Local Economy

Food processing also promotes sustainability by reducing waste and maximizing the use of agricultural products. For example, by-products from one process can be utilized in another, such as using peels and seeds in animal feed or bioenergy production. Additionally, local sourcing of raw materials minimizes transportation costs and carbon emissions, further enhancing the town's commitment to green practices.

The presence of a food processing industry can attract ancillary businesses such as packaging suppliers, logistics companies, and distribution networks, creating a ripple effect that boosts the local economy. Moreover, processed food products can be marketed under a local brand, generating additional revenue and enhancing the town's identity. The mission of these Cities of Hope will incentivize buyers to prefer these food products as everyone wants to support eradicating the homelessness issue.

Strategic Partnerships and Market Reach

Strategic partnerships with local farmers, cooperatives, and other stakeholders are essential to ensure the food processing industry's success. These partnerships can help secure a steady supply of raw materials and ensure that the products meet quality standards. Additionally, marketing strategies can be developed to reach wider markets, including neighboring towns, cities, and even international markets.

In summary, the food processing industry within these Cities of Hope offers a robust solution to local economic development while promoting sustainability and food security. It creates jobs, adds value to agricultural products, and establishes the town as a vital player in the regional economy.

Manufacturing of Animal Food (Cat and Dog Food)

Introduction to Animal Food Manufacturing

Manufacturing animal food, specifically cat and dog food, is another viable and strategic business line for Cities of Hope. This industry complements the agricultural and food processing sectors and taps into a lucrative and growing market. With the increasing number of pet owners across the United States and the rising demand for high-quality pet food, establishing a pet food manufacturing facility within these towns presents significant economic opportunities.

Market Potential and Economic Impact

The pet food industry in the U.S. is a multi-billion-dollar market, with consumers increasingly seeking premium, nutritious, and sustainable options for their pets. By focusing on the production of both dry and wet cat and dog food, as well as specialized treats, these towns can capture a share of this booming market. The facility could produce a range of products, from budget-friendly options to high-end, organic, and grain-free formulas.

The manufacturing process involves sourcing high-quality ingredients, including meats, grains, vegetables, and vitamins. These ingredients can be sourced locally, from the town's agricultural zones, or through partnerships with regional suppliers. This ensures freshness and quality and supports the local agricultural economy.

Employment and Skill Development

Animal food manufacturing offers numerous employment opportunities across various levels of expertise. Roles range from entry-level positions in production and packaging to more specialized roles in product development, quality assurance, and supply chain management. Industry also provides opportunities for research and development, particularly in creating new formulations that cater to specific dietary needs or market trends.

Training programs can be developed to equip residents with the necessary skills to work in this industry, including food safety, machinery operation, and quality control. This ensures that the workforce is well-prepared to maintain high standards of production, which is crucial for building a reputable brand in the competitive pet food market.

Sustainability and Innovation

Sustainability can be a key differentiator for the pet food products manufactured in these towns. By focusing on environmentally friendly practices, such as sourcing organic ingredients, using recyclable packaging, and minimizing waste, the town can appeal to the growing segment of eco-conscious consumers. Innovation in product formulations, such as plant-based proteins or grain-free recipes, can further enhance the town's competitive edge.

Moreover, the waste products from the food processing industry can be repurposed as ingredients for animal food, thereby reducing waste and creating a closed-loop system that benefits both industries.

Strategic Partnerships and Distribution

The pet food manufacturing facility can establish partnerships with major retailers, online platforms, and pet specialty stores to maximize market reach. Branding the products under a unique, locally inspired label can also create a distinct market presence. Furthermore, collaborations with veterinarians and animal nutritionists can help develop products that meet specific health needs, adding credibility and value to the product line.

In conclusion, manufacturing cat and dog food within these Cities of Hope offers a profitable business opportunity that complements existing industries. It creates jobs, supports local agriculture, and taps into a growing market, all while maintaining a focus on sustainability and innovation.

Catering Services for Adjacent Towns, Cities, and Businesses

Introduction to Catering Services

Establishing a catering service industry within Cities of Hope represents a strategic initiative that generates revenue, fosters community engagement, and supports local economies. Catering services can be developed to serve a wide range of clients, including businesses, federal offices, schools, and other institutions in adjacent towns and cities. This industry leverages the town's food processing capabilities and workforce, providing high-quality, affordable meals while creating employment opportunities for residents.

Economic and Employment Impact

Catering services offer diverse job opportunities, from chefs and kitchen staff to delivery drivers and administrative personnel. By employing residents in these roles, the industry helps reduce unemployment and provides valuable skills training. The catering service can operate on a large scale, providing meals for corporate events, government offices, schools, hospitals, and community gatherings in neighboring towns and cities.

The catering business can also operate on a flexible basis, offering daily meal services, event-specific catering, and customized menu planning. This flexibility allows the service to cater to a variety of clients, from small businesses to large institutions, ensuring a steady stream of revenue.

Sustainability and Local Sourcing

The catering service's key focus can be sustainability and the use of locally sourced ingredients. The catering service can ensure freshness, quality, and traceability by utilizing products from the town's agricultural and food processing sectors. This supports local farmers and producers and reduces the carbon footprint associated with transporting ingredients from distant locations.

Menus can be designed to highlight seasonal produce, promote healthy eating, and accommodate dietary restrictions, thereby appealing to a broad clientele. Additionally, the catering service can adopt eco-friendly practices, such as using biodegradable packaging and minimizing food waste through careful planning and portion control.

Strategic Partnerships and Market Reach

The catering service can establish partnerships with local businesses, government agencies, and non-profit organizations to expand its market reach. These partnerships can lead to long-term contracts for meal services, providing a stable revenue base. The catering service can also collaborate with local schools and hospitals to offer healthy meal options, further embedding itself into the community's daily life.

Marketing efforts can emphasize the service's commitment to quality, sustainability, and community support, differentiating it from competitors and building a loyal customer base. By branding the service as a community-driven initiative, the catering business can attract clients who value social responsibility and local economic development.

Operational Efficiency and Innovation

Catering services can leverage modern technology to enhance operational efficiency. Online ordering systems, meal planning software, and efficient logistics management can streamline operations, reduce costs, and improve customer satisfaction. Innovation in menu offerings, such as themed meals, gourmet options, and subscription-based meal plans, can further boost the service's appeal.

In summary, the catering service industry within these Cities of Hope offers a dynamic business opportunity that supports local economies, creates jobs, and strengthens community ties. It leverages the town's existing resources and industries, contributing to the community's overall sustainability and economic vitality.

Social Project: Free Lunch Program for School Kids

Introduction to the Free Lunch Program

The Free Lunch Program is a social initiative that builds on the catering services these Cities of Hope offer. This program aims to provide free, nutritious meals to schoolchildren in adjacent towns and cities, ensuring no child goes hungry during their school day. The program addresses child hunger, promotes healthy eating habits, and supports academic performance. By leveraging the catering facilities within the Cities of Hope, the Free Lunch Program can operate efficiently and sustainably.

Economic and Social Impact

Child hunger is a pressing issue that affects millions of children across the United States, impacting their ability to learn and thrive in school. The Free Lunch Program addresses this issue head-on by providing daily meals to children in need. This initiative not only improves the health and well-being of students but also alleviates the financial burden on low-income families who may struggle to provide consistent, nutritious meals.

The program can be financed through a combination of sources, including the industrial town's overall revenues, contributions from federal and state governments, support from non-governmental organizations (NGOs), and corporate sponsorships. This multi-source funding model ensures the program's sustainability and scalability, allowing it to reach more children over time.

Operational Structure

The Free Lunch Program would be managed by the catering services within the Cities of Hope,

> Progressive Thought:
>
> I am developing an innovative model with my associate, Clinton G. Bryan, a blockchain expert, that leverages blockchain technology to enhance the value for buyers of products and services from these businesses. This model will allow buyers to earn points, similar to credit card loyalty programs, which can be redeemed across various programs and enterprises. With nationwide support and incentivization, these Cities of Hope will be poised for success. The "Pay it Forward" initiative will offer buyers additional perks and benefits, allowing them to use earned points for discounts and other advantages. Supported by federal and state governments, this program could also provide tax benefits through tax credits, further encouraging participation and stimulating economic growth.

'

Job Creation and Workforce Development

Addressing the issue of homelessness is more than just providing a roof over someone's head. Sustainable change requires creating pathways to stable employment and equipping individuals with the necessary skills to get a job and thrive in it. Job creation and workforce development are critical components of the industrial town's concept, which is designed to offer lasting solutions to economic instability and joblessness.

Job Training Programs

A cornerstone of our approach involves comprehensive job training programs. These programs are tailored to meet the specific needs of the industries present within the Cities of Hope. Whether it's manufacturing, agriculture, or green energy production, training modules will be designed to equip participants with the necessary technical skills and knowledge.

The job training programs aim to be as inclusive and flexible as possible, using a combination of hands-on workshops, online courses, and mentorship opportunities. The goal is to accommodate all participants' diverse backgrounds and learning styles. Initial training phases will focus on basic skills, gradually moving to more specialized areas as participants progress.

Skilling and Reskilling

Today's labor market demands initial job skills and the ability to adapt and reskill as industries evolve. Our workforce development strategy includes ongoing educational opportunities for both skilling and reskilling. Keeping pace with technological advancements, further training programs will be provided to help workers transition from outdated techniques to modern practices.

Reskilling initiatives are particularly important for adapting to innovations in automation and new technologies that continuously reshape industries. For example, workers who start in basic manufacturing roles might later be trained for advanced positions involving automated systems and smart technology. This allows for a dynamic workforce that's ready to meet future demands.

Collaboration with Trade Schools and Community Colleges

Partnerships with local trade schools and community colleges will be fundamental to our workforce development efforts. These institutions offer both theoretical and practical knowledge that aligns well with the needs of Cities of Hope. Collaboration can occur in various forms, including co-designed curricula, dual-enrollment opportunities, and internships.

Such partnerships expand educational resources and provide a broader range of credentials and certifications. This ensures that participants receive industry-recognized qualifications that enhance their employability. Moreover, these educational institutions can act as feeder systems, continually supplying a stream of well-prepared workers.

Beyond technical skills, collaboration can help instill other essential skills such as communication, teamwork, and problem-solving. As a result, individuals are job-ready and fit comfortably into various roles within a community-driven industrial ecosystem.

- Integration of Apprenticeship Programs

- Funding for Continuing Education

- Career Counseling and Placement Services

In conclusion, the strategies outlined in this chapter lay the groundwork for an effective job creation and workforce development system within Cities of Hope. By focusing on comprehensive job training, constant reskilling, and strong partnerships with educational institutions, we aim to create a resilient, adaptable, and empowered workforce. This not only helps to eradicate the issue of homelessness but also fosters the growth of vibrant, self-sustaining communities.

Job Training Programs

Job training programs are pivotal in bridging the gap between homelessness and stable employment. These programs are essential for equipping individuals with the skills needed to thrive in the diverse industries that will form the backbone of our envisioned Cities of Hope. A well-structured job training framework enhances employability and garners sustainable employment outcomes, which are crucial for eradicating homelessness and fostering community growth.

Firstly, it's important to recognize potential residents' diverse educational levels and backgrounds. Customized training modules should be designed to accommodate varying skill levels, from basic literacy and numeracy to advanced technical skills. Programs should align closely with the required competencies of the sectors prevalent in the Cities of Hope, such as manufacturing, agriculture, textile production, recycling, and green energy production. This alignment ensures that training is immediately applicable and beneficial to local industries.

Effective job training programs should also focus on skilling and reskilling. For individuals who have been unemployed for an extended period, reskilling can provide the necessary education to transition into emerging industries. Workshops, vocational classes, and hands-on training sessions will be essential components of these programs. Such training can be administered through collaboration with trade schools, community colleges, and local businesses. Partnerships with these institutions can provide a seamless transition from education to employment, offering internships and apprenticeships that give real-world experience.

Moreover, training programs should incorporate soft skills development. Interpersonal skills, communication, problem-solving, and teamwork are all critical in maintaining long-term employment. These skills can be taught through coaching sessions, role-playing activities, and group projects, ideally integrated into the broader technical training. Soft skills training ensures individuals can adapt and excel in diverse work environments.

To support the success of these programs, it is essential to provide wraparound services. **These services may include career counseling, financial literacy education, and mental health support, which create a holistic development approach**. Providing a supportive environment boosts self-confidence and mitigates barriers that may hinder job retention and career advancement.

Additionally, leveraging technology can enhance the reach and effectiveness of job training programs. Online training portals, virtual classrooms, and digital learning resources can increase accessibility, particularly for those who may face mobility or transportation challenges. These digital platforms can offer flexible learning schedules, ensuring that people can learn at their own pace and convenience.

Furthermore, continuous feedback mechanisms are vital for evolving and improving job training programs. Engage participants in surveys and focus groups to gather insights and adapt the programs accordingly. This iterative approach ensures the training remains relevant and meets the evolving needs of both the workforce and the industries.

Through well-designed job training programs, we can establish a robust workforce ready to contribute to the success of Cities of Hope. These programs provide individuals with the tools necessary for meaningful employment and cultivate a sense of community, purpose, and economic resilience. Ultimately, job training programs are a cornerstone in eradicating homelessness and building prosperous, self-sustaining towns.

Skilling and Reskilling

In the context of Job Creation and Workforce Development, skilling and reskilling are indispensable for the success of Cities of Hope. These towns aim not only to provide immediate employment but also to offer avenues for career growth and stability, ensuring that residents do not become obsolete in a rapidly changing job market.

The advent of new technologies and changing economic landscapes necessitates a workforce that can adapt swiftly. This requires a strong focus on both skilling for new entrants into the workforce and reskilling for existing workers whose jobs may evolve or become redundant. A structured skilling and reskilling program is a cornerstone in facilitating these adaptations.

Firstly, skilling initiatives need to be tailored to the industries operational within the Cities of Hope. These may include manufacturing, green energy production, recycling, and textile production, among others. Practical, hands-on training programs will be established to equip residents with the necessary skills. Partnerships with local trade schools and community colleges will be leveraged to create curriculum and certification programs that align with industry needs.

Reskilling, on the other hand, emphasizes continuous learning and career pivoting. It focuses on older or displaced workers who need to acquire new skill sets to remain employable. By offering evening classes, online courses, and flexible schedules, the Cities of Hope will cater to the diverse needs of their adult workforce. This will enable workers to transition smoothly into new roles without significant downtime or financial strain.

Moreover, the integration of technology in skilling and reskilling programs can't be overlooked. For instance, virtual reality (VR) simulations can provide effective training in a controlled, replicable environment. Likewise, online learning platforms can offer courses ranging from basic skills to advanced certifications, making education accessible to everyone.

A key component is the establishment of mentorship and support networks. Experienced professionals can offer guidance and share insights, fostering an environment of continuous development and peer learning. These networks will help in skill acquisition and boost morale and community spirit. **Some of the employees coming from the novel visa program will be employed full-time in this function**.

Veterans can also serve as invaluable mentors in the Cities of Hope, offering guidance, support, and leadership based on their rich experiences and disciplined training. Their unique perspectives, shaped by their service and resilience, make them particularly effective in mentoring roles. They can help others navigate challenges, instill a sense of purpose, and foster community spirit, making them essential contributors to the Cities of Hope mentorship programs.

Lastly, skilling programs must be regularly evaluated and updated. The dynamic nature of industries means that today's relevant skills might become outdated tomorrow. Therefore, a feedback loop involving industry experts, educators, and residents will ensure that the training modules remain effective and relevant.

Cities of Hope can build a resilient workforce capable of thriving in a modern economy through strategic skilling and reskilling initiatives. This will create immediate employment opportunities and pave the way for sustainable growth and personal development, ultimately contributing to the larger goal of eradicating homelessness and fostering profitable, thriving communities.

Collaboration with Trade Schools and Community Colleges

Collaboration with trade schools and community colleges is pivotal for Job Creation and Workforce Development to be truly effective. These institutions are the cornerstone of practical education and technical training, providing students with the skills necessary to thrive in various industries. By partnering with trade schools and community colleges, Cities of Hope can create a steady pipeline of skilled labor, ensuring that local businesses and industries have access to a workforce that is adequately trained and continuously improving.

One of the most tangible benefits of these partnerships is the alignment of curriculum with local industry needs. Trade schools and community colleges can tailor their programs to focus on the specific skills required by the businesses operating within these Cities of Hope. This bespoke approach enhances employability, increases job satisfaction, and reduces turnover, as workers are well-prepared for their roles from the outset. Collaboration could extend to internships, co-op programs, and onsite training, giving students hands-on experience and fostering a seamless transition from education to employment.

Moreover, these partnerships can drive innovation through joint ventures in research and development. Trade schools and community colleges often have facilities and expertise that can be leveraged for pilot projects, problem-solving, and creative solutions to industry challenges. By working closely with educational institutions, industries can stay ahead of technological advancements and continually refine their processes and products.

In addition to preparing students for immediate employment, these collaborations can support ongoing education and reskilling efforts. As industries evolve, the need for workers to upgrade their skills becomes critical. Offering continuing education programs and professional development courses through these institutions helps ensure that the workforce remains adaptable and competitive. Lifelong learning becomes a practical reality, contributing to both individual growth and community prosperity.

From a community perspective, the benefits are equally compelling. Trade schools and community colleges offer accessible education opportunities to local residents, promoting social mobility and reducing barriers to employment. This can be particularly transformative in communities facing high unemployment rates or where access to higher education has historically been limited. The presence of these institutions can also attract families and young professionals, fostering a vibrant and diverse community culture.

Establishing strong, ongoing relationships with trade schools and community colleges requires deliberate planning and commitment from all stakeholders. This includes regular communication between educational administrators and industry leaders, joint committees to oversee collaborative projects, and shared investment in facilities and resources. By making these partnerships a strategic priority, Cities of Hope can ensure a well-equipped, highly skilled workforce that is essential for sustainable economic growth and community well-being.

Housing and Community Services

Creating a thriving community involves more than just providing jobs; it requires a holistic approach that addresses housing, healthcare, education, and recreational needs. So, let's delve into how Cities of Hope can address these crucial aspects effectively.

Affordable Housing Models

At the heart of any community is where its citizens live. Affordable housing serves as the cornerstone for this initiative. Multiple housing models can be deployed to ensure that everyone has a place to call home. These range from high-density apartment complexes to single-family homes, each designed considering efficiency and cost-effectiveness.

Utilizing modular construction methods and sustainable materials will help reduce costs and build time. This will allow for staying within budget and on time, considering the criticality of addressing this problem as urgent as possible.

Healthcare Facilities

No community can thrive without access to healthcare, especially in this delicate situation concerning our homeless citizens. These towns will be equipped with comprehensive healthcare facilities, including primary care clinics, specialized medical units, and emergency services. By incorporating telehealth services, we can extend specialized care to remote areas, ensuring all residents have access to necessary medical treatment.

Partnerships with educational institutions can also facilitate continuous medical education programs for healthcare providers, keeping them updated on the latest medical practices and technologies.

Educational Institutions

Education is another pillar of community service. By establishing a range of educational institutions, from pre-schools to community colleges, the towns can cater to the educational needs of all age groups. Vocational training centers and trade schools will further support workforce development, aligning educational programs with industry needs.

These educational institutions can also serve as hubs for community activities, hosting workshops, seminars, and events that foster a sense of community.

Recreational & Belief Centers

A balanced life includes time for leisure and recreation. Recreational centers with facilities for sports, arts, and outdoor activities will help enhance the quality of life for residents. These centers can also include community meeting spaces, supporting social interaction and community engagement.

Parks and green spaces within the town offer relaxation and physical activities, promoting mental and physical well-being. Incorporating cultural and arts programs can additionally enrich the community's social fabric. Religious centers such as Churches, Synagogues, and Mosques will also be added.

In conclusion, Cities of Hope must provide comprehensive housing and community services to support their residents. Affordable housing, accessible healthcare, quality education, and leisure activities are critical to not just attract people but to help them build fulfilling lives.

Affordable Housing Models

Achieving affordable housing in Cities of Hope is critical to addressing homelessness and ensuring long-term financial sustainability. In this context, we need to consider a variety of housing models that cater to different income levels, family sizes, and the needs of our homeless citizens. Emphasis should be placed on financial viability and creating vibrant, inclusive communities.

One of the primary models to consider is **mixed-income housing**. Mixed-income communities include a range of housing options, from high-end to subsidized units. This approach fosters social integration and stabilizes the local housing market. With such a model, market-rate housing can subsidize lower-cost units, making the overall financial framework more sustainable. In the model of Homelessness transformation towns, the residents who are able to work and generate monthly income will be positioned in higher-end housing, whereas the residents who are not in a position to work due to various reasons but are taken care of by the overall community revenues generated from the businesses will be housed in lower end housing units. **This approach will serve both equality and equity at the same time.**

Another effective strategy is the adoption of **modular and prefabricated housing**. These methods significantly reduce construction time and costs. Prefabricated units are built off-site and then transported to the housing location, ensuring consistent quality and minimizing construction waste. This decreases the initial investment needed and reduces the environmental footprint.

Micro-apartments and **co-housing** are also worth exploring. Micro-apartments, typically ranging from 250 to 400 square feet, provide affordable living spaces for individuals and small households. These units can be designed to maximize functionality and comfort despite their size. Co-housing, on the other hand, offers shared living spaces such as kitchens and communal areas, reducing individual housing costs while enhancing community bonds.

Adaptive reuse of existing buildings can be another cost-effective solution. Underutilized warehouses, office buildings, and old schools can be converted into residential units. These structures often have historical or architectural value, adding character to the community while also minimizing resource use for new construction.

Lastly, **community land trusts (CLTs)** present a model where the community collectively owns the land, but individual buildings can be owned or rented. This setup keeps land ownership in the hands of the community, helping to control housing costs and ensuring long-term affordability. By removing the land cost from the equation, housing costs can be kept within the budget of the overall program.

Implementing a mix of these models can help create a diverse and resilient housing landscape in Cities of Hope. The goal is not just to provide shelter but to build communities where people can thrive economically, socially, and emotionally. Achieving this will require collaboration between government entities, private investors, non-profits, and the community members themselves.

Although the model I am proposing will not require some of the above options, I wanted to mention these models for further scalability and adaptation to different needs that might arise in society in the future. (an example would be to adapt this model for distressed communities that will focus on manufacturing industries to achieve the revitalization of those communities through tax incentives and advantages (Opportunity zone districts)

The chapter on cost analysis and funding sources further details these models' financial feasibility. However, the practicality of these housing solutions hinges on comprehensive planning, inclusive policy-making, and robust public engagement. By cultivating a multidisciplinary approach, affordable housing in Cities of Hope becomes a possibility and a reality.

Healthcare Facilities

The healthcare facilities in our proposed Cities of Hope are a cornerstone in ensuring the well-being of all residents. Accessible and comprehensive healthcare services are not just a necessity; they are a right that can dramatically influence the productivity and quality of life within any community. In the context of creating viable Cities of Hope that tackle homelessness and spur economic growth, the integration of well-planned healthcare services becomes even more crucial.

Our vision includes both immediate and long-term healthcare solutions. At the outset, each town will have at least one well-equipped health center, providing both primary care and emergency medical services. The goal is to offer a safety net for residents, many of whom may have previously had limited or no access to healthcare.

These health centers will feature general practitioners, pediatricians, and nurses, ensuring that families and individuals can receive adequate medical attention swiftly. To address more specific medical needs, including mental health services, our facilities will also employ specialists who are accessible through regular on-site visits or telehealth options. The provision of mental health care is particularly pertinent, given the trauma and stress associated with homelessness and job insecurity.

Moreover, healthcare in these towns will transcend beyond illness treatment to encompass preventative care. Regular health check-ups, vaccinations, wellness programs, and health education workshops will be instrumental. Adopting a proactive approach can mitigate common health problems and reduce long-term medical costs.

Collaboration with nearby hospitals and medical schools will bolster these efforts, providing internship opportunities for medical students while augmenting the towns' medical service capabilities. Additionally, partnerships with pharmaceutical companies and non-profit organizations can help ensure a steady supply of medications, vaccines, and other essential health supplies at reduced costs.

Foreigners coming to work in these Cities of Hope through the novel visa program will be employed in these healthcare facilities together with their American colleagues. The novel visa program will enable the selection of applicants according to their profession, and healthcare professionals will hold a substantial percentage of this visa program.

A sustainable healthcare model also necessitates the inclusion of facilities supporting public health initiatives. Clean water supply, proper sanitation, and waste management systems are essential components that will be integrated into the town's infrastructure. These are not just about maintaining hygiene but are critical to preventing the spread of diseases.

Furthermore, leveraging technology will play a significant role in enhancing our healthcare framework. Electronic Health Records (EHRs) will be implemented to ensure streamlined and efficient patient care management. This digital approach can significantly reduce paperwork, improve accuracy, and ease coordination between different healthcare providers.

Lastly, training programs for residents interested in pursuing careers in healthcare will also be established. This addresses employment and ensures that the healthcare system remains resilient and self-sustaining. These programs can provide certifications and hands-on training, encouraging residents to contribute directly to their community's health and well-being.

In conclusion, establishing robust healthcare facilities within these Cities of Hope is essential for eradicating homelessness and building a sustainable and thriving community. By providing comprehensive, accessible, and proactive healthcare services, we can create an environment where residents are healthy, happy, and capable of contributing meaningfully to their community.

Educational Institutions

Educational institutions play a pivotal role in the fabric of Cities of Hope, serving both as a foundation for community development and a crucial element in breaking the cycle of homelessness. By establishing robust educational systems, Cities of Hope can provide essential skills and knowledge to their residents and foster a sense of community and long-term economic growth.

The goal of incorporating educational institutions within Cities of Hope is multifaceted. Primarily, these institutions aim to equip residents with the skills needed to participate in the local economy, ensuring that the workforce remains skilled and adaptable. This includes traditional K-12 schools, vocational training centers, community colleges, and partnerships with higher education institutions. Each of these components plays a unique role in nurturing a well-rounded and skilled populace.

K-12 schools form the bedrock of the educational framework, providing children with a comprehensive education that covers fundamental subjects and essential life skills. By integrating these schools within the community, children benefit from a stable and supportive environment that encourages academic achievement and personal growth. Smaller class sizes and targeted support for students who may have faced educational disruptions are crucial to ensuring no child is left behind.

Vocational training centers and community colleges are the next key elements. These institutions focus on job-specific skills and provide certifications in fields such as manufacturing, agriculture, green energy, and more. By aligning their curricula with the needs of local industries, these centers ensure that residents can immediately contribute to the workforce upon completion of their training. This alignment facilitates a seamless transition from education to employment, which is critical in maintaining the town's economic sustainability.

Partnerships with higher education institutions further enhance the educational landscape. These collaborations can provide advanced training and research opportunities, driving innovation within the community. By hosting satellite campuses or offering distance learning programs, universities can contribute to a culture of lifelong learning and continuous professional development.

Moreover, education in Cities of Hope extends beyond traditional academic and vocational training. Lifelong learning programs, adult education classes, and technology literacy initiatives are integral to ensuring that all residents, regardless of age, have the opportunity to improve their skills and knowledge base. These programs not only enhance employability but also contribute to personal development and community engagement.

Ultimately, the inclusion of comprehensive educational institutions within Cities of Hope is a cornerstone in creating a self-sustaining, resilient community. By investing in education at all levels, these towns can cultivate a skilled workforce, foster innovation, and provide residents with the tools they need to lead fulfilling lives. In turn, this approach helps to eradicate homelessness and creates a pathway to economic and social stability for all members of the community.

Recreational & Belief Centers

Recreational centers play a crucial role in fostering a strong sense of community and promoting the overall well-being of residents in Cities of Hope. These centers are not just hubs of physical activity but also spaces where social bonds can be forged, cultural activities can be enjoyed, and mental health can be enhanced.

Given the multifaceted benefits they offer, recreational centers should be conducive to a variety of activities catering to all age groups. Facilities like gyms, swimming pools, sports courts, and open fields can provide opportunities for physical exercise, which is essential for maintaining good health. Regular physical activity helps reduce the risk of chronic diseases and can lower healthcare costs in the long run.

More than just physical benefits, recreational centers offer a venue for social interaction. Organized community events—such as sports leagues, arts and crafts workshops, and music festivals—can bring people together, helping to build a closer-knit community. Social cohesion is a vital component in creating a safe and welcoming environment, especially for those transitioning out of homelessness.

Integrating spaces for relaxation and mindfulness, like meditation rooms or gardens, can also significantly impact mental well-being. Providing such facilities can lower stress levels and enhance residents' overall quality of life. Additionally, these centers can serve as platforms for educational workshops and life skills training, empowering individuals with new knowledge and skills.

Operational efficiency and sustainability should be guiding principles when planning and maintaining recreational centers. Applying green building practices and leveraging renewable energy sources can make these centers eco-friendly and cost-effective. Collaboration with local non-profits and businesses can aid in the funding and management of these facilities, ensuring they remain vibrant and functional.

The importance of recreational centers cannot be overstated. They are instrumental in attracting residents and retaining them by significantly enhancing their quality of life. An investment in such centers is an investment in the social fabric of Cities of Hope, making them more resilient and sustainable in the long term.

Churches, Synagogues, and Mosques

Religious institutions such as churches, synagogues, and mosques can play a pivotal role in Cities of Hope's social and spiritual fabric. These places of worship are not only centers of faith but also serve as vital community hubs where residents can find spiritual solace, moral guidance, and social support.

In the context of Cities of Hope, these institutions can contribute significantly to community building by offering services that extend beyond religious activities. They can provide essential social services, counseling, and support groups, especially for those transitioning out of homelessness. Moreover, they can organize community events, charity drives, and volunteer programs, fostering a spirit of giving and solidarity among residents.

In addition to their spiritual functions, religious institutions can collaborate with recreational centers to offer programs that promote mental well-being, such as meditation sessions, community discussions, and educational workshops. This collaboration can enhance these institutions' overall impact by providing a holistic approach to community care—addressing residents' physical, mental, and spiritual needs.

Furthermore, churches, synagogues, and mosques can act as platforms for interfaith dialogue and cultural exchange, enriching the diversity of the town and promoting inclusivity. These institutions can help build a more cohesive and resilient community by encouraging mutual respect and understanding among different faith groups.

Just like recreational centers, religious institutions should also consider sustainable practices in their operations. By incorporating energy-efficient systems and eco-friendly designs, they can contribute to the town's environmental sustainability. Partnerships with local businesses and non-profits can support these efforts, ensuring that these institutions remain vibrant and active participants in the community.

In conclusion, the inclusion of churches, synagogues, and mosques as central components of Cities of Hope is crucial for fostering a well-rounded, supportive, and inclusive community. These institutions, together with recreational centers, can significantly enhance the quality of life for residents, making the town a more attractive and sustainable place to live.

Financial Feasibility Considerations

Financial feasibility is a cornerstone for the successful implementation of Cities of Hope, aimed at eradicating homelessness and fostering economic development. A meticulously structured financial plan ensures these towns' viability and inspires confidence among potential investors, stakeholders, and government bodies. In this chapter, we'll break down the costs, analyze operational expenses, and identify potential revenue streams that make this ambitious project achievable.

Cost Analysis for Building the Towns

Constructing Cities of Hope involves significant initial investment. Key areas of expenditure include land acquisition, infrastructure development, building construction, and the setup of basic utilities. Let's consider each of these components:

- **Land Acquisition:** Securing land in strategic locations is crucial. The cost can vary significantly based on geography, zoning laws, and current market conditions.

- **Infrastructure Development:** Roads, sewage systems, electrical grids, and water supply networks are fundamental for any town's operation. These need to be planned meticulously to scale efficiently with the growth of the town.

- **Building Construction:** This includes residential units, industrial facilities, schools, healthcare centers, and recreational areas. Utilizing modern construction techniques and sustainable practices can help manage costs and improve long-term sustainability.

- **Utility Setup:** Initial setup costs for essential services like electricity, water, and internet connectivity are significant but vital for ensuring livable conditions.

Operational Costs

While initial costs are substantial, operational costs must be carefully managed to ensure ongoing feasibility. These costs include, but are not limited to:

- **Maintenance and Upkeep:** Regular infrastructure and facilities maintenance is essential for longevity and operational efficiency.

- **Salaries and Wages:** Skilled labor for administration, healthcare, education, and law enforcement needs to be adequately compensated to maintain high service standards.

- **Utility Bills:** Continuous utility supply is a recurrent cost that needs a sustainable financial model.

- **Community Services:** Funding for healthcare, education, and recreational activities needs to be allocated to ensure the holistic well-being of residents.

Revenue Streams

To balance the investment and operational costs, Cities of Hope must generate sustainable revenue. Potential revenue streams include:

- **Industrial Operations:** Manufacturers, agricultural projects, textile producers, and green energy facilities generate revenue through the sale of goods and services.

- **Government Grants and Subsidies:** Securing grants and subsidies can provide essential funding, especially during the initial phases of development.

- **Public-Private Partnerships:** Collaborations with private entities can unlock additional revenue and investment opportunities. These partnerships can drive innovation and efficiency while sharing financial risk.

By methodically assessing these financial components, it's clear that the development of Cities of Hope can be both practical and profitable. Careful planning, judicious spending, and diversified revenue streams form the financial backbone needed to realize this vision.

Cost Analysis for Building the Towns

Analyzing the cost of building these Cities of Hope is critical to determining their financial feasibility. While the vision is grand, understanding the economic requirements at different stages will help ensure successful implementation.

The initial capital expenditure includes land acquisition, infrastructure development, and the construction of housing, commercial spaces, and community services. The first significant cost is acquiring suitable land that meets zoning regulations and environmental standards. This process can vary greatly depending on location, but average costs for land range from $5,000 to $100,000 per acre, considering variations in urban and rural areas. In coordination with Federal and State Authorities as well as NGOs and private corporations, the acquisition of land can be free for these towns (if structured properly)

Infrastructure development follows, encompassing roads, utilities, and digital networks. Utilities—water, electricity, and sewage—require substantial upfront investment, potentially reaching upwards of $50 million for a mid-sized town. Digital infrastructure, including internet and communication networks, could add another $5 million to $10 million. Depending on the extent and quality, road construction can range from $1 million to $5 million per mile.

Next comes the construction of buildings. Residential units, healthcare facilities, educational institutions, and recreational centers are essential components. Construction costs for residential units vary widely based on materials and design but generally fall between $100 and $200 per square foot. Due to their specialized requirements, community services, such as healthcare and education buildings, could see costs ranging from $300 to $500 per square foot.

Including contingency funds for unexpected expenses is crucial, typically estimated at 10-20% of the total budget. This fund acts as a buffer against unforeseen expenditures and cost overruns.

Operational costs begin once the town is built. These include maintenance, security, healthcare, education, and other community services. Annual operational expenses can range from $10 million to $30 million, depending on the scale and services provided. Factoring in salaries for educators, medical staff, and maintenance personnel is also necessary. The average yearly expense per professional fluctuates based on local labor markets but generally hovers around $50,000 to $100,000 per individual.

Technological integration for smart city functionalities—like automated waste management, energy-efficient systems, and data analytics—demands a separate allocation. Initial installation costs for these technologies generally range from $5 million to $15 million but can offer long-term savings on operational efficiencies.

Ultimately, while the costs are substantial, the investment in building these Cities of Hope is justifiable because of their potential to eliminate homelessness, foster employment, and stimulate economic growth. Careful cost planning and strategically allocating funds will be essential in translating this ambitious vision into reality.

I have outlined the general cost perceptions in this section. However, my construction, cost optimization, and financial skills give me a different view of the real costs. In the following chapters, I will provide my personal cost assumptions to provide an alternative perspective on the cost analyses.

Operational Costs

Understanding the operational costs associated with the development and maintenance of Cities of Hope is crucial for assessing their financial feasibility. These costs encompass a wide range of expenditures, including but not limited to utility expenses, personnel salaries, maintenance of infrastructure, and the procurement of raw materials and essential services.

Firstly, utility expenses form a significant portion of the operational costs. These include electricity, water, gas, and waste management services. Given the aim to incorporate green energy production, initial costs may be higher, but the long-term benefits of energy efficiency and sustainability can balance these expenditures.

Personnel salaries and wages are another major component. From healthcare professionals to educators and technicians, a diverse workforce is necessary to manage the day-to-day operations of the industrial town. Competitive salaries must be offered to attract and retain skilled labor, ensuring high service standards and operational efficiency.

Infrastructure maintenance cannot be overlooked. Routine and preventive maintenance of housing units, healthcare facilities, educational institutions, recreational centers, and industrial equipment ensures longevity and functionality. Neglecting these can lead to higher costs down the line due to unplanned repairs and replacements.

Procuring raw materials and essential services is also a recurring cost. This includes everything from construction materials for ongoing development projects to medical supplies for healthcare facilities. Implementing efficient procurement strategies and building strong supplier relationships can help minimize these costs over time.

Most of these services can be fulfilled by workers coming via the Novel Visa program.

Moreover, investing in technology and data analytics for continuous improvement can yield cost savings. Smart city technologies can optimize utilities, enhance security, and improve overall operational efficiency, which can lead to cost reductions in the long run. However, these technologies come with their own set of operational costs that need to be managed effectively.

Lastly, administrative costs such as legal fees, insurance, and regulatory compliance are pivotal to the smooth functioning of an industrial town. Ensuring compliance with various regulations will require a dedicated administrative workforce, whose operational costs must be factored into the overall budget.

In conclusion, while the operational costs are substantial, they are essential investments for Cities of Hope's long-term viability and success. A detailed understanding of these costs and strategic financial planning can make the dream of eradicating homelessness through profitable Cities of Hope a tangible reality.

Revenue Streams

The success of our proposed Cities of Hope hinges on identifying diverse and sustainable revenue streams that will ensure the project's financial viability. Establishing these revenue sources is crucial for covering initial construction costs and ongoing operational expenses and generating profits that can be reinvested into the project for continuous improvement and expansion.

The primary source of revenue will be the sale of locally produced goods and services. Manufacturing and agricultural output from the Cities of Hope can be marketed locally, regionally, and even globally, creating a steady inflow of funds. The revenue streams from waste to energy projects, Call Center Services, and other industries to be added will create the backbone of revenue streams that will cover the repayment of the HUD bonds to be issued for financing the CAPEX of these towns in addition to the Novel Visa program lottery application fees.

Commercial leases from businesses and industries operating within the town will also form a robust revenue stream. Establishing industrial parks will encourage businesses to set up operations, thereby creating jobs and contributing lease payments.

By offering competitive lease and partnership terms, modern facilities, and tax advantages, these Cities of Hope will attract a mix of manufacturing, agriculture, textile production, recycling, and green energy companies.

Though primarily designed for resident well-being, Recreational centers and community services will also have revenue-generating capabilities. Membership fees, sponsorship activities, event hosting, and recreational activities will create consistent and diversified income opportunities. These facilities will enhance the quality of life for residents, making the town more attractive to potential new residents and businesses. As these towns gradually advance, more economic activity will occur due to supply chain necessities and the organic growth that comes with these developments.

Lastly, strategic public-private partnerships and collaborations with non-profit organizations will open opportunities for grants and funding aimed at specific projects like green energy installations or community health programs. These additional funds will supplement our primary revenue streams, facilitating further improvements and innovations within the town.

By diversifying revenue streams and creating a robust financial model, Cities of Hope can become self-sustaining and generate surpluses that will bolster long-term growth and resilience. Each source of income reinforces the others, creating a synergistic effect that enhances the town's overall economic stability and ability to address the homeless crisis effectively.

Economic Impact Analysis

In this chapter, we will delve into the potential economic impact of establishing Cities of Hope aimed at solving the homeless crisis. The focus will be on job creation metrics, economic multipliers, and long-term financial projections. By understanding these factors, we can make a compelling case for why this model is not only feasible but also immensely beneficial for both the individuals it serves and the broader economy.

Job Creation Metrics

One critical metric to consider is job creation. The establishment of Cities of Hope will create numerous job opportunities across various sectors. These jobs won't just be limited to the industrial activities central to each town—whether it's manufacturing, agriculture, or green energy production—but will also extend to essential community services like healthcare, education, and retail.

The initial phase of developing these towns will create construction jobs, ranging from unskilled labor to specialized roles. Post-construction, the operational phase will require a permanent workforce to run the industries, manage community services, and maintain infrastructure. By providing wide-ranging employment opportunities, these towns aim to attract a diverse labor force, thereby contributing to a reduction in the national unemployment rate.

Economic Multipliers

Economic multipliers are an effective way to understand the broader economic impact. They measure an initial investment or job creation event's ripple effect on the broader economy. For instance, when a new factory opens and hires 100 people, the income of these employees generates additional demand in the local economy. They spend their earnings on goods and services, which, in turn, supports further job creation.

Cities of Hope's construction and operational phases will generate significant initial and secondary economic activity. Local businesses, like retail stores, restaurants, and service providers, will likely see a surge in demand as new residents and employees spend their incomes. This process will result in a cycle of economic growth, driving further investment and job creation in and around these communities.

Long-term Financial Projections

The long-term financial success of Cities of Hope hinges on several factors, including sustained employment, community satisfaction, and ongoing operational efficiency. Financial projections should account for the revenue generated through industrial and commercial activities, government grants, and private investments.

With sound financial management, towns can be self-sufficient in the mid-run. The initial capital outlay for construction and setup might be substantial, but the long-term revenue streams, ranging from industrial output to service fees, can make these towns profitable.

Additionally, the Cities of Hope's focus on sustainable and green industries can attract environmental grants, subsidies, and investment. This can further incentivize diverse financial backers to involve themselves in this socially responsible and economically viable initiative.

By adopting a multi-faceted approach to economic impact analysis, we can confidently argue that the establishment of Cities of Hope could be a game-changer in addressing homelessness while providing substantial economic benefits. The positive ripple effects on job creation, local economies, and long-term financial sustainability offer a compelling case for why this model should be adopted nationally.

Job Creation Metrics

When assessing the economic impact of Cities of Hope, one of the critical metrics to consider is job creation. Job creation serves as a primary indicator of economic health and social stability within these newly developed communities. It addresses unemployment and stimulates local economies by increasing consumer spending and generating revenue through various channels.

Firstly, let's break down the types of jobs that will be generated. The basic industries for employment discussed previously form the backbone of job opportunities in the Cities of Hope. These include but are not limited to manufacturing, agriculture, textile production, recycling, waste management, Call Centers, Animal Food Production, Catering Services, and green energy production. Each of these sectors has the potential to create a diverse range of positions, from entry-level labor to highly skilled technical roles.

For instance, manufacturing facilities might require operators, engineers, supervisors, and quality control experts. Agriculture offers roles like farm laborers, management positions, and technicians skilled in modern farming techniques. Textile production can generate positions for machinists, designers, and logistics coordinators. Similarly, green energy projects need electricians, planners, and renewable energy experts.

In evaluating job creation metrics, we must delve into several key indicators:

1. **Employment Rate:** The primary indicator measuring the increase in the number of employed individuals within the town.

2. **Job Diversity:** The variety of job types available ensures a range of opportunities for different skill levels and career paths.

3. **Income Levels:** Track average incomes to ensure that jobs improve residents' standard of living.

4. **Stability and Growth:** Evaluating how many of these jobs offer long-term stability and opportunities for career advancement.

Additionally, we need to consider secondary economic benefits. Every job created typically supports additional employment through economic multipliers. For example, new manufacturing plants need suppliers, maintenance services, and logistical support, further expanding job opportunities beyond the primary sectors.

Another essential factor is the impact of job creation on the community's social fabric. Employment provides financial benefits and contributes to social stability, individual self-worth, and overall mental health. Stable jobs reduce crime rates, increase educational attainment, and foster a stronger sense of community.

Effective job creation metrics also involve monitoring workforce development programs, which are critical, as discussed in the previous chapter. Training and skilling initiatives play an essential role in preparing residents for these new job opportunities. Collaboration with trade schools and community colleges ensures a continuous pipeline of qualified candidates, tailoring education and training programs to meet industry-specific needs.

In conclusion, evaluating job creation metrics provides a comprehensive view of the economic impact that Cities of Hope can achieve. By focusing on employment rates, job diversity, income levels, and secondary benefits, we can paint a detailed picture of how these towns address unemployment and foster economic prosperity. This, in turn, underscores the long-term viability of the industrial town model as a solution to the homelessness crisis and broader urban economic challenges.

Economic Multipliers

Economic multipliers play a crucial role in assessing the broader impact of establishing new Cities of Hope to address homelessness and stimulate local economies. This concept is essential in measuring how initial spending in the town generates additional economic activity beyond the initial investment.

At its core, an economic multiplier is a factor that quantifies the additional economic activity resulting from an initial spending event. Spending money to build housing, establish industries, or develop community services in these new towns triggers a chain reaction of spending throughout the economy. Consequently, this ripple effect amplifies the initial investment's total impact, making it larger than the sum of its parts.

Consider the construction phase for an industrial town. The initial expenditure on materials, labor, and services creates jobs and increases demand for local businesses. Construction workers and contractors spend their earnings locally on goods and services such as food, entertainment, and healthcare. These local businesses, in turn, need to hire more staff and purchase additional supplies, perpetuating the cycle of economic benefits.

The multiplier effect extends beyond the construction phase. Once operational, the town's industries generate employment opportunities, increasing household incomes and improving purchasing power. Residents spend their earnings in local shops, restaurants, and service providers, further stimulating the economy. As industries thrive, they may attract ancillary businesses, creating additional job prospects and bolstering the economic base.

The magnitude of the multiplier effect can vary based on several factors, including the type of industries established, the local economy's current state, and the residents' spending patterns. Generally, industries with strong local linkages—those that source materials and labor locally—tend to have higher multipliers.

Government grants and investments have a vital role in amplifying these multipliers. Public funds can leverage additional economic activity when used strategically to complement private investments. For instance, spending on infrastructure like roads, public transit, and utilities enhances the town's connectivity and attractiveness for businesses and residents alike, thus increasing the multiplier effect.

Moreover, economic multipliers must be considered in long-term financial projections. Understanding these effects can help policymakers and stakeholders make informed decisions about funding allocations and project the potential economic benefits of the industrial town initiative. By quantifying these impacts, we can demonstrate the feasibility and profitability of eradicating homelessness through the establishment of such towns, thereby encouraging governmental and citizen action.

In summary, economic multipliers are indispensable tools for evaluating the economic impact of new Cities of Hope. By generating additional economic activity from initial investments, they provide a compelling argument for the viability and benefits of this transformative approach.

Long-term Financial Projections

When evaluating the feasibility and sustainability of Cities of Hope (Cities of Hope), it's crucial to consider long-term financial projections. These projections provide a roadmap for understanding these towns' economic viability and financial health over an extended period. Analyzing long-term financial projections involves predicting revenue stream expenditure patterns and assessing potential economic impacts on a broader scale.

The primary sources of revenue for these Cities of Hope include profits from industrial activities and service fees. Industries such as manufacturing, agriculture, and green energy production are expected to generate significant income, thereby reducing dependency on external funding sources. Job creation within these sectors will boost local employment rates and stimulate ancillary businesses, creating a multiplier effect that benefits the entire community.

Expenditures encompass a wide range of areas, including operating costs, maintenance of infrastructure, and provision of community services like healthcare, education, and recreational facilities. Forecasting these costs accurately is essential to ensure that the towns remain financially viable. Regular updates and audits can help ensure that the expenditure remains aligned with financial planning, preventing resource misallocation and inefficiencies.

Another critical aspect to consider in long-term financial projections is the potential economic impact on the surrounding regions. Developing Cities of Hope is expected to alleviate the homeless crisis by offering stable employment and affordable housing, reducing the financial burden on urban areas struggling with homelessness. The increased economic activity will likely attract new investments, leading to further economic growth.

Scenario analysis can be a helpful tool to anticipate various future developments. Planners can prepare for different economic conditions and adjust their strategies by creating best-case, worst-case, and most-likely scenarios. This flexibility is vital for navigating uncertain economic climates and for making informed decisions that ensure the long-term stability of the towns.

To engage both the government and citizens in this initiative, it's important to communicate these financial projections transparently and regularly. Stakeholders need to be aware of the tangible benefits and potential risks associated with the project. Continuous community involvement and feedback will also play a role in fine-tuning financial plans to meet the evolving needs of the residents and ensure that the project adheres to its long-term objectives.

In conclusion, long-term financial projections are a cornerstone of the economic impact analysis for Cities of Hope. They offer invaluable insights into the sustainability and economic benefits of the project. By carefully forecasting revenues, expenditures, and economic impacts, and remaining adaptable to changing conditions, we can create financially robust towns that mitigate the homeless issue and foster thriving communities and economic prosperity.

Case Studies of Successful Industrial Towns

Examining real-world examples of thriving Industrial Towns can offer valuable insights for those looking to replicate their success. Across the globe, various towns have transformed local economies and social structures through well-thought-out industrial projects. This chapter will spotlight a few international examples and draw lessons from their experiences.

International Examples

Let's delve into a couple of well-documented case studies from different parts of the world where Industrial Towns have met and exceeded expectations.

- **Songdo, South Korea:** An ultra-modern city built from scratch, Songdo showcases the potential of integrating technology with industry. Designed as a "smart city," it features advanced technological infrastructure, automated systems, and a focus on sustainability. This emphasis on innovation has attracted numerous businesses and residents, turning Songdo into a model for future Industrial Towns.

- **Tietê, Brazil:** Originally an agricultural town, Tietê strategically repositioned itself as a hub for small and medium-sized enterprises (SMEs). Through incentives and infrastructure development, the town now hosts a diverse range of industries, including textiles, food processing, and metalwork. The economic diversification has significantly reduced unemployment rates and boosted local income levels.

- **Kalundborg, Denmark:** Known for its eco-industrial park, Kalundborg exemplifies industrial symbiosis, where the waste byproduct of one company becomes a resource for another. This approach has led to substantial cost savings and reduced environmental impact. The success of Kalundborg's model has inspired similar projects worldwide, demonstrating the feasibility of eco-friendly industrial development.

Lessons Learned

The case studies above yield several critical lessons that can be applied to new industrial town projects:

1. **Integrated Planning and Design:** The success of any industrial town depends on careful planning that integrates residential, commercial, and industrial areas. Ensuring ease of access, efficient transport networks, and the availability of essential services can enhance the town's appeal and functionality.

2. **Technology Integration:** Incorporating advanced technology, such as automated systems and smart grids, can improve efficiency and attract high-tech industries. This element was key to Songdo's success and can be crucial for future developments.

3. **Diversification and Flexibility:** Economic diversification helps mitigate risks associated with market volatility. Tietê's transformation from an agricultural base to a manufacturing and services hub illustrates the benefits of maintaining a flexible, diversified economic strategy.

4. **Community Engagement:** Involving local stakeholders from the outset fosters a sense of ownership and can help tailor the project to meet community needs. Public-private partnerships and active community participation were instrumental in Kalundborg's success.

5. **Environmental Sustainability:** Emphasizing sustainability through practices like industrial symbiosis reduces costs and aligns the project with global environmental standards. This factor is increasingly important for attracting both businesses and residents who prioritize ecological responsibility.

By analyzing these case studies, it's evident that the successful implementation of Cities of Hope hinges on thoughtful planning, technological innovation, economic diversification, community involvement, and environmental stewardship. Bureaucrats, technicians, and other stakeholders can derive actionable insights from these examples to build and sustain prosperous Cities of Hope, tackling issues like homelessness and unemployment while creating profitable ventures.

International Examples

Exploring successful Industrial Towns around the globe provides valuable insights that can be adapted to address the homeless crisis in the United States while generating profitable economic zones. Learning from these international examples highlights best design, implementation, and management practices that have led to sustainable and thriving communities.

One prominent example is the city of **Songdo** in South Korea. Built from the ground up on reclaimed land, Songdo is often cited as a "smart city" that seamlessly integrates technology with urban planning. The city's infrastructure supports a balanced mix of residential, commercial, and industrial sectors. Songdo's focus on green spaces, connected services, and advanced waste management systems demonstrates a holistic approach to city planning, ensuring environmental sustainability and high quality of life for residents. By leveraging the efficient use of technology, Songdo has managed to reduce operational costs and attract significant foreign investment, providing a model for financial feasibility.

Another successful case is the **Hüttendorf** model in Switzerland. Hüttendorf towns were developed to mitigate housing shortages and unemployment in post-World War II Europe. These towns were built around core industries, such as manufacturing and woodworking, providing immediate employment opportunities for residents. The integration of on-site training centers facilitated workforce development, skilling, and reskilling, ensuring that the community could adapt to changing industrial needs. The Swiss model emphasizes community services and social cohesion, featuring affordable housing, healthcare facilities, and recreational centers. The Hüttendorf approach underscores the importance of comprehensive planning and community engagement in the success of Cities of Hope.

In **Tianjin**, China, the Binhai New Area illustrates the successful development of an industrial town with a focus on innovation and technology. Originally a barren coastal area, Binhai has transformed into a hub of economic activity, specializing in aerospace, biotechnology, and renewable energy industries. Significant collaboration with universities and research institutes has created a pipeline of skilled labor and fostered a culture of continuous improvement. The Tianjin case shows how targeted investments in education and industry can create robust economic ecosystems capable of sustaining long-term growth.

Furthermore, the **Emilia-Romagna** region of Italy offers another compelling example with its network of small-to-medium enterprises (SMEs) that power the local economy. This region excels in sectors like automotive, ceramics, and agri-food. A supportive local government and strong cooperative culture among businesses and residents have played crucial roles in the region's success. Emilia-Romagna's emphasis on collaboration and community-driven initiatives provides a roadmap for overcoming the isolation and fragmentation often observed in US cities grappling with homelessness.

Each of these international examples demonstrates that the concept of Cities of Hope is feasible and highly adaptable. By examining the diverse strategies employed in these successful models, stakeholders in the United States can develop a tailored approach to create Cities of Hope that address homelessness, spur economic growth, and foster community well-being. Whether through the integration of smart technologies, embedding job training programs, or encouraging public-private partnerships, the lessons learned from these global examples can drive the design and implementation of effective solutions to complex social and economic challenges.

Lessons Learned

Examining case studies of successful Industrial Towns reveals several crucial lessons that can be applied to developing and implementing new towns designed to tackle homelessness and create economic opportunities. These lessons can guide both policymakers and stakeholders in making informed decisions to ensure the feasibility and sustainability of such projects.

First and foremost, the importance of **community engagement** cannot be overstated. Successful Industrial Towns have consistently shown that active and continuous involvement of residents, local businesses, and other stakeholders is key to creating a thriving, cohesive community. Engaging with the community in the planning stages and maintaining open communication channels can help address concerns, gather local insights, and foster a sense of ownership and pride among residents. This inclusivity contributes significantly to the town's long-term success.

Another pivotal lesson revolves around the **diversification of industries**. Relying on a single industry can make a town vulnerable to economic downturns associated with that sector. The case studies demonstrate that incorporating a mix of manufacturing, agriculture, green energy, and other industries creates a robust employment base and enhances economic resilience. This diversification ensures that job opportunities are available across various skill levels and helps mitigate risks associated with market fluctuations.

The integration of **education and job training programs** has proven to be a critical factor in the success of these towns. Establishing partnerships with trade schools, community colleges, and other educational institutions can provide residents the necessary skills and reskilling opportunities. This focus on education ensures that the workforce remains adaptable and skilled, meeting the evolving demands of the job market and fostering upward mobility for residents.

Affordable housing and comprehensive **community services** are other essential components highlighted by the case studies. Providing accessible housing options and essential services such as healthcare, education, and recreational facilities contribute to the overall well-being of the community. These amenities improve residents' quality of life and attract businesses and workers to the area, further boosting economic activity.

Financial viability is another critical consideration. The case studies emphasize the need for a well-thought-out financial plan that includes diverse funding sources such as government grants, private investments, and public-private partnerships. A sustainable financial model also involves careful cost analysis and identifying revenue streams to ensure that the towns are self-sufficient and profitable in the long run.

Lastly, the role of **effective governance** and **administration** cannot be ignored. A solid governance structure that includes clear policies, transparent decision-making processes, and strong leadership is essential for the successful management of Cities of Hope. Establishing mechanisms for continuous improvement and adapting to emerging challenges ensures that the towns remain vibrant and responsive to the needs of their residents.

By learning from these examples, stakeholders can develop strategic plans that incorporate these key elements, increasing the likelihood of creating successful Cities of Hope that address homelessness and generate economic opportunities. The lessons learned serve as a blueprint, demonstrating that with careful planning, collaborative efforts, and sustainable practices, the vision of eradicating homelessness and building profitable, inclusive communities is indeed achievable.

Implementation Strategies

The development and execution of Cities of Hope to tackle homelessness in the United States is an ambitious yet plausible vision. This chapter focuses on the strategies essential for turning the concept into a tangible reality. Implementation strategies must be meticulously designed to ensure the success of this multifaceted project.

Phased Rollout Plan

The rollout of Cities of Hope can't be accomplished overnight. A phased approach is pivotal for managing resources effectively and ensuring smooth operations. The initial phase would involve extensive planning and feasibility studies. This includes conducting environmental impact assessments, securing land, and obtaining necessary permits.

The second phase would focus on infrastructure development. Establishing basic utilities like water, electricity, and road access is critical. Concurrently, industrial facilities must be constructed and equipped. The third phase would include establishing residential units and community services such as healthcare and educational facilities.

Subsequent phases would involve gradual scaling, incorporating lessons learned from pilot projects, and improving infrastructure and services based on feedback. This iterative approach ensures adaptability and sustainability.

Risk Management

Every large-scale project comes with its own set of risks. Effective risk management strategies are needed to address financial uncertainties and operational hiccups. Comprehensive risk assessments should be conducted periodically to identify potential vulnerabilities.

As discussed in earlier chapters, financial risks can be mitigated through diversified funding sources. Operational risks require strict quality control measures and regular performance evaluations. Another critical aspect involves developing contingency plans to handle unforeseen events like economic downturns or natural disasters. Contingency planning ensures that the project remains resilient against various disruptions.

Stakeholder Engagement

Engaging stakeholders is indispensable for the project's long-term success. Multiple groups must be aligned with the project goals, including government bodies, private investors, non-profits, and the public. Maintaining clear and transparent communication channels helps build trust and secure ongoing support.

Government bodies might require regular updates and reports to ensure compliance with regulations. Private investors and non-profits would appreciate detailed financial reports showcasing the viability and sustainability of their investments. The public should be engaged through community meetings and feedback mechanisms, particularly future residents. This inclusive approach fosters a sense of ownership and commitment to the collective goal.

Lastly, collaboration with local authorities and organizations can facilitate smoother transitions. Local municipalities and community leaders can provide valuable insights and help in addressing location-specific challenges.

In conclusion, implementing Cities of Hope as a solution to homelessness in the U.S. requires a well-coordinated strategy. Adopting a phased rollout plan, implementing robust risk management protocols, and engaging stakeholders effectively can transform the vision into a reality. Furthermore, leveraging the **Interagency Council on Homelessness,** which possesses the ultimate reach, access, resources, and means, is crucial for achieving a successful implementation strategy. With their comprehensive capabilities, the Interagency can guide the initiative to ensure that the ambitious goal of eradicating homelessness while creating profitable and sustainable communities becomes achievable.

Phased Rollout Plan

Implementing the concept of Cities of Hope on a broad scale requires a carefully structured phased rollout plan. This strategic approach ensures smooth transitions, manageable risk, and maximized chances for success. The complexities of constructing entire towns demand diligent planning and execution, particularly when the aim is to address homelessness while generating profitability.

The phased rollout plan can be segmented into distinct stages, each focusing on specific milestones and objectives:

- **Initial Pilot Phase**: The first phase involves selecting a small number of pilot locations. These sites serve as proving grounds where concepts can be tested and refined. Evaluation metrics include initial cost estimates, logistical considerations, and preliminary economic impact assessments. Engaging with local authorities and community leaders from the onset is critical. Their input helps tailor the project to the unique needs of the area.

- **Development Phase**: Once the pilot towns demonstrate viability, the development phase scales up the construction and integration processes. During this phase, more cities are developed concurrently, leveraging lessons learned from the pilots. Emphasis is placed on securing necessary permits, finalizing designs, and establishing initial industries. Workforce development initiatives begin from the outset to ensure residents are ready for employment when the towns become operational.

- **Expansion Phase**: With established successful operations in multiple towns, the expansion phase focuses on broader geographical spread. This phase aims to create a network of interconnected Cities of Hope. Standardizing procedures, sharing resources, and creating economic linkages between towns can foster regional development. This interconnectedness can enhance economies of scale and create a more resilient system capable of handling setbacks.

- **Sustainability Phase**: Finally, the sustainability phase solidifies the long-term viability of the Cities of Hope. Efforts during this period involve continuous monitoring, fine-tuning operations, and integrating advanced technologies for efficiency. Policies to ensure ongoing maintenance, resident engagement, and adaptive strategies are crucial. Creating community leadership programs and facilitating public-private partnerships support the towns' continuing growth and development.

Throughout the phased rollout, constant evaluation and feedback loops are imperative. Data-driven decision-making helps to adapt strategies in real-time, ensuring flexibility and responsiveness. Building a transparent communication channel with stakeholders, including government agencies, private investors, and the public, fosters trust and collaboration.

It is also essential to anticipate and mitigate potential risks at each phase. Risk management strategies encompass financial safeguards, regulatory compliance, and community acceptance. Proactive engagement with all partners and a robust contingency plan prepares the project to weather unexpected challenges.

> **A phased rollout plan provides a structured and strategic approach to implementing Cities of Hope. We can ensure a smooth and effective deployment by breaking down the process into manageable segments, each with clear objectives and milestones. This methodical progression from pilot projects to long-term sustainability stands as a testament to this concept's feasibility and transformative potential in eradicating homelessness while fostering economic growth.**

Risk Management

Effective risk management is crucial to the successful implementation of Cities of Hope, particularly given the scale and complexity of this undertaking. It's imperative to identify potential risks early and develop strategies to mitigate them, ensuring the initiative's goals are met without significant disruptions.

Identifying Potential Risks

First, conducting a comprehensive risk assessment that considers various factors, such as financial constraints, regulatory hurdles, and community resistance, is important. Potential risks can stem from unexpected cost overruns during construction, legal challenges, environmental impacts, and even fluctuations in the job market that could affect the sustainability of employment opportunities within the towns.

Financial Risks

Managing financial risks involves careful planning and resource allocation. We can reduce dependence on any single revenue stream by diversifying funding sources, including government grants, private investments, and public-private partnerships. Implementing rigorous financial oversight and regular audits can also help detect and address financial discrepancies early, ensuring that funds are utilized efficiently.

Regulatory Risks

Navigating the regulatory landscape is another significant challenge. Ensuring compliance with zoning laws, environmental regulations, and labor laws requires meticulous planning and ongoing consultation with legal experts and regulatory bodies. Establishing a proactive compliance framework can help anticipate regulatory changes and adapt accordingly, minimizing legal risks.

Community Resistance

Community buy-in is critical for the success of Cities of Hope. Resistance may arise due to misconceptions about the project's impact or concerns over changes to local demographics. Engaging in transparent communication, conducting community meetings, and incorporating feedback will help build trust and mitigate opposition.

Environmental Risks

Environmental sustainability is a major concern that cannot be overlooked. Potential environmental risks must be assessed and managed, including pollution, resource depletion, and negative impacts on local ecosystems. Adopting green building practices, investing in renewable energy sources, and implementing waste reduction initiatives can significantly mitigate these risks.

Operational Risks

Operational risks pertain to the day-to-day functioning of these towns. Ensuring operational sustainability involves robust planning for infrastructure maintenance, staffing for essential services, and establishing contingency plans for emergencies such as natural disasters or economic downturns. Continuous monitoring and data analytics can provide insights into operational performance, enabling proactive adjustments.

Planning for Uncertainty

Lastly, it's essential to create adaptive strategies that allow for flexibility in the face of unexpected challenges. This includes developing crisis management protocols and maintaining an agile approach to project management, where plans can be adjusted swiftly in response to unforeseen events. Cities of Hope can remain viable and adaptive to changing circumstances by fostering a culture of resilience and adaptability.

In summary, managing risks effectively involves a multifaceted approach that includes financial planning, regulatory compliance, community engagement, environmental stewardship, and operational resilience. Through vigilant oversight and adaptive strategies, we can navigate the complexities of establishing Cities of Hope, ultimately contributing to eradicating homelessness and creating thriving, profitable communities.

Stakeholder Engagement

The successful implementation of Cities of Hope necessitates a robust strategy for engaging stakeholders. This involves identifying and collaborating with key individuals and groups whose interests and expertise can positively influence the project. Stakeholder engagement ensures a comprehensive approach, incorporating diverse perspectives and fostering a sense of shared ownership and commitment.

First and foremost, building strong partnerships with local governments is crucial. These entities will significantly facilitate regulatory approvals, secure land, and provide infrastructural support. Establishing an open line of communication with municipal and state authorities can streamline bureaucratic processes and mitigate potential legal hurdles.

Engaging the private sector is equally essential. Businesses and investors can provide critical funding, resources, and expertise. Collaborating with companies across multiple industries—from manufacturing to green energy production—can boost the towns' employment opportunities and economic growth. Additionally, public-private partnerships can harness innovative technologies and practices that improve operational efficiency and sustainability.

Non-profit organizations and community groups should also be integral to the stakeholder engagement strategy. These organizations can offer invaluable insights into the needs and challenges of the homeless population, ensuring that the towns are designed to address these effectively. The initiative can benefit from grassroots support and advocacy by involving these groups in planning and decision-making processes.

Academia and research institutions can contribute significantly by conducting feasibility studies, impact analyses, and best practice research. Their involvement can provide data-driven insights that inform all phases of development—from design and layout to workforce development and community services. Collaborations with trade schools and community colleges will be particularly beneficial for job training and skill enhancement programs.

Public engagement is another critical component. It is important to involve current and future residents in the planning process. Mechanisms for gathering feedback, such as town hall meetings and surveys, can help ensure that the community's needs and preferences are reflected in the project's design and implementation.

Transparent and consistent communication with all stakeholders is paramount. This involves regular updates, clear articulation of goals and progress, and addressing concerns promptly. Effective communication builds trust and fosters a collaborative environment where stakeholders feel valued and invested in the project's success.

In conclusion, stakeholder engagement involves a multi-faceted approach that leverages the strengths and insights of various groups and individuals. By fostering strong partnerships and maintaining open communication, the initiative to develop Cities of Hope can create sustainable, inclusive, and economically viable communities that address homelessness and drive societal progress.

Regulatory and Policy Considerations

When establishing Cities of Hope to eradicate homelessness and create profitable, self-sustained communities, navigating the regulatory and policy landscape is paramount. This chapter delves into key regulatory and policy considerations that will guide the development and operationalization of these towns. Compliance is crucial for obtaining necessary approvals and avoiding potential legal pitfalls.

Zoning Laws

Zoning laws dictate how parcels of land can be used within a jurisdiction, directly impacting the development of Cities of Hope. It's essential to collaborate with local zoning boards to ensure the land designated for these towns is appropriately zoned for mixed-use, industrial, and residential purposes.

Understanding zoning classifications and restrictions will inform the feasibility of various town components, such as manufacturing plants, housing units, and recreational facilities. Rezoning efforts may be required to align with the town's vision. This process involves detailed proposals and often public hearings, requiring thorough preparation and stakeholder engagement.

Environmental Regulations

Industrial activities and construction projects must comply with a myriad of environmental regulations, including those enforced by the Environmental Protection Agency (EPA). Key areas include:

- Air Quality: Permits are required for operations emitting pollutants. Technologies to minimize emissions must be incorporated.

- Water Quality: Proper waste treatment systems should be in place to prevent contamination of nearby water bodies.

- Hazardous Waste: Protocols for handling, storage, and disposal of hazardous materials must be followed to avoid legal ramifications and ensure public safety.

Meeting these environmental standards ensures legal compliance and enhances the town's sustainability credentials, attracting green investments and support from environmental advocacy groups.

Labor Laws

The cornerstone of Cities of Hope is creating employment opportunities. Therefore, compliance with federal and state labor laws is non-negotiable. Aspects to consider include:

1. Minimum Wage: Ensuring all employees receive fair wages in accordance with federal and state guidelines.

2. Working Conditions: Compliance with OSHA standards to ensure a safe working environment.

3. Workers' Rights: Upholding workers' rights to organize, collectively bargain, and engage in workplace decision-making is crucial for fostering a supportive community.

Failure to adhere to these labor laws can result in penalties and undermine the project's social mission. Moreover, fair labor practices contribute to job satisfaction and retention, which are integral to the town's long-term success.

In conclusion, navigating regulatory and policy considerations is an intricate but essential part of developing Cities of Hope. Adhering to zoning laws, environmental regulations, and labor laws ensures a smooth, legally compliant operation, laying the groundwork for a sustainable and profitable community. As we move forward, the following chapters will delve into technological integration, community building, and environmental sustainability, each playing a critical role in the town's holistic development.

Zoning Laws

Understanding zoning laws is crucial for the successful implementation of Cities of Hope, especially when aiming to address homelessness and create economically viable communities. These regulations govern how land can be used in different areas, dictating the types of buildings, their purposes, and the activities that can take place within specified zones.

Zoning laws vary substantially from one jurisdiction to another, reflecting local priorities and geographic considerations. At their core, they exist to ensure that different land uses—residential, commercial, industrial, and agricultural—can coexist to enhance the overall quality of life. For Cities of Hope, particular attention must be paid to zones allocated for industrial activities, residential areas, and mixed-use developments, all while ensuring regulatory compliance.

One of the first steps in developing Cities of Hope involves identifying suitable land parcels that are either already zoned for industrial use or could be reclassified through rezoning applications. This requires thorough coordination with local planning boards and regulatory agencies. Successful rezoning can often be achieved by demonstrating the potential economic benefits that the industrial town will bring to the community, such as job creation.

Moreover, zoning regulations will impact the design and layout of the town. Industrial activities typically require large tracts of land and must be located at a reasonable distance from residential areas to mitigate noise, air pollution, and other environmental concerns. Buffer zones, such as parks or green spaces, can serve as transitional areas between industrial and residential zones, thereby enhancing the community's livability.

In addition to the physical layout, zoning laws will also influence the types of buildings that can be constructed. For example, affordable housing must comply with residential zoning requirements but might also require special permits if high-density housing or multi-family units are to be included.

Understanding these nuances ensures that the community can meet its housing and industrial development goals.

Further complicating matters, zoning laws often require adherence to specific environmental regulations to protect natural resources and promote sustainability. Cities of Hope must thus balance economic development with environmental stewardship, ensuring that industrial activities do not degrade local ecosystems. This requires careful planning and, often, the integration of green technologies and practices.

Zoning laws can also affect the provision of essential services within the town. For instance, educational institutions, healthcare facilities, and recreational centers must be appropriately zoned and strategically placed to serve the community effectively. Ensuring these elements fit within the three-way residential, commercial, and industrial zones framework is critical for creating a self-sustaining, functioning town.

In summary, navigating zoning laws is a multifaceted task requiring collaboration with local authorities, careful planning, and a thorough understanding of regulatory requirements and community needs. By adhering to these regulations while demonstrating Cities of Hope's economic and social benefits, stakeholders can foster supportive environments conducive to eradicating homelessness and building profitable, sustainable communities.

Clear communication and transparent processes are essential for policymakers, bureaucrats, and professionals involved in this initiative. Aligning zoning strategies with the overarching goals of industrial town development will ensure regulatory compliance and tangible benefits to residents.

Environmental Regulations

When tackling the ambitious project of building Cities of Hope to eradicate homelessness and promote economic sustainability, adhering to environmental regulations is paramount. These regulations serve not only to protect ecosystems but also to ensure the health and well-being of future residents. Understanding and complying with these laws can mitigate potential legal challenges and foster community trust.

The construction and operation of Cities of Hope should align with federal, state, and local environmental statutes. This includes the Clean Air Act (CAA), the Clean Water Act (CWA), and the National Environmental Policy Act (NEPA). Each of these laws has specific requirements that must be addressed to prevent air and water pollution, manage waste, and protect endangered species and habitats.

Industrial activities within these towns, such as manufacturing and recycling, may emit pollutants. Proper permits are necessary to control these emissions and reduce harmful impacts. Additionally, integrating green energy production, such as solar or wind power, can help towns comply with greenhouse gas emission limits and contribute to wider environmental goals.

Water management is another critical concern. The CWA mandates that any discharge into water bodies must meet stringent quality standards. This requires comprehensive planning for wastewater treatment facilities within the towns. Innovative water recycling and conservation techniques should be employed to ensure that the towns' water usage is sustainable.

Construction projects need to undergo Environmental Impact Assessments (EIA) and, where necessary, acquire Environmental Impact Statements (EIS) as mandated by NEPA. These assessments evaluate the potential environmental effects of proposed actions and consider alternatives that might lessen negative impacts. This process promotes transparency and community involvement, identifying and addressing potential issues early.

Incorporating sustainable building practices can also contribute significantly to environmental compliance. Using materials with lower environmental footprints, improving energy efficiency, and integrating green spaces can make a substantial difference. Not only do these practices help meet regulatory requirements, but they also enhance the quality of life for residents.

Finally, continuous monitoring and adaptation are critical. Establishing protocols for regular environmental audits and being proactive about compliance will help maintain adherence to regulations. This also involves educating residents and workers on environmental best practices and fostering a community's sustainability culture.

By addressing these environmental regulations comprehensively, Cities of Hope can achieve their dual goals of providing a sustainable solution to homelessness and creating ecologically responsible communities. This balanced approach will set a standard for future projects and inspire confidence among stakeholders, paving the way for broader adoption and lasting impact.

Labor Laws

In establishing Cities of Hope, understanding and adhering to labor laws is crucial for compliance and the workforce's well-being. These towns will create a variety of jobs across different sectors. Therefore, labor laws come into play to ensure fair wages, safe working conditions, and equitable treatment of all employees.

Labor laws in the United States are designed to protect workers' rights and ensure they have a safe and fair working environment. For Cities of Hope to be successful and sustainable, adherence to these laws isn't just about legal compliance; it's about building a community where workers are treated with dignity and respect. This contributes to higher morale, improved productivity, and the long-term viability of the town itself.

Several key labor laws impact the operations of Cities of Hope:

- **Fair Labor Standards Act (FLSA):** Establishes minimum wage, overtime pay eligibility, recordkeeping, and child labor standards. Ensuring compliance with FLSA helps maintain fair compensation structures.

- **Occupational Safety and Health Act (OSHA):** Mandates the creation of workplace safety and health standards. Implementing OSHA guidelines in the industrial settings of these towns can prevent injuries and illnesses, promoting a safe working environment.

- **Family and Medical Leave Act (FMLA):** Entitles eligible employees to take unpaid, job-protected leave for specified family and medical reasons. This ensures workers can manage personal and family health issues without fear of losing their jobs.

- **National Labor Relations Act (NLRA):** Protects employees' rights to organize, join labor unions, and collectively bargain. Respecting these rights can foster a cooperative atmosphere between workers and management.

Child labor laws and anti-discrimination statutes, such as the Equal Employment Opportunity Commission (EEOC) guidelines, must also be strictly enforced to make certain that no worker faces exploitation or unfair treatment. Cities of Hope can encourage a more engaged and dedicated workforce by fostering a culture of equity and inclusivity.

Compliance with these labor laws isn't just about avoiding fines and legal trouble. It's about creating a thriving community where workers are respected and valued. Moreover, state-specific labor laws must be examined and adhered to, as they may impose additional requirements beyond federal mandates.

Training programs and continuous education on labor rights can empower employees and ensure that management is up to date on regulatory changes. Labor law compliance audits and regular inspections can serve as tools for maintaining adherence to these laws. Establishing a transparent reporting mechanism for grievances will also help in addressing concerns efficiently.

Moving forward, it will be essential to collaborate with labor organizations, legal experts, and government agencies to review and update policies regularly. This will ensure that Cities of Hope are compliant and model communities that value their workforce. Ensuring robust labor law adherence will lead to a more stable, happy, and productive community, laying the foundation for the town's lasting success.

Technological Integration

The successful integration of technology is essential for the viability and efficiency of Cities of Hope. Emerging technologies can enhance residents' quality of life and ensure the towns are sustainable, productive, and competitive in the modern economy. This chapter explores various facets of technological integration, emphasizing smart city technologies, automation, and data analytics. Understanding and implementing these technologies can maximize operational efficiency, reduce costs, and create a more livable environment for inhabitants.

Smart City Technologies

Smart city technologies are at the forefront of urban development and crucial for Cities of Hope. These include IoT (Internet of Things) devices, sensors, and interconnected systems that monitor and manage essential services such as water supply, waste management, and energy consumption. Leveraging these technologies can optimize resource use, reducing both costs and environmental impact.

For example, smart grids can manage electricity distribution more efficiently, minimizing outages and enabling the integration of renewable energy sources. Smart water management systems can detect leaks and monitor water quality in real-time, ensuring a reliable and safe water supply. These tools contribute to creating sustainable Cities of Hope that use resources judiciously while maintaining high living standards.

Automation and Efficiency

Automation is another critical aspect of technological integration. Cities of Hope can significantly boost productivity by automating repetitive and time-consuming tasks. Key areas for automation include manufacturing, agriculture, and administrative processes.

In manufacturing, robotics and AI-driven machinery can handle complex tasks with precision and consistency, minimizing errors. Similarly, automated farming techniques can increase agricultural yields and reduce labor costs. Drones and IoT devices can monitor crop health and soil conditions, allowing for timely interventions and optimized use of fertilizers and water.

Administrative automation can streamline bureaucratic processes, making it easier for residents to access services and for administrators to manage the town's operations. Automated reporting, for instance, can simplify compliance with environmental and labor regulations, ensuring that the town remains in good legal standing.

Data Analytics for Continuous Improvement

Data analytics is the cornerstone of continuous improvement in Cities of Hope. By collecting and analyzing data from various sources, towns can identify trends, pinpoint inefficiencies, and make informed decisions. This data-driven approach can lead to significant enhancements in both operational and strategic areas.

For instance, analyzing energy consumption patterns can reveal opportunities for reducing waste and lowering costs. Data on traffic flow can inform the design of more efficient transportation networks, reducing congestion and improving safety. In the realm of healthcare, data analytics can identify public health trends, enabling proactive measures to tackle potential issues before they become widespread.

The implementation of data analytics requires a robust digital infrastructure and skilled personnel capable of interpreting and acting on the insights provided by the data. Training programs and partnerships with academic institutions can help build this capacity, ensuring that Cities of Hope remains at the cutting edge of technological innovation.

- IoT Devices and Sensors

- Smart Grids and Water Management

- Automated Farming and Manufacturing

- Robotics in Industrial Processes

- Data Analytics for Process Optimization

In conclusion, integrating smart city technologies, automation, and data analytics is not just a luxury but a necessity for the development and sustainability of Cities of Hope. These technologies offer tangible benefits, from increased operational efficiency to enhanced quality of life, and are central to the vision of eradicating homelessness and creating profitable, self-sufficient communities. By prioritizing technological integration, we can build towns that are not only economically viable but also model environments for sustainable and inclusive living.

Smart City Technologies

In the context of creating Cities of Hope to eradicate homelessness and generate profitable, sustainable communities, integrating smart city technologies is essential. These technologies serve as catalysts, enabling streamlined operations, improved service delivery, and enhanced quality of life for residents. By emphasizing

Smart city technologies encompass a variety of electronic methods and sensors that collect data. Insights derived from these data streams enable proactive management of resources and infrastructure. Key areas include:

1. **Internet of Things (IoT):** IoT devices, such as sensors and smart meters, can monitor utility consumption, environmental conditions, and infrastructure integrity in real time. This data enables efficient resource management and quick response to issues.

2. **Smart Grids:** Smart grids enhance energy efficiency by balancing supply and demand in real-time. They enable the integration of renewable energy sources, ensuring a stable and sustainable power supply for industrial operations and residential needs.

3. **Intelligent Transportation Systems:** Implementing smart traffic lights, public transportation systems, and autonomous vehicles can dramatically reduce congestion, lower emissions, and improve overall mobility within the industrial town.

4. **Smart Waste Management:** IoT-enabled waste bins can optimize collection routes and schedules based on fill levels. This reduces operational costs and minimizes environmental impact.

5. **Advanced Communication Networks:** High-speed internet and reliable communication networks form the backbone of smart cities. They enable seamless connectivity for residents, businesses, and public services.

The deployment of these technologies requires a robust data analytics framework capable of processing vast amounts of information. Machine learning algorithms and artificial intelligence play crucial roles in predictive maintenance, resource allocation, and optimizing various aspects of city management.

Economic and Social Benefits

From an economic standpoint, smart city technologies attract investment and create job opportunities, both in tech-centric sectors and through the improved efficiency of traditional industries. Additionally, enhanced infrastructure and public services contribute to a higher quality of life, thus fostering a more resilient and engaged community.

Moreover, these technologies help in reducing operational costs, thus allowing for the scalable implementation of Cities of Hope across different regions. For bureaucrats and policymakers, this means a higher return on investment and more effective use of public funds.

Implementation Considerations

While the benefits are substantial, planning and executing smart city initiatives require careful consideration of several factors:

- **Interoperability:** Ensuring that different technologies and systems can seamlessly work together is critical for the overall efficacy of the smart city ecosystem.

- **Security and Privacy:** Protecting the data gathered by smart city technologies is paramount. Measures must be in place to prevent breaches and ensure resident privacy.

- **Community Engagement:** It's essential to involve residents in the planning and implementation phases to ensure the technologies meet their needs and improve their daily lives.

- **Regulatory Compliance:** Adhering to existing regulations and preparing for future legislative changes can mitigate risks and support sustainable development.

In conclusion, integrating smart city technologies into the Cities of Hope framework provides a transformative approach to solving homelessness and creating self-sustaining, prosperous communities. By leveraging technology, these towns can become models of modern living, showcasing how strategic investments in infrastructure and services can yield significant social and economic returns.

Automation and Efficiency

In the modern age, the integration of automation and efficient technologies can be the backbone of any large-scale, sustainable community initiative, particularly in the context of building Cities of Hope to address homelessness and create economic opportunities. The seamless incorporation of automation allows for the optimization of resources, minimizing waste and reducing the need for manual labor in repetitive tasks. This approach frees up human capital for more complex and intellectually engaging work, contributing to residents' personal and professional growth.

One immediate benefit of automation in Cities of Hope is its impact on production processes. Whether in manufacturing, agriculture, recycling, or green energy production, automated systems can enhance productivity by operating around the clock with minimal errors. This level of efficiency ensures a steady supply of goods and services and helps maintain competitive pricing, thus making the industrial town self-sustaining and economically viable.

For the workforce, the introduction of automated processes necessitates robust job training programs. Rather than eliminating jobs, automation transforms them. Workers who previously performed manual tasks can be upskilled to manage and maintain automated systems, handle data analytics, and engage in supervisory roles. This transition is facilitated through collaboration with trade schools and community colleges, which can offer specialized courses and certifications tailored to the town's needs.

Moreover, automation contributes to the efficiency of essential services such as healthcare, transportation, and utility management. For instance, automated healthcare systems can streamline patient management and healthcare delivery, thus ensuring timely and efficient medical services. In transportation, the implementation of automated public transit systems can reduce traffic congestion and improve connectivity within and outside the town. Similarly, smart utility management systems can optimize electricity, water, and waste services, reducing operational costs and environmental impact.

The role of automation extends to the town's administrative functions as well. Automated data analytics enables continuous monitoring and optimization, ensuring that resources are used effectively and the community's needs are consistently met. This level of oversight supports the long-term sustainability of the towns, making them adaptable to changing conditions and resilient against potential challenges.

Finally, the ethical considerations of automation and efficiency should not be overlooked. It's essential to ensure that the implementation of these technologies does not lead to social inequities or exacerbate existing disparities. Policies should be in place to guarantee fair labor practices and protect the rights of workers, ensuring that the benefits of automation are shared equitably among all residents.

In conclusion, automation and efficiency are pivotal elements in the technological integration of Cities of Hope. They hold the potential to revolutionize how we address homelessness and create economic viability while promoting the growth and well-being of the community. By embracing these technologies, we can create towns that are not only profitable but also inclusive and sustainable, driving both social and economic progress.

Data Analytics for Continuous Improvement

In the dynamic realm of technological integration, data analytics serves as an indispensable tool for ensuring the continuous improvement of Cities of Hope. For bureaucrats, technicians, academics, students, professionals, and the general public, understanding the role of data analytics in this context is crucial for these initiatives' sustainable development and financial success.

Data analytics provides a systematic approach for tracking and evaluating the performance of various operational sectors within Cities of Hope. By collecting and analyzing data from numerous sources, such as employment rates, housing occupancy, healthcare utilization, and educational attainment, we can make informed decisions leading to better resident outcomes. These decisions can range from improving workforce development programs to enhancing community services.

One key advantage of data analytics is its ability to identify trends and patterns that might not be immediately apparent. For instance, data from manufacturing and green energy production sectors can be used to identify productivity bottlenecks or forecast future workforce needs. This predictive capability allows for proactive measures, thereby avoiding potential crises and ensuring the smooth running of the town's economy.

Moreover, data analytics facilitates the measurement and optimization of resource allocation. Financial resources, for example, can be directed more efficiently when data reveals which areas yield the highest return on investment. This aspect is particularly critical for maintaining the financial feasibility of Cities of Hope, as it ensures that funds are used effectively and contribute to the community's long-term economic stability.

Another layer of continuous improvement is stakeholder engagement. By analyzing feedback from residents and workers, data analytics can provide insights into community satisfaction and areas that require attention. This fosters a culture of transparency and accountability, as stakeholders can see the real-time impacts of their input and the subsequent improvements made.

The integration of smart city technologies further amplifies the benefits of data analytics. For instance, Internet of Things (IoT) devices can collect real-time data on energy usage, traffic patterns, and other critical infrastructure metrics. This data can then be analyzed to optimize energy efficiency, reduce traffic congestion, and enhance overall quality of life for residents.

In conclusion, data analytics stands as a cornerstone for the continuous improvement of Cities of Hope. By leveraging the power of data, we can create adaptive, efficient, and thriving communities that address the homeless issue and pave the way for sustainable and profitable towns. The path forward involves embracing these technologies today to build a better tomorrow.

Social and Psychological Benefits

Creating Cities of Hope not only offers economic solutions to the homelessness crisis but also brings profound social and psychological benefits. A carefully designed town fosters an environment where community building, mental health support, and an increased sense of self-worth and dignity can flourish.

Community Building

A strong, cohesive community provides the backbone for social stability and individual well-being. In Cities of Hope, carefully planned community activities and public spaces encourage residents to socialize and collaborate. These towns will feature communal areas such as parks, recreational centers, and community halls where people can gather and form meaningful relationships. Furthermore, consistent community engagement programs will help to knit together the social fabric, making residents feel a part of something larger and more significant than themselves.

Mental Health Support

Addressing mental health is crucial, especially in populations that have experienced the trauma of homelessness. Cities of Hope will include accessible and comprehensive mental health services. Clinics and support groups will be available, providing therapy, counseling, and other mental health care services. These resources will help residents to manage stress, anxiety, and other related issues, contributing to both individual and community health. Social initiatives like peer support networks can also enable residents to support each other, creating a web of mutual care and understanding.

Increased Self-Worth and Dignity

A stable job and a secure home are fundamental to one's self-worth and dignity. Cities of Hope offer stable employment opportunities, allowing individuals to contribute to their community and earn a living. This sense of purpose can significantly improve one's mental outlook and foster a positive self-image. Living in a safe, well-maintained environment further enhances this sense of dignity. Feeling valued and respected, each resident can better engage with and contribute to the community.

All these elements—community building, mental health support, and increased self-worth—collectively form the bedrock of a socially thriving industrial town. By focusing on these social and psychological benefits, we can create environments where every individual feels supported and valued, thus turning the tide on the homelessness crisis while building prosperous communities.

Community Building

A cornerstone of the Cities of Hope concept is the emphasis on community building. Creating a strong, supportive community environment addresses the immediate needs of housing and employment for the homeless and **fosters a sense of belonging and mutual support**. When we talk about community building, we're referring to more than just placing people in proximity to one another; it involves creating networks of support, collaboration, and shared purpose that can uplift an entire town.

First and foremost, these towns will prioritize inclusive and participatory planning. Residents will have a voice in decision-making processes, ensuring that community needs are met and they feel a meaningful connection to their surroundings. This approach encourages a sense of ownership and responsibility among community members, which is essential for long-term sustainability.

Social cohesion can be further promoted through the establishment of community centers, recreational areas, and shared spaces where residents can gather, socialize, and engage in various activities. These centers will serve as hubs for educational programs, skills training, cultural activities, and social services. By offering a range of community services and activities, we can cater to diverse interests and needs, helping build a more resilient and integrated community.

> **I have personally witnessed the strong social bonds that form among our homeless population as they support one another to endure the harsh conditions they face daily. This unique social cohesion, which is often absent in other types of cities, is something I expect to flourish in these new communities. I am confident that homeless citizens will value this opportunity and collaborate to ensure that these Cities of Hope become true success stories. While challenges and tensions may arise during the transition and initial stabilization phases, I firmly believe these can be effectively managed.**

Another crucial element of community building is fostering a culture of mutual support and cooperation. Initiatives such as communal gardens, cooperative businesses, and volunteer programs can create opportunities for residents to contribute to and benefit from their community. These activities provide practical benefits like food security and economic opportunities, strengthen social bonds, and promote a culture of giving back.

Mentorship programs and peer support groups can also play a vital role in community building. We can create a powerful support network by connecting individuals who have successfully transitioned out of homelessness with those currently making the transition. These mentors can provide guidance, share experiences, and offer much-needed emotional support, which can significantly enhance the well-being and resilience of new residents.

It's also important to consider the role of local governance in community building. Establishing local councils or committees comprised of residents can ensure that the community's voices are heard and considered in governance. These bodies can oversee various aspects of the town's operations, from organizing events to addressing grievances, thereby fostering a more democratic and engaged community.

Lastly, partnerships with existing community organizations, nonprofits, and local businesses can enhance the range of services and opportunities available to residents. By leveraging these partnerships, Cities of Hope can offer a more comprehensive support system and provide residents with access to resources that might otherwise be unavailable.

In summary, community building is an integral part of the concept of Cities of Hope. By creating an environment that promotes inclusivity, social cohesion, and mutual support, we can address the immediate issues of homelessness and build strong, vibrant communities that thrive in the long term. This comprehensive approach ensures that everyone, from individuals to families, finds a home and a community they can contribute to and be proud of.

Mental Health Support

Mental health plays a crucial role in the overall well-being of individuals and communities, especially within the context of addressing homelessness. By integrating mental health support into the fabric of Cities of Hope, we can create a community environment that not only meets the physical needs of individuals but also addresses their psychological and emotional needs.

One of the foundational aspects of mental health support in these towns will be accessible and comprehensive mental health services. These services can range from emergency crisis intervention to ongoing counseling and therapy. By hiring a team of professionals, including psychologists, counselors, and social workers, we can ensure residents have the support they need to manage mental health conditions effectively.

A key to successful mental health support is reducing the stigma associated with seeking help. Community-wide education programs can raise awareness about mental health issues and promote a culture of understanding and support. This approach encourages individuals to seek help without fear of judgment or discrimination.

Additionally, integrating mental health services with other community services can provide a holistic approach to well-being. For example, mental health professionals working in tandem with healthcare providers, job training programs, and housing services can offer a more cohesive support system. This integrated model ensures that mental health is not an isolated aspect of care but part of a broader strategy to improve quality of life.

Preventative measures are just as important as direct mental health services. Regularly scheduled workshops and seminars on stress management, emotional resilience, and healthy coping mechanisms can empower residents with tools to maintain their mental health. Offering activities such as mindfulness sessions, yoga classes, and peer support groups can also create a supportive and proactive environment.

Moreover, the physical design of these Cities of Hope should include spaces that nurture mental well-being. Parks, recreational areas, and communal spaces provide residents with opportunities to unwind, connect with nature, and build social connections, which are all vital for mental health.

By focusing on mental health support within the context of Cities of Hope, we not only address immediate psychological needs but also foster a healthier, more resilient community. This approach can play a significant role in breaking the cycle of homelessness and enabling individuals to thrive in a stable, supportive environment.

Increased Self-Worth and Dignity

For individuals experiencing homelessness, the struggle isn't just about finding shelter—it's about grappling with a loss of self-worth and dignity that often accompanies their situation. Addressing this psychological and social impact is paramount in the creation of Cities of Hope. By providing stable employment, affordable housing, and a supportive community, these towns can significantly enhance residents' sense of self-worth and dignity.

Employment opportunities in these towns serve as more than just a source of income; they are a gateway to personal empowerment. Unlike the instability of gig work or temporary jobs, the positions offered within Cities of Hope are designed to be sustainable and to provide room for career growth. When individuals take part in meaningful work, particularly in industries that contribute to social good, they experience a renewed sense of purpose and contribution. This fosters a positive self-image and pride in their accomplishments.

Moreover, the dignity derived from having a place to call home cannot be understated. Affordable and secure housing within these communities eradicates the stigma of homelessness. Residents can engage in daily life's simple yet profound routines, such as maintaining their homes, participating in community activities, and fostering social relationships. These elements contribute significantly to their overall sense of dignity and personal value.

The design of Cities of Hope also encourages community involvement and self-governance. When residents actively participate in decision-making processes and see their contributions shaping their environment, it creates a sense of ownership and belonging. Their voices are not only heard but acted upon, reinforcing their importance within the community. Enhanced self-worth transcends to other areas of their lives, leading to better mental health outcomes and a drive for continuous self-improvement.

In essence, the Cities of Hope model does more than provide economic stability—it reinstates the essential human need for dignity and self-worth. This holistic approach is integral to ensuring that residents not only survive but thrive, reinforcing that this initiative is viable and beneficial on both an individual and societal level.

While it might initially seem that the primary focus of these transformation towns is to offer support and assistance to the homeless, the broader impact on the United States will be profound and far-reaching. These towns are not merely charitable ventures; they are about providing a second chance—empowering individuals to play an active role in the revitalization of our nation.

By developing new, vibrant communities in areas that are currently underutilized, these individuals will help attract skilled talent to the U.S. and generate significant economic value. Moreover, their engagement in social programs, such as free lunch initiatives for school children and other community-focused projects, will deliver lasting benefits to society as a whole.

> **Homeless citizens will realize that, in the long run, their contributions to the nation will far outweigh the initial support they receive through the Cities of Hope Initiative. This understanding will foster a deep sense of self-dignity and self-confidence as they recognize their vital role in the nation's growth. This is the right approach for them and the broader society, as it ensures a mutually beneficial outcome for all involved.**

Environmental Sustainability

Creating sustainable environments within Cities of Hope is not just a noble goal; it's essential for the long-term success and viability of the project. By integrating green principles into every aspect of the town's design and operation, we can ensure that these towns contribute positively to the environment while offering their residents a higher quality of life.

Green Building Practices

In laying the groundwork for environmentally sustainable Cities of Hope, it is crucial to incorporate green building practices from the outset. These practices include using sustainable materials, enhancing energy efficiency, and minimizing waste throughout construction. By leveraging innovations in building technology, such as the use of prefabricated components and modular design, we can significantly reduce the environmental footprint of constructing new homes and facilities.

A key element of green building practices is proper insulation and energy-efficient windows, which help in reducing heating and cooling demands. Additionally, buildings can be designed to take advantage of natural light, reducing the need for artificial lighting during the day. Implementing green roofs and walls not only aids in insulation but also supports local biodiversity and improves urban air quality.

Renewable Energy Sources

The backbone of a sustainable industrial town is its energy system. Prioritizing renewable energy sources over fossil fuels will reduce carbon emissions and promote energy independence. Solar panels, wind turbines, and geothermal energy systems should be integral components of the town's energy infrastructure. Government incentives and subsidies can help offset the initial costs of these renewable technologies, making them more accessible and appealing to investors and developers.

Integrating microgrids that combine renewable sources with advanced battery storage systems is also beneficial. These microgrids can ensure a reliable power supply, even when renewable sources fluctuate. This decentralization of energy production enhances resilience and empowers local communities by giving them greater control over their energy use.

Waste Reduction Initiatives

Aiming for zero waste is another vital aspect of environmental sustainability in Cities of Hope. This begins with a robust waste management system that emphasizes the reduction, reuse, and recycling of materials. By creating a **circular economy** within the town, we can minimize the volume of waste that ends up in landfills and promote the sustainable use of resources.

Implementing comprehensive recycling programs is a must. These programs should cover a wide range of materials, from household waste to industrial by-products. Composting organic waste will reduce landfill usage and produce valuable fertilizer that can support the town's agriculture initiatives. Companies within the industrial parks should be encouraged to adopt manufacturing processes that generate less waste and make use of recycled materials whenever possible.

Public awareness campaigns and educational programs can significantly ensure that residents and businesses buy into these waste reduction initiatives. Encouraging behaviors such as eliminating single-use plastics, participating in community clean-up efforts, and responsible consumption can contribute significantly to maintaining a sustainable community.

In conclusion, integrating environmental sustainability into the fabric of Cities of Hope isn't just about protecting the planet; it's about creating thriving communities that are built to last. By adopting green building practices, utilizing renewable energy sources, and implementing effective waste reduction initiatives, we lay the foundation for economically viable, socially equitable, and environmentally sound towns. As government officials, technocrats, academics, and members of the public, our collective action and support are paramount in making this vision a reality. Together, we can build a sustainable future where Cities of Hope addresses homelessness and sets a benchmark for environmental stewardship.

Green Building Practices

Green building practices are essential for achieving environmental sustainability in the development of Cities of Hope. Adopting these practices minimizes the ecological footprint and creates healthier living conditions for residents. Below are key principles and strategies that can guide the implementation of green building practices in Cities of Hope.

Energy Efficiency

One of the most crucial elements of green building is energy efficiency. Incorporating energy-efficient designs and technologies, such as high-performance insulation, energy-efficient windows, and advanced HVAC systems, can significantly reduce energy consumption. Using energy-efficient appliances and lighting further cuts down energy use. Implementing smart grid technologies allows for optimal energy management, reducing wastage and promoting sustainability.

Use of Sustainable Materials

Selecting sustainable construction materials is another vital aspect of green building practices. Materials that are recycled, renewable, or have low environmental impact should be prioritized. For example, bamboo flooring, reclaimed wood, and recycled metal can be used in various construction phases. These materials reduce resource depletion and lower the carbon footprint associated with manufacturing and transportation.

Water Conservation

Water is a precious resource, and its conservation is a significant concern in green building practices. Incorporating low-flow fixtures, rainwater harvesting systems, and greywater recycling can lead to substantial water savings. Landscaping with drought-resistant plants and using efficient irrigation systems are additional measures that contribute to water conservation.

Indoor Environmental Quality

Maintaining a high indoor environmental quality (IEQ) is critical for the health and well-being of residents. This involves using non-toxic, low-VOC (volatile organic compounds) paints and finishes, ensuring proper ventilation, and maximizing natural light. Improving IEQ enhances resident comfort, promotes productivity, and reduces health issues related to poor indoor air quality.

Renewable Energy Integration

Integrating renewable energy sources such as solar, wind, and geothermal energy into building designs can make Cities of Hope more self-sufficient and environmentally friendly. Installing solar panels on rooftops, creating small wind farms, and utilizing geothermal heat pumps are effective strategies to harness renewable energy. These initiatives reduce reliance on fossil fuels and decrease greenhouse gas emissions.

Waste Reduction

Reducing waste during construction and operation is a fundamental component of green building. Implementing waste management plans that prioritize recycling and reuse can significantly lower the volume of waste sent to landfills. Encouraging the use of modular construction techniques, which allow for easy disassembly and reuse, further promotes sustainability.

In conclusion, adopting green building practices in the development of Cities of Hope addresses environmental concerns and creates economic and social benefits. By implementing energy-efficient designs, using sustainable materials, conserving water, ensuring high indoor environmental quality, integrating renewable energy sources, and focusing on waste reduction, Cities of Hope can set a new standard for sustainable urban development. These practices will ultimately contribute to creating a more viable, resilient, and prosperous community for all residents.

Renewable Energy Sources

Renewable energy sources play an indispensable role in our pursuit of environmental sustainability within Cities of Hope. Leveraging renewable energy aligns with global efforts to combat climate change and ensures a sustainable and economically viable energy future for these towns. This section examines various renewable energy sources, their implementation, and their impact on both the environment and the economic stability of Cities of Hope.

Firstly, solar energy stands out as a prominent renewable resource due to its widespread availability and decreasing costs. Modern photovoltaic (PV) panels convert sunlight directly into electricity. Installing solar farms on unused land or integrating solar panels into building designs can significantly decrease reliance on non-renewable energy. For Cities of Hope, solar energy can meet a substantial portion of energy needs, simultaneously reducing utility costs and carbon footprints.

Wind energy is another viable option, especially in regions with consistent and strong wind patterns. Wind turbines can be established both onshore and offshore. The initial investment in wind turbines is often balanced by low operational costs and long lifespans, making wind power an attractive option for long-term sustainability. Furthermore, technological advancements continue to enhance turbine efficiency and energy output.

Hydropower, derived from flowing or falling water, offers another robust option, particularly for towns situated near rivers or water bodies. Small-scale hydroelectric plants can support the energy grid while having minimal environmental impact compared to larger dams. However, evaluating potential ecological disruptions and community impacts is crucial before choosing this energy source.

Another promising source is geothermal energy, which harnesses heat from the Earth's core. Geothermal plants provide a stable and continuous energy supply, relatively unaffected by weather or seasons. Geothermal energy can be a reliable and clean source for Cities of Hope located in geologically favorable regions.

Biomass energy, produced from organic materials like plant and animal waste, offers a way to convert waste into valuable energy. Biomass systems can generate electricity, heat, or even fuel, contributing to waste reduction efforts while providing energy. Integrating biomass facilities within the Cities of Hope can create a closed-loop system where waste products aid in sustaining energy needs.

Implementing a mix of these renewable energy sources ensures resilience and adaptability. This hybrid approach can safeguard industries and residents against energy shortages and price fluctuations, enhancing the economic stability of the towns. Additionally, investments in renewable energy infrastructures create job opportunities in the construction, operation, and maintenance fields, thus contributing to job creation and workforce development.

Government incentives and policies are crucial in facilitating the transition to renewable energy. Furthermore, public awareness and education on the benefits of renewable energy can foster community support and participation.

The integration of renewable energy sources into the design and operation of Cities of Hope exemplifies a commitment to environmental sustainability. Through careful planning and strategic investments, these towns can serve as models for balancing economic growth with ecological responsibility, inspiring action and participation from both government entities and citizens in the United States.

Waste Reduction Initiatives

Effective waste reduction is a cornerstone of environmental sustainability in the development of Cities of Hope. It's a crucial element for minimizing the ecological footprint and a potential avenue for generating employment and fostering community engagement. This section delves into various waste reduction strategies, focusing on practicality and the potential to create tangible benefits for both residents and the environment.

One of the primary aspects of waste reduction is the implementation of robust recycling programs. By categorizing waste into recyclable, compostable, and non-recyclable segments, Cities of Hope can drastically cut down on the amount of waste destined for landfills. These programs should be supported by comprehensive education campaigns designed to inform residents about the importance and benefits of proper waste segregation. The goal here is environmental stewardship and the creation of jobs within the recycling sector, from waste collectors to sorting facility operators.

In addition, composting offers another effective method for waste reduction. Organic waste, when handled correctly, can be converted into useful compost that benefits local agriculture. This cycle diminishes landfill dependency and provides a sustainable nutrient source for the town's agricultural initiatives. Setting up community composting centers can involve residents directly, increasing the sense of ownership and responsibility towards waste management.

Furthermore, adopting a zero-waste approach in industrial operations can substantially decrease the amount of industrial waste. Encouraging businesses to evaluate their processes and materials for opportunities to reuse by-products and reduce overall waste aligns with broader sustainability goals. This initiative can be supported through policy incentives and partnerships with organizations specializing in sustainable industrial practices.

Encouraging the reduction of single-use plastics is another critical initiative. Establishing policies limiting or banning single-use plastics and promoting alternatives can reduce waste significantly. Towns can implement these policies in conjunction with awareness programs to ensure community buy-in. Businesses within the town can be incentivized to switch to sustainable packaging solutions, thus fostering a culture of environmental responsibility.

Lastly, public awareness campaigns and community engagement are vital. Residents must understand the broader benefits of waste reduction and how their actions contribute to the town's sustainability goals. This can be achieved through workshops, community challenges, and educational outreach. Cities of Hope can pave the way for long-term environmental health and economic vitality by fostering a collective mindset centered on sustainability.

Governance and Administration

Effective governance and administration are critical for Cities of Hope's successful implementation and sustainability. This chapter delves into the framework needed to administer these towns efficiently, ensuring they meet their economic, social, and environmental objectives.

Local Government Structures

The governance of Cities of Hope should be rooted in robust local government structures. To foster a collaborative environment, these structures must integrate various stakeholders, including residents, businesses, and government officials. Local government bodies should be responsible for:

- **Regulatory Oversight:** Ensuring compliance with zoning, labor, and environmental regulations.
- **Service Provision:** Managing essential public services like water, electricity, waste management, and healthcare.
- **Economic Development:** Facilitating job creation, supporting local businesses, and attracting new investments.

Establishing a council comprising elected representatives from different sectors of the community can provide a democratic means of governance. Regular town hall meetings can also serve as platforms for dialogue between the government and the residents, offering transparency and accountability.

Community Leadership Programs

Engaging the community through leadership programs is crucial for fostering a sense of ownership and responsibility among residents. These programs should aim to develop leaders who can address local issues and contribute to the town's long-term vision. Key components include:

- **Training and Development:** Offering workshops and courses on leadership, conflict resolution, and community organizing.
- **Youth Engagement:** Creating opportunities for young people to take on leadership roles in community projects and initiatives.
- **Volunteerism:** Encouraging residents to participate in volunteer programs builds community solidarity and resilience.

Leadership programs not only empower residents but also ensure that the community has a pool of knowledgeable and skilled individuals who can step in when needed.

Public-Private Partnerships

The success of Cities of Hope hinges on effective public-private partnerships (PPPs). These collaborations leverage the strengths of both sectors to achieve shared goals. Essential aspects of PPPs include:

- **Shared Investment:** Pooling resources for infrastructure development, such as roads, utilities, and public facilities.

- **Operational Efficiency:** Private entities bringing in managerial expertise and efficiency, particularly in areas like healthcare, education, and waste management.

- **Innovation and Technology:** Facilitating the adoption of the latest technologies and innovative solutions for enhanced service delivery.

Successful PPPs require clear agreements that delineate public and private entities' responsibilities, financial commitments, and performance metrics. These partnerships can drive economic growth, improve service delivery, and enhance City of Hope's overall quality of life.

In conclusion, a well-structured governance framework encompassing local government structures, community leadership programs, and public-private partnerships is essential for the administration of Cities of Hope. This approach ensures efficient management and fosters community involvement and sustainable development, paving the way for successful Cities of Hope.

Local Government Structures

The foundation of Cities of Hope rests on a robust local government structure. Effective governance is paramount in ensuring the sustainability and success of these communities. Given Cities of Hope's unique demographic and economic makeup, local governments must be adaptable, forward-thinking, and nimble in their operations.

Local government structures in these towns should prioritize inclusivity and community engagement. A key strategy is the establishment of councils composed of government representatives, business leaders, and residents. This tripartite system ensures varied perspectives are considered in decision-making processes, fostering a sense of ownership and accountability across all community levels.

Formal governance frameworks should include entities like a Town Council, Planning and Zoning Boards, and Public Health Committees. Each body must have clearly defined roles and responsibilities to avoid redundancy and inefficiency. The Town Council, for instance, could focus on overarching policy implementation and budget oversight, while Planning and Zoning Boards would handle land use and infrastructure development.

In addition, implementing Community Leadership Programs can significantly enhance local governance. By offering residents leadership training and capacity-building workshops, towns can cultivate a pool of skilled individuals ready to take on governance roles. This democratizes the decision-making process and ensures a continuous supply of knowledgeable leaders as the community evolves.

Public-Private Partnerships (PPPs) are another critical element in the administrative framework. Collaboration between government entities and private sector stakeholders can bring in much-needed expertise and financial resources for town development projects. When adequately regulated and transparent, PPPs can bridge gaps in public funding and expedite infrastructural and service-related projects.

Local governments must also adopt modern technological systems to streamline operations. This includes the implementation of e-governance platforms that can facilitate everything from public service requests to real-time updates on town projects. Automation in administrative tasks can lead to significant cost savings and improved efficiency, ensuring that governance keeps pace with the needs of the community.

Moreover, inter-town collaboration should be promoted to share best practices and resources. Forming regional alliances can help Cities of Hope mitigate common challenges such as environmental concerns, healthcare services, and emergency responses. This pooled resource approach can lead to collective bargaining advantages and knowledge-sharing opportunities that benefit all involved parties.

In summary, the success of Cities of Hope heavily relies on robust, adaptable local government structures. These towns can create an efficient and inclusive governance model by fostering community engagement, leveraging public-private partnerships, and embracing technology. Ultimately, strong local governance will not only ensure the towns' operational success but also enhance the quality of life for all residents, making the vision of eradicating homelessness and creating profitable communities a tangible reality.

Community Leadership Programs

Community leadership programs are vital to the success and sustainability of Cities of Hope. These programs enable local residents to take an active role in governance and decision-making processes, fostering a sense of ownership and responsibility within the community. By empowering individuals, we create a more resilient and engaged population capable of addressing both immediate and long-term challenges.

The primary goal of these programs is to build a cadre of local leaders who are well-versed in their communities' unique needs and opportunities. Local leaders can act as liaisons between the residents and the town's administration, ensuring that the voices of the people are heard and considered in governance decisions. To achieve this, community leadership programs should focus on several key components:

1. **Training and Development:** Structured training sessions are essential to equip potential leaders with the necessary skills and knowledge. These sessions can cover a wide range of topics, from public speaking and conflict resolution to project management and financial literacy.

2. **Mentorship Opportunities:** Connecting emerging leaders with experienced mentors can provide invaluable guidance and support. Mentors can share their insights and experiences, helping new leaders navigate the complexities of community governance.

3. **Inclusion and Diversity:** Ensuring that leadership programs are accessible to all residents, regardless of their background, is crucial. Diverse leadership can provide broader perspectives and more innovative solutions to community issues.

4. **Community Projects:** Hands-on projects allow potential leaders to apply what they've learned in real-world settings. These projects can bring tangible community benefits while providing practical leadership experience.

5. **Feedback Mechanisms:** Regular feedback sessions with residents can help leaders understand the community's evolving needs and aspirations. This fosters a culture of continuous improvement and responsiveness.

Effective community leadership programs create a ripple effect, strengthening the individuals who participate directly and the broader community. When residents see their neighbors taking initiative and making positive changes, they are more likely to become engaged and proactive themselves. This engagement is crucial for the long-term viability of Cities of Hope, as it drives collective action towards shared goals.

Moreover, community leadership programs can help bridge the gap between the government and its citizens. By cultivating leaders from within the community, these programs ensure that governance remains rooted in local realities and responsive to the people it serves. This alignment is particularly important in the context of Cities of Hope, where the close-knit nature of the community can be a significant asset if leveraged appropriately.

In conclusion, community leadership programs are indispensable components of Cities of Hope's governance and administration framework. By fostering local leadership, these programs enhance community resilience and ensure that governance structures are more responsive, inclusive, and effective. This creates a solid foundation for addressing the homeless crisis and building thriving, sustainable communities where every resident has the opportunity to contribute and succeed.

Public-Private Partnerships

The development of Cities of Hope to tackle homelessness and foster economic growth hinges on effective cooperation between the public and private sectors. Public-private partnerships (PPPs) are essential for leveraging the strengths and resources of both sectors to create sustainable and profitable communities.

In a PPP, the public sector typically provides regulatory support, land, and initial funding, while the private sector contributes expertise, efficiency, and additional investment. For Cities of Hope, this collaboration can streamline project development, reduce costs, and distribute risks more evenly. Moreover, the strategic alliance between government entities and private companies ensures that projects align with public interests while maintaining the dynamism of private enterprise.

One of the core advantages of PPPs in this context is their ability to undertake the development of essential infrastructure and services. This includes the construction of affordable housing, healthcare facilities, educational institutions, and recreational centers—all key components of a thriving industrial town. By sharing the financial burden and operational responsibilities, public and private partners can deliver these facilities more effectively than they could alone. **In addition to the overall funding model I am proposing, private capital can join the government concerning the investments for funding the businesses and industrial complexes essential for Cities of Hope.**

Furthermore, PPPs are instrumental in job creation and workforce development. Private companies participating in these partnerships often bring with them opportunities for employment, training programs, and career advancement for residents. This symbiotic relationship not only addresses immediate employment needs but also enhances the long-term economic stability of the town.

Another critical role of PPPs is in the realm of technological integration and innovation. Smart city technologies, data analytics, and automation can significantly improve the efficiency and sustainability of Cities of Hope. Private sector firms specializing in these areas can offer cutting-edge solutions and continuous improvements, supported by public sector policies encouraging technological uptake.

Effective governance and administration of PPPs require clear frameworks and transparent processes. This includes well-drafted contracts, performance monitoring mechanisms, and dispute resolution strategies. Additionally, stakeholder engagement is crucial. Regular consultations with community members, local businesses, and other relevant parties help ensure that the direction of development aligns with the needs and expectations of all stakeholders.

Lastly, a successful PPP model fosters a sense of shared purpose and community ownership. When residents see the tangible benefits of public-private collaborations—such as improved living conditions, job opportunities, and accessible services—they are more likely to support and participate in the town's long-term sustainability efforts.

In conclusion, public-private partnerships are a fundamental aspect of the governance and administration of Cities of Hope. By combining public oversight with private sector efficiency and innovation, PPPs can create viable, profitable, and community-oriented solutions to homelessness and economic development.

Transportation and Infrastructure

Effective transportation and infrastructure form the backbone of any thriving industrial town. To ensure these towns are not only sustainable but also economically viable, robust planning and investment in transportation networks and infrastructure are imperative. This chapter delves into the elements that make such systems functional and efficient, fostering ease of movement and connectivity.

Public Transit Systems

A comprehensive public transit system is essential for connecting residents to job opportunities, community services, and other critical amenities. By integrating various modes of transit—such as buses, trams, and bicycles—the towns can offer affordable and efficient transportation options for all residents. These systems should prioritize accessibility and reliability, ensuring that they meet the needs of different demographics and facilitate seamless travel within and between Cities of Hope.

Creating transport hubs that link various modes of transit can significantly reduce commute times and improve overall quality of life. Additionally, adopting green transit solutions, such as electric buses or solar-powered trams, aligns with the broader goals of environmental sustainability discussed in previous chapters. Public transit systems can also mitigate traffic congestion and lower pollution levels by reducing reliance on personal vehicles.

Road and Utility Networks

The backbone of any industrial town is its road and utility network. An efficiently designed road system enhances access to industrial parks, commercial zones, and residential areas. Well-maintained roads are crucial for the smooth operation of businesses and the safe, swift movement of goods and people.

Beyond roads, utility networks—comprising water supply, sewage systems, electricity, and telecommunication lines—are vital for the daily operation of both households and industries. Initial planning should incorporate future growth and development, ensuring that the infrastructure can accommodate increasing demand over time. Implementing smart grids and advanced utility management technologies can enhance the efficiency and reliability of these systems, providing cost savings and operational benefits.

Digital Infrastructure

In today's digital age, robust digital infrastructure is a necessity rather than a luxury. High-speed internet access is crucial for businesses, educational institutions, healthcare facilities, and individuals. Investment in fiber optic networks and 5G technology can provide the high-speed connectivity required for modern digital applications and services.

Furthermore, digital infrastructure plays a pivotal role in the implementation of smart city technologies. Sensors, data analytics, and IoT (Internet of Things) devices can optimize resource use, improve public safety, and enhance service delivery. For instance, smart traffic management systems can reduce congestion and travel times, while real-time data analytics can help maintain utilities more efficiently.

By fostering digital literacy and providing access to digital tools and resources, Cities of Hope can enhance educational and economic opportunities for residents. Collaborations with tech companies and educational institutions can facilitate community training programs, ensuring residents are equipped to thrive in a digital economy.

In conclusion, transportation and infrastructure are integral to the success and sustainability of Cities of Hope. We can create connected, efficient, and resilient communities by investing in effective public transit systems, robust road and utility networks, and state-of-the-art digital infrastructure. These efforts improve residents' quality of life and attract businesses and investors, driving economic growth and ensuring long-term feasibility.

As we move forward, stakeholder engagement and continuous assessment will be key to adapting and refining these systems, ensuring they meet evolving needs and challenges. With the insights gathered here, we will discuss long-term sustainability plans, community involvement, and methods for continuous improvement in the subsequent chapters.

Public Transit Systems

Public transit systems play a pivotal role in the overall transportation and infrastructure framework of Cities of Hope. These systems are essential not only for facilitating the daily commute of residents but also for promoting environmental sustainability by reducing the reliance on personal vehicles. Effective public transit systems can significantly enhance the livability and economic vitality of these towns, making them attractive to both businesses and residents.

One of the primary objectives of establishing a robust public transit system is to ensure connectivity within the town and to neighboring regions. This connectivity is crucial for enabling residents to access employment hubs, educational institutions, healthcare facilities, and recreational centers without undue delay or expense. A well-integrated public transit system can thus serve as the backbone of the town, ensuring seamless movement and fostering a sense of community. This is critical as industrial complexes will hire other Americans who will commute from other towns.

- **Accessibility:** Public transit options must be accessible to all residents, including the elderly, disabled, and economically disadvantaged. This can be achieved through the provision of features such as low-floor buses, audio-visual announcements, and strategically placed transit stops.

- **Affordability:** Keeping the cost of public transit low is crucial to its adoption. Subsidized fare structures (because the Cities of Hope can afford it thanks to the profits the businesses will generate) can help ensure that transportation costs do not become a barrier for residents, particularly for those in lower-income brackets.

- **Frequency and Reliability:** High-frequency and reliable transit schedules are vital for ensuring that residents can depend on public transit for their daily needs. Implementing real-time tracking technologies and rigorous maintenance schedules can reduce wait times and enhance service reliability.

Investment in diverse modes of public transit, such as buses, light rail, and bike-sharing programs, can provide residents with multiple options for navigating the town. Integrating these modes into a cohesive network enhances convenience and flexibility, facilitating door-to-door transportation solutions. For larger towns, a multi-modal transit hub can serve as the nexus for different transit options, ensuring smooth transitions from one mode to another.

Another critical aspect is the incorporation of environmentally friendly practices within the public transit system. This includes using electric or hybrid buses, bike-sharing programs, and infrastructure supporting walking. Such initiatives can considerably reduce the town's carbon footprint, aligning with broader goals of environmental sustainability outlined in other sections of this book.

Collaboration with regional transit authorities and private transportation providers can further expand the reach and efficiency of public transit systems. Public-private partnerships (PPPs) can also be instrumental in attracting the expertise and capital necessary for large-scale transit projects.

Ultimately, a well-planned and executed public transit system is indispensable for the success of Cities of Hope. It ensures the smooth movement of people and goods and enhances the overall quality of life for residents. By fostering economic activity and reducing environmental impact, an efficient public transit system contributes to these vibrant communities' long-term sustainability and growth.

Integrating public transit with broader transportation and utility networks, as elaborated in the following sections, will create a comprehensive infrastructure that supports the multifaceted needs of the Cities of Hope.

Road and Utility Networks

Effective road and utility networks are the backbone of any thriving community, and this holds especially true for the proposed Cities of Hope. These networks not only facilitate smooth transport and logistics but also ensure that essential utilities like water, electricity, and telecommunications are seamlessly provided. The design and implementation of these networks require meticulous planning and coordination to support both residential life and industrial activities.

The primary goal for road networks in Cities of Hope is to enable efficient movement of goods, services, and people. This includes integrating various types of roads, such as main thoroughfares, secondary streets, and pathways for non-motorized transport. Key factors to consider in the layout include connectivity to major highways, ease of access to industrial parks, and minimal traffic congestion within the town. Additionally, suitable road surfaces and maintenance plans are crucial to ensure longevity and reliability, reducing long-term costs and inconvenience.

Utility networks, on the other hand, make sure that residents and industries have constant access to essential services. Potable water supply, sewage systems, electricity, and high-speed internet are some of the critical utilities that need robust infrastructure. Special attention needs to be given to sustainability; for instance, smart grids can be employed to optimize electricity use, and renewable energy sources can be integrated into the town's design. The utility network should be resilient to disruptions and designed to support the projected growth of the community.

The coordination between road and utility networks can't be overstated. For example, the placement of underground utilities should be planned in tandem with road construction to avoid future complications. Furthermore, adopting smart city technologies can result in more efficient management of both road and utility networks. From intelligent traffic systems to real-time utility usage monitoring, technological integration plays a significant role in the modern infrastructure landscape.

Overall, well-designed road and utility networks are pivotal in achieving the vision of Cities of Hope. They enhance industries' operational efficiency and improve residents' quality of life. By investing in advanced, sustainable, and resilient infrastructure, it's possible to create communities that eradicate homelessness and set the standard for future urban development.

Digital Infrastructure

In today's interconnected world, a robust digital infrastructure is crucial for any industrial town's success. This section will explore the components and integrations necessary to create a seamless and efficient digital environment in these new communities. A digital infrastructure supports various facets of daily life, from essential services and business operations to community engagement and innovation.

The foundation of a digital infrastructure begins with high-speed internet connectivity. Reliable broadband access is no longer a luxury but a necessity for both residents and businesses. It facilitates online education, telemedicine, remote work, and continuous learning opportunities. To achieve this, Cities of Hope must partner with internet service providers to ensure comprehensive coverage, including in rural and underdeveloped areas. Investing in fiber-optic networks and 5G technology can provide the required speed and bandwidth to support a growing digital ecosystem.

Next, consider the role of smart city technologies. These include Internet of Things (IoT) devices, sensors, and data analytics platforms that enhance the efficiency and quality of municipal services. Smart lighting, waste management systems, and energy grids can drastically improve operational efficiencies and reduce costs. For example, smart grids can help manage energy consumption more effectively, ensuring that industrial operations and residential areas alike are energy-efficient and sustainable.

Moreover, digital infrastructure extends to public safety and emergency response. Enhanced communication networks allow for quicker response times and better coordination among emergency services. Implementing smart surveillance systems and emergency alert mechanisms can help ensure the safety and security of residents.

Another key component is the integration of digital platforms for government services. E-governance platforms allow residents to access a range of public services online, from applying for permits to paying utility bills. These platforms enhance transparency and reduce administrative burdens for citizens and government employees. User-friendly design and accessibility standards must be prioritized to ensure that everyone, regardless of their technical proficiency, can benefit from these digital services.

In terms of education and workforce development, a strong digital infrastructure facilitates access to online courses, training programs, and professional development resources. Collaboration with educational institutions and online platforms can provide residents with the tools they need to acquire new skills and adapt to changing job markets, fostering a culture of lifelong learning.

Finally, community engagement can be significantly enhanced through digital means. Social media, community forums, and mobile apps can serve as platforms for residents to voice their opinions, participate in local governance, and foster a sense of community. These digital tools also provide a means for government officials to communicate updates and gather feedback efficiently.

In conclusion, establishing a comprehensive digital infrastructure is not just about technology; it's about creating a resilient, efficient, and inclusive environment that benefits all aspects of an industrial town. The integration of high-speed internet, smart technologies, e-governance, and digital community platforms will play a pivotal role in achieving the vision of sustainable and thriving Cities of Hope.

Long-term Sustainability

Ensuring the long-term sustainability of Cities of Hope is paramount not only for eradicating homelessness but also for creating thriving, self-sufficient communities. This chapter focuses on three crucial aspects that contribute to the enduring success of these towns: maintenance plans, community involvement, and continuous improvement mechanisms.

Maintenance Plans

The first step in safeguarding the longevity of Cities of Hope involves comprehensive maintenance plans. These plans must cover all aspects of the town's infrastructure, including housing, industrial facilities, public spaces, and services. Regular inspections and timely repairs are essential to prevent the deterioration of physical assets.

Creating a maintenance schedule that includes routine checks and preventive measures can go a long way. For instance, housing units should undergo periodic evaluations to ensure they meet safety standards and are comfortable for residents. Industrial facilities must be maintained to comply with regulations and to function efficiently. Public spaces and recreational centers should be regularly cleaned and upgraded to ensure they remain inviting and usable.

Funding for these maintenance activities can be sourced from various channels, including local government allocations, community contributions, and partnerships with private entities. A sustainable financial model, integrating these diverse funding sources guarantees that maintenance activities will not stall due to budgetary constraints.

Community Involvement

Community involvement is pivotal for the sustainability of Cities of Hope. Engaging residents in the upkeep and development of their community fosters a sense of ownership and responsibility. Several strategies can be employed to nurture this involvement:

- **Resident Committees:** Establish resident committees dedicated to various aspects such as neighborhood watch, public space maintenance, and event organization. These committees can act as a bridge between the administration and the community, ensuring that residents' voices are heard.

- **Volunteer Programs:** Encourage volunteer programs where community members contribute their time and skills for the betterment of the town. This can include activities like teaching, organizing clean-up drives, or providing free services.

- **Feedback Mechanisms:** Implement robust feedback mechanisms to gather residents' input on ongoing projects and future plans. Surveys, town hall meetings, and suggestion boxes are effective tools to collect and address concerns.

- **Local Events:** Hosting local events such as festivals, sports competitions, and cultural nights fosters community spirit and helps bond residents.

An engaged community is resilient and adaptive, ready to confront challenges and contribute to solutions. This level of participation is crucial for sustaining the town's vibrancy and functionality over the long term.

Continuous Improvement Mechanisms

No system is perfect from the outset, and Cities of Hope is no exception. Continuous improvement mechanisms ensure that the town's development is dynamic and responsive to changing needs and challenges. These mechanisms should include:

- **Performance Monitoring:** Establish a set of key performance indicators (KPIs) to monitor various aspects of the town's operations and quality of life. Frequent evaluation of these KPIs can help identify areas needing improvement.

- **Innovation Adoption:** Stay updated on technological advancements and integrate smart city technologies to enhance efficiency and improve residents' quality of life. Technologies in waste management, energy efficiency, and digital communication are particularly beneficial.

- **Policy Reviews:** Regularly review and update policies governing the town. This iterative approach ensures that the town's rules and regulations remain relevant and effective.

- **Training Programs:** Offer continuous training programs for town administrators and other key personnel. Keeping staff updated with the latest skills and knowledge ensures the town is managed effectively.

Cities of Hope can remain adaptable, progressive, and sustainable by setting up these continuous improvement mechanisms. The objective is to create a scalable model that can evolve with time, ensuring both immediate and future needs are met.

In conclusion, the long-term sustainability of Cities of Hope hinges on a well-rounded approach incorporating meticulous maintenance plans, active community involvement, and robust continuous improvement mechanisms. These elements work together to form a resilient, evolving community capable of overcoming challenges and thriving for generations to come.

Maintenance Plans

For the long-term sustainability of Cities of Hope, the implementation of robust maintenance plans is critical. Effective maintenance ensures that infrastructure remains functional, safe, and efficient, thus prolonging the lifecycle of various facilities and systems within these towns. By prioritizing regular upkeep, we can mitigate the costs and disruptions associated with unexpected failures or extensive repairs.

The maintenance plans for Cities of Hope should encompass several core areas:

- **Infrastructure Maintenance:** Regular inspections and timely repairs are essential for roads, bridges, and utility networks. Advanced monitoring technologies can be employed to detect wear and tear early, allowing for preemptive action.

- **Building and Facility Upkeep:** This includes residential housing, educational institutions, healthcare facilities, and recreational centers. Implementing a system for routine checks and minor repairs can prevent larger, more costly issues down the line.

- **Public Spaces and Amenities:** Parks, playgrounds, and other communal areas require consistent attention to ensure they remain safe and welcoming. Landscaping, waste management, and facility repairs should be scheduled regularly.

- **Essential Services Maintenance:** This includes the continuous operation and servicing of water supply, waste management, and energy systems. Renewable energy installations, in particular, need constant monitoring and maintenance to function optimally.

To effectively execute these plans, several strategies should be adopted:

1. **Comprehensive Maintenance Scheduling:** Creating a detailed calendar that outlines specific maintenance tasks, along with their frequency, ensures that no aspect of town infrastructure is neglected.

2. **Training and Workforce Development:** Skilled personnel are crucial for the implementation of maintenance plans. Ongoing training programs ensure that maintenance staff are knowledgeable about the latest techniques and technologies.

3. **Budget Allocation:** Setting aside sufficient financial resources is essential for timely maintenance. Budget planning should account for both routine maintenance and unexpected repairs.

4. **Community Involvement:** Engaging community members in maintenance efforts fosters a sense of ownership and responsibility. Volunteers can assist with minor tasks, and their feedback can highlight maintenance needs that might otherwise be overlooked.

5. **Technological Integration:** Utilizing data analytics and smart technologies can streamline maintenance processes. IoT sensors, for instance, can provide real-time data on infrastructure integrity, helping to identify issues before they escalate.

In summary, the longevity and sustainability of Cities of Hope hinge on meticulous and proactive maintenance plans. By incorporating regular inspections, skilled workforce training, proper budget allocation, community engagement, and technological tools, we can ensure that these towns remain viable and profitable for years to come.

Community Involvement

Long-term sustainability is a cornerstone of the Cities of Hope concept, and nowhere is this more evident than in community involvement. Engaging residents in the ongoing development and governance of these towns ensures not only their immediate success but also their endurance over the years.

Residents ' active participation fosters a sense of ownership and responsibility. By involving community members in decision-making processes, from planning town policies to organizing local events, we create an empowered populace that's invested in the well-being of their environment. This not only enhances the quality of life but also reduces the dependency on external agencies for town upkeep.

One effective approach is the formation of community committees that bring together diverse groups of residents. These committees can focus on various aspects of town life, such as safety, environmental preservation, and social activities. Through these platforms, community members can voice their opinions and collaborate on solutions tailored to their specific needs.

Volunteering opportunities also play a crucial role in community involvement. By encouraging residents to contribute their time and skills, we can address various needs within the town, from maintaining public spaces to mentoring young residents. Volunteer initiatives supplement municipal efforts and strengthen the social fabric by promoting a culture of mutual support and cooperation.

Additionally, partnerships with local organizations, schools, and businesses can amplify community engagement. Collaborating with educational institutions, for instance, can support lifelong learning programs that empower residents with new skills, thereby contributing to personal growth and community resilience. Local businesses, in return, benefit from a committed workforce and a loyal customer base, creating a symbiotic relationship that bolsters the town's economy.

Community events and recreational activities are also vital. Festivals, sports leagues, and cultural programs offer residents platforms to connect, celebrate, and share experiences. These activities are critical for fostering a sense of community and belonging, which are essential for long-term sustainability.

In summary, community involvement is indispensable for the long-term sustainability of Cities of Hope. By encouraging active participation, fostering collaboration, and promoting volunteerism, we can create resilient communities that thrive socially, economically, and environmentally. It's a collective effort where everyone has a role to play in achieving and maintaining the vision of sustainable, inclusive, and prosperous towns.

Continuous Improvement Mechanisms

Ensuring the long-term sustainability of Cities of Hope requires more than just initial planning and implementation. To thrive over time, these towns must adopt continuous improvement mechanisms that allow for ongoing assessment, adaptation, and enhancement. This dynamic approach addresses emerging challenges and embraces new opportunities for growth and efficiency.

A primary tool for continuous improvement is **regular performance evaluation**. Periodic assessments using predefined Key Performance Indicators (KPIs) will help gauge the success of various initiatives—from housing and employment to community services and environmental sustainability. These evaluations will provide actionable insights, highlighting areas where interventions are needed. Using data analytics, trends can be identified early, enabling proactive measures rather than reactive fixes.

Resident Feedback Loop systems play a crucial role. Direct input from town residents offers invaluable perspectives on day-to-day living conditions and emerging issues. Establishing multiple channels for feedback—such as town hall meetings, digital platforms, and community surveys—ensures that all residents have a voice. The collected data must be systematically reviewed and incorporated into decision-making processes, closing the gap between administration and community needs.

A commitment to **innovative adaptation** is essential. Integrating new technologies can enhance operational efficiency and community well-being as technological advancements continue to evolve. Automation in industries, smart city infrastructure, and renewable energy innovations must be continually explored and adopted as appropriate. Partnerships with tech companies and academic institutions can pave the way for pilot projects and cutting-edge solutions that keep the towns at the forefront of progress.

Stakeholder Engagement mechanisms are another pillar. Collaborating closely with various stakeholders—including local businesses, non-profits, academic institutions, and governmental bodies—ensures a comprehensive approach to town management. Regular stakeholder meetings and collaborative workshops can foster a shared vision and collective problem-solving, leveraging the strengths and resources of each participating entity.

Lastly, **ongoing education and training programs** are vital for sustaining a skilled workforce and informed citizenry. Continuous learning opportunities for residents and employees help to address skill gaps and prepare the community for future challenges. Programs should be tailored to the evolving needs of the town's industries and should promote lifelong learning as a principle for all residents.

By embedding these mechanisms into the fabric of Cities of Hope, we create a robust framework that supports long-term sustainability. It's not just about maintaining what we have built but continuously evolving and adapting to improve the quality of life for all residents. These continuous improvement mechanisms ensure that Cities of Hope are not only viable today but will flourish well into the future.

Marketing and Public Relations

Marketing and public relations form the backbone of any successful initiative and play particularly crucial roles in the establishment and promotion of Cities of Hope to combat homelessness. This chapter outlines strategic approaches to create awareness, engage the broader community, and maintain transparency with both residents and investors.

Awareness Campaigns

Conveying the vision and benefits of Cities of Hope effectively starts with robust awareness campaigns. It's essential to reach various demographics through multiple channels. Social media platforms like Facebook, Twitter, and Instagram offer widespread reach and allow for targeted advertising based on geographic and demographic data. Additionally, traditional media such as newspapers, radio, and television can be used to capture the attention of a broader audience.

A successful awareness campaign should include:

- **Clear Messaging:** Consistently communicate the goals, benefits, and long-term vision of Cities of Hope. Highlight how these towns solve the homeless crisis while providing economic and social benefits to the wider community.

- **Storytelling:** Share success stories and testimonials from individuals who have benefited from similar initiatives. Real-life examples can be powerful motivators and can humanize abstract concepts.

- **Visual Branding:** Develop a cohesive visual identity for the campaign, including logos, color schemes, and graphics that resonate with the target audience. Consistent branding builds recognition and trust.

Engagement with Media

Media engagement is essential for building credibility and gaining public support. Establishing relationships with journalists and media outlets can help secure coverage in news stories, feature articles, and opinion pieces. Here are key strategies for effective media engagement:

- **Press Releases:** Regularly distribute press releases to announce major milestones, new partnerships, and significant achievements. Ensure that press releases are well-written and newsworthy.

- **Media Kits:** Prepare comprehensive media kits that include background information, key statistics, high-quality images, and contact details. A well-prepared media kit can make it easier for journalists to cover your story.

- **Events and Press Conferences:** Organize events and press conferences to make major announcements. These provide opportunities for face-to-face interactions with reporters and can generate significant media coverage.

Transparency with Residents and Investors

To build and maintain trust, transparency with both residents and investors is paramount. Open communication channels and regular updates can foster a sense of ownership and involvement among all stakeholders.

For residents:

- **Community Meetings:** Hold regular community meetings to discuss progress, address concerns, and gather feedback. Transparency in decision-making processes can alleviate fears and build trust.

- **Newsletters:** Distribute monthly or quarterly newsletters that provide updates on project milestones, upcoming events, and other relevant information. These can be distributed both digitally and in print.

- **Feedback Mechanisms:** Implement accessible channels for residents to voice their concerns, suggestions, and feedback. This could include suggestion boxes, online platforms, and dedicated hotlines.

For investors:

- **Regular Reports:** Provide detailed financial and operational reports on a regular basis. Transparency in the use of funds and progress toward goals can help build investor confidence.

- **Investor Meetings:** Arrange periodic meetings with investors to discuss performance, challenges, and future plans. Open dialogue can strengthen relationships and encourage ongoing support.

- **Transparency Portals:** Develop online portals where investors can access real-time project performance and financial data. This kind of transparency can help in early identification of issues and foster a collaborative approach to problem-solving.

The combined use of awareness campaigns, media engagement, and transparent communication will create a strong foundation for marketing and public relations efforts. By fostering trust and building a positive public image, stakeholders at all levels will be encouraged to support and participate in the ambitious endeavor to establish Cities of Hope as a viable solution to homelessness.

Awareness Campaigns

Effective awareness campaigns are crucial for the success of Cities of Hope. They serve to inform the public, potential investors, and stakeholders about the project's benefits and goals, creating momentum and support for lasting change. **Given the complexities of addressing homelessness and developing an entirely new community model, a multi-faceted approach to awareness is essential.**

First, it's important to focus on **clear, concise messaging**. The narrative should articulate the vision of Cities of Hope as a feasible and impactful solution to homelessness while also emphasizing economic and social benefits for the wider community. Utilizing various platforms, including social media, traditional media, and community outreach programs, can maximize reach and engagement.

Partnering with influencers, celebrities, and well-respected figures can significantly amplify the campaign's impact. Their endorsement can lend credibility and attract attention from diverse audience segments. Similarly, engaging with local leaders and community organizations can foster grassroots support, ensuring the message resonates on a personal level.

Educational initiatives play a critical role in awareness campaigns. Hosting webinars, workshops, and town hall meetings can provide in-depth understanding and answer any lingering questions. These forums allow for direct engagement with the community and stakeholders, fostering a sense of participation and commitment.

A strong online presence is essential. Developing a comprehensive website and regularly updating blogs, videos, and newsletters can keep interested parties informed and encouraged. Social media campaigns, leveraging hashtags and interactive content, can create viral moments that further disseminate the message.

To maintain transparency and build trust, timely and honest communication about project milestones, successes, and challenges is vital. Regular updates can be shared via email newsletters, press releases, and social media posts. Transparency ensures continued support and demonstrates accountability, which is crucial for attracting long-term investments and partnerships.

Effective use of visual aids – infographics, videos, and interactive content – can make complex information accessible and engaging. Visual storytelling can capture the community's imagination, showing tangible benefits and real-life impacts of Cities of Hope.

Moreover, collaborating with local educational institutions for research and outreach can strengthen campaigns. Academic studies validating the project's benefits can provide empirical support, enhance credibility, and attract academic and policy attention.

Finally, monitoring and evaluating the impact of awareness campaigns is necessary for continuous improvement. Collecting data on engagement levels, public sentiment, and stakeholder feedback will inform future initiatives, ensuring they remain effective and relevant.

By implementing these strategies, awareness campaigns can build widespread support, ensuring that the vision for Cities of Hope becomes a shared mission driven by collective commitment and action.

Engagement with Media

Engaging with media is a pivotal tactic within the broader scope of marketing and public relations. The power of media in shaping public perception and influencing decision-makers cannot be overstated. When it comes to the concept of Cities of Hope aimed at eradicating homelessness and generating profitable communities, a well-planned media engagement strategy can effectively communicate the vision, progress, and benefits of the project to a wide audience.

The first step in engaging with media involves identifying relevant media outlets and platforms that can amplify the message. Traditional media, such as newspapers, television, and radio, offer a broad reach and can significantly impact public opinion. Additionally, digital media platforms, including social media, blogs, and news websites, play an increasingly crucial role in disseminating information quickly and interactively. A comprehensive media engagement plan should encompass both traditional and digital media to maximize outreach and impact.

Crafting compelling stories and narratives is essential for capturing media interest and the public's attention. The Cities of Hope project must be presented not just as a solution to the homeless crisis but as a transformative initiative that brings economic, social, and environmental benefits. Incorporating human interest stories, success anecdotes, and testimonials can make the project relatable and inspire action. Journalists and content creators are more likely to cover stories that are emotionally resonant and demonstrate a tangible impact on individuals and communities.

Building relationships with media professionals is another important aspect. Regular press releases, media briefings, and exclusive interviews with key stakeholders can keep journalists informed and engaged. Providing timely updates on milestones, developments, and successes can help maintain media interest over the long term. Establishing a dedicated media contact person or team ensures that inquiries are promptly addressed and accurate information is disseminated.

Social media engagement is particularly critical in today's digital age. Platforms like Twitter, Facebook, LinkedIn, and Instagram can be leveraged to reach diverse audience segments, including policymakers, potential investors, community leaders, and the general public. Regular updates, multimedia content, and interactive posts can generate buzz and foster a sense of community around the Cities of Hope initiative. Engaging with followers through comments, shares, and direct messages can also enhance transparency and build trust.

Public campaigns and media events are effective ways to generate public interest and media coverage. Organizing events such as ground-breaking ceremonies, open houses, and community forums can provide journalists with opportunities for on-the-ground reporting and firsthand experiences. Partnering with well-known public figures, advocates, and influencers can further amplify the message and reach a broader audience.

Finally, monitoring media coverage and public sentiment allows for continuous improvement in media engagement strategies. Analyzing media reports, social media metrics, and public feedback can provide valuable insights into the effectiveness of the media strategy and areas for enhancement. Adjusting messaging, improving communication channels, and addressing any misinformation or concerns can help maintain a positive public perception and support for the Cities of Hope project.

Engaging with media is not just about promoting the project; it is about building a narrative that resonates with people and encourages active participation from all stakeholders. By effectively leveraging media channels, the Cities of Hope initiative can gain the visibility, support, and momentum needed to realize its vision of eradicating homelessness and creating sustainable, profitable communities.

Transparency with Residents and Investors

Effective marketing and public relations are essential for the successful implementation of Cities of Hope, which aims to eradicate homelessness and create profitable communities. One key aspect of this strategy is maintaining transparency with both residents and investors. This involves not only establishing a continuous dialogue but also ensuring that all stakeholders are fully informed about the project's progress, financial health, and long-term sustainability.

For Residents:

For residents, transparency builds trust and a sense of ownership. Regular updates on the town's developments, financial status, and future plans should be made accessible. This can be achieved through town hall meetings, community newsletters, and digital platforms. By keeping residents informed, we foster a collective effort toward achieving the town's goals.

- **Open Communication Channels:** Establish multiple communication channels such as suggestion boxes, online forums, and mobile apps to gather residents' feedback and address their concerns.

- **Financial Transparency:** Provide residents with a clear understanding of how funds are allocated and spent. Regular financial reports and community briefings should be part of this transparency initiative.

- **Progress Updates:** Residents are regularly updated on milestones and upcoming projects. This could include everything from new employment opportunities to advancements in infrastructure.

For Investors:

Investors require clarity to understand the project's feasibility and potential returns. Detailed financial reports, risk assessments, and progress updates should be shared consistently.

- **Financial Reporting:** Regular financial statements and audits should be provided to investors. This ensures that they are fully aware of the financial health and performance of the project.

- **Risk Transparency:** Clearly outline any potential risks and the strategies in place to mitigate them. This includes economic downturns, regulatory changes, and other unforeseen challenges.

- **Performance Metrics:** Share key performance indicators (KPIs) that illustrate the project's success. Metrics could include job creation numbers, housing occupancy rates, and economic impact statistics.

Ensuring transparency with both residents and investors not only builds trust but also strengthens the overall credibility of the industrial town model. By maintaining open lines of communication, we can ensure that all stakeholders are aligned in their efforts to create sustainable and profitable communities capable of addressing homelessness.

In conclusion, the commitment to transparency is a pivotal component of our marketing and public relations strategy. Keeping residents and investors well-informed and engaged will drive Cities of Hope's long-term success and replicability across the United States.

Contingency Planning

Contingency planning is a pivotal element in the grand scheme of establishing Cities of Hope to combat homelessness while fostering economic growth. It is essential to acknowledge that no project, regardless of its scale or preparation, is immune to unforeseen challenges. Contingency planning ensures that these Cities of Hope can weather crises and adapt quickly to changing circumstances.

Crisis Management

Effective crisis management is the cornerstone of any robust contingency plan. It starts with identifying potential crises that could impact the Cities of Hope, such as natural disasters, economic downturns, public health emergencies, and social unrest. To mitigate these risks, it is crucial to develop comprehensive response strategies tailored to each potential scenario.

Key components of crisis management include:

- **Risk Assessment:** Regular, thorough assessments to identify vulnerabilities and potential threats.

- **Emergency Response Plans:** Clearly defined procedures for immediate action during a crisis, including evacuation routes, emergency contacts, and first aid strategies.

- **Communication Protocols:** Efficient, transparent communication channels to ensure swift dissemination of information to residents, staff, and stakeholders.

- **Training and Drills:** Regular training sessions and drills for residents and employees to ensure preparedness and effective execution of emergency plans.

Adaptive Strategies

Adaptive strategies focus on the long-term resilience of the Cities of Hope. These strategies are designed not only to address immediate crises but also to build flexibility and scalability into the town's operational framework.

Important aspects of adaptive strategies include:

- **Resource Diversification:** Reducing dependency on a single industry or supply chain by diversifying resources and revenue streams.

- **Flexible Infrastructure:** Designing infrastructure that can be quickly modified or repurposed to respond to new challenges, such as converting facilities for different types of production or adapting housing units for various needs.

- **Continuous Learning:** Implementing a feedback loop where lessons learned from each crisis are documented, analyzed, and used to improve future planning and responses.
- **Partnerships and Collaboration:** Building strong relationships with governmental bodies, NGOs, private sector partners, and the local community to create a support network that can offer aid and resources during crises.

Adaptive strategies also extend to financial planning. Establishing emergency funds and securing insurance policies to cover various risks can provide a financial safety net, ensuring that unexpected events do not derail the town's progress.

The Role of Technology

Technology plays a critical role in both crisis management and adaptive strategies. Utilizing advanced data analytics, AI, and IoT (Internet of Things) can greatly enhance the capability to predict, monitor, and respond to crises. For instance, data analytics can identify emerging patterns that signal potential threats, while IoT devices can provide real-time monitoring of environmental conditions and infrastructure health.

Moreover, digital platforms can facilitate seamless communication among residents, administrators, and external stakeholders. Mobile apps, social media, and dedicated websites can serve as immediate information dissemination tools, ensuring everyone stays informed and connected during a crisis.

Conclusion

While the vision of Cities of Hope is ambitious and promising, it is paramount to plan for adversities that could disrupt this vision. Contingency planning, encapsulating crisis management, and adaptive strategies provide a framework to navigate and mitigate risks effectively. By embracing a proactive and flexible approach, these towns can survive crises and emerge stronger, ensuring long-term sustainability and success.

Contingency Planning

Crisis Management

The establishment and operation of Cities of Hope, which aim to alleviate homelessness and foster economic growth, necessitate robust crisis management strategies. Effective crisis management involves identifying potential threats, devising plans to mitigate risks, and ensuring swift recovery from any unforeseen events that could jeopardize the town's stability and sustainability.

First and foremost, it's crucial to develop a comprehensive risk assessment. This includes evaluating natural disasters, economic downturns, social unrest, and public health emergencies. Disaster response teams should be trained and equipped to handle a wide range of scenarios. Collaboration with city governments, emergency services, and healthcare providers is essential to ensure a coordinated response.

Second, communication plays a pivotal role in crisis management. Clear and timely communication with residents, staff, and stakeholders can minimize panic and facilitate organized evacuation or sheltering processes if required. Utilizing modern communication platforms, such as mobile alerts and social media, can help disseminate information quickly and efficiently.

Moreover, financial resilience should be built into the planning stage. Establishing emergency funds and securing insurance for key assets can provide significant support during crises. Financial stability ensures that the industrial town can continue operations and recover more quickly.

Infrastructure resilience is another key component. Buildings and facilities should be constructed to withstand natural disasters, and utility services should have redundancies built into their systems. This might involve backup generators, water sources, and alternative transportation routes to maintain functionality during a crisis.

Furthermore, the mental health and well-being of residents cannot be overlooked. During a crisis, providing immediate mental health support and counseling can help mitigate long-term psychological effects. Creating community support networks and training staff to provide psychological first aid can be invaluable.

In addition, continuous training and drills for all stakeholders, including residents, employees, and management, can ensure everyone is prepared for various types of emergencies. These exercises should include evacuation procedures, first aid training, and crisis communication protocols.

Lastly, post-crisis evaluation is vital for continuous improvement. After any incident, conducting a thorough review to understand what worked, what didn't, and what could be improved will help refine crisis management plans. This feedback loop ensures that the town is always evolving and better prepared for future challenges.

In conclusion, effective crisis management is a cornerstone of the success and sustainability of Cities of Hope. By proactively planning and preparing for potential crises, the towns can not only protect their residents and assets but also reinforce the goal of creating secure, thriving communities for those in need.

Adaptive Strategies

In the realm of contingency planning for Cities of Hope aimed at eradicating homelessness and fostering economic viability, adaptive strategies hold a crucial role. Regardless of how well we plan, unforeseen events are bound to occur, and being prepared to adapt is key. Flexibility, coupled with a keen understanding of potential roadblocks, will enable these communities to thrive even when faced with unexpected challenges.

First, adaptive strategies should include a robust feedback loop. By continuously gathering data from residents, employees, and other stakeholders, the town's management can identify emerging issues and respond promptly. This involves setting up regular town hall meetings, surveys, and digital platforms where real-time feedback can be collected and analyzed.

Another essential adaptive strategy is cross-training the workforce. By ensuring that employees are skilled in multiple areas, the town can maintain operational continuity even if specific sectors face temporary shutdowns or labor shortages. For instance, workers trained in both agriculture and manufacturing could switch roles as needed, mitigating employment volatility and keeping key industries operational.

It's also vital to establish emergency funds and resources. These can be supported by a mix of public and private investments. Having a dedicated financial reserve ensures that critical services, such as healthcare facilities and housing, remain functional during crises like economic downturns, natural disasters, or pandemics. This financial cushion will safeguard the community's health and stability.

Implementing a dynamic resource allocation system can further enhance adaptability. This refers to fluidly shifting resources, such as personnel, equipment, or funding, to areas where they are most needed at any given time. By doing so, the town can efficiently address emergent needs without straining its overall system.

On a technological front, leveraging smart city technologies can significantly contribute to adaptive strategies. Real-time data analytics on utilities, traffic, and public health can provide early warnings about potential issues, allowing for swift intervention. Automating routine processes can free up human resources for more complex tasks, and data-driven insights can lead to more informed decision-making.

Furthermore, fostering strong community ties can improve resilience. When residents feel a sense of belonging and mutual support, they're more likely to pull together during tough times. Community-building activities, mental health support systems, and inclusive governance can enhance social cohesion and collective problem-solving.

Lastly, the establishment of strong partnerships is critical. Engaging with local and state governments, non-profits, and private entities can provide additional support and flexibility. These collaborations can help share the burden during crises and open new avenues for innovation and resource acquisition.

Adaptive strategies are not a sign of weak planning; rather, they reflect strong, resilient planning that anticipates change and uncertainty. By integrating these various approaches, Cities of Hope can navigate difficulties while continuing to offer a stable and prosperous environment for all residents.

The Role of Technology in Scaling

As we venture deeper into the intricacies of establishing Cities of Hope as a viable solution to the homeless crisis, one can't overlook the indispensable role that technology plays. Technology serves as the engine that drives scaling, efficiency, and long-term sustainability. By integrating advanced technological solutions, we can ensure that our vision of building profitable, self-sustaining towns does not remain a utopian dream but becomes a tangible, scalable reality.

Digital Platforms for Management

First and foremost, digital platforms are pivotal for the management of these Cities of Hope. Comprehensive digital platforms can facilitate a wide array of functions ranging from urban planning to daily administrative tasks. For instance, smart city management systems can monitor infrastructure, track energy consumption, and even predict maintenance needs through predictive analytics. Such platforms enable decision-makers to operate with real-time data, thereby enhancing the overall efficiency and responsiveness of town management.

Furthermore, these platforms can consolidate various administrative functions such as housing allocation, healthcare services, and employment tracking. By creating a consolidated digital ecosystem, we enable seamless coordination between different departments, thereby minimizing bureaucratic delays and inefficiencies. This integration is crucial when scaling from one industrial town to multiple, ensuring uniformity and consistency in service delivery.

Innovation in Automation and Logistics

Automation is another area where technology makes a significant impact. Automation can dramatically improve productivity in the industries central to these towns—such as manufacturing, agriculture, and recycling. Automated machinery and robots can handle repetitive tasks with precision and speed, allowing human workers to focus on more complex and value-added activities. This not only optimizes labor costs but also enhances the quality and consistency of output. **Careful planning of automation will be essential to balance the need for employment as well as achieving efficiency.**

In the realm of logistics, technology offers innovative solutions for supply chain management and distribution. With the implementation of Internet of Things (IoT) devices, we can track and manage inventory in real time. Autonomous vehicles and drones can further streamline the delivery process, making sure that goods and services are distributed efficiently within and beyond the industrial town.

Moreover, **blockchain technology** can bring transparency and security to supply chains, ensuring that all transactions are recorded immutably. This kind of transparency is vital for garnering trust from both residents and external stakeholders, contributing to the overall credibility and attractiveness of the Cities of Hope.

Futureproofing Through Continuous Improvement

In a rapidly changing technological landscape, the ability to adapt and upgrade is paramount. Continuous improvement mechanisms must be embedded into the foundational principles of our Cities of Hope. Regular audits and updates to technological systems will ensure that we are not left behind as new innovations emerge. Predictive maintenance for infrastructure, data analytics for performance tracking, and periodic technology assessments can help fine-tune operations and preemptively address potential issues.

Additionally, creating an environment conducive to innovation is essential. Establishing research and development (R&D) centers within these towns can foster a culture of continuous technological advancement. Collaboration with tech firms, academic institutions, and research bodies can drive innovations tailored to the specific needs of Cities of Hope, ensuring they remain at the cutting edge of technological progress.

Scalability and Replication

One of the primary advantages of leveraging technology is the ease of scalability and replication. Digital platforms and automated systems can be easily duplicated and customized to fit the unique requirements of different locations. **This modularity ensures that once a prototype is successfully developed and tested, it can serve as a blueprint for future towns.**

Standardized technological solutions also facilitate training and skill development. Technicians and administrators trained in one industrial town can easily transition to another, thereby reducing the learning curve and enhancing operational efficiency across multiple towns. Furthermore, standardized digital platforms enable more effective data collection and benchmarking, providing invaluable insights for continuous improvement across the board.

- 1. Implementation of digital platforms for urban management
- 2. Automation in baseline industries for heightened efficiency
- 3. Innovative logistics solutions for streamlined distribution
- 4. Continuous improvement mechanisms for adaptation and upgrading
- 5. Scalability and replication leveraging standardized solutions

In conclusion, the role of technology in scaling Cities of Hope cannot be overstated. From digital platforms and automation to continuous improvement and scalability, technology serves as the foundational cornerstone that will transform our vision into a scalable, sustainable reality. By harnessing the power of technological innovation, we build resilient communities and set the stage for a future where homelessness is eradicated and prosperity is within reach for all. Let's embrace this technological revolution and pave the way for a brighter, more inclusive future.

Digital Platforms for Management

In the modern age, the ability to manage large-scale projects like Cities of Hope hinges significantly on our adeptness with digital platforms. For scaling these towns effectively, digital platforms offer a centralized and efficient way to oversee various operational facets. Whether it's coordinating construction projects, managing resources, or maintaining community services, digital platforms are indispensable.

One of the primary benefits of digital platforms is their capacity to centralize data. From housing records and employment statistics to financial transactions and healthcare services, everything can be monitored in real-time. This centralization leads to better decision-making because it provides a comprehensive overview of all operations. Digital dashboards, coupled with data analytics, empower managers to identify bottlenecks, allocate resources efficiently, and adopt a proactive approach in addressing potential issues.

Moreover, digital platforms facilitate greater transparency. Utilizing **blockchain technology,** for instance, can make financial transactions and records immutable and easily auditable. These foster trust among investors, government bodies, and residents alike. Given that transparency and accountability are critical for the success of any large-scale initiative, these platforms serve as an invaluable asset in garnering support and maintaining integrity.

Automation, another significant feature of digital platforms, can bring about substantial improvements in efficiency. Routine tasks such as scheduling maintenance, tracking inventory, and even some aspects of healthcare can be automated to reduce human error and speed up processes. Automation also frees up human resources to focus on more complex and strategic initiatives, further enhancing productivity and innovation within the Cities of Hope.

Collaboration tools integrated into digital management platforms are equally important. In a project involving multiple stakeholders—including government agencies, private investors, non-profits, and the local community—facilitating seamless communication is vital. Platforms like Slack, Trello, or custom-built solutions can streamline project management and communication, enabling swift and coordinated action.

Another pivotal aspect is the use of Geographic Information Systems (GIS). GIS can be instrumental in urban planning, environmental management, and even in emergencies. By mapping out resources, infrastructure, and environmental data, GIS allows planners and managers to make data-driven decisions that improve both the efficiency and quality of life within these towns.

Lastly, digital platforms can play a crucial role in continuous improvement. By incorporating feedback loops, these systems can gather input from residents, employees, and other stakeholders. This information can be analyzed to implement changes that enhance operations, improve living conditions, and adapt to the evolving needs of the community.

In summary, digital platforms are not just tools for managing Cities of Hope; they are integral to scaling and sustaining these communities effectively. They centralize data, enhance transparency, automate routine tasks, facilitate communication, and enable continuous improvement. Thus, investing in robust digital management systems is essential for ensuring the long-term success and viability of Cities of Hope.

Innovation in Automation and Logistics

Scaling the concept of Cities of Hope to effectively address homelessness and create profitable, sustainable communities hinges significantly on the implementation of cutting-edge technology in automation and logistics. By streamlining operations and resource management, we can vastly improve efficiency and scalability, ensuring that these towns are economically viable and self-sustaining over the long term.

The integration of automation in manufacturing and other basic industries is pivotal. Automated systems and robotics can significantly reduce the cost of production while increasing output and consistency. For example, advanced robotics in agricultural practices can revolutionize food production, making it more efficient and less labor-intensive. This is especially important as it can provide employment opportunities that focus on managing and maintaining these automated systems rather than the traditional manual labor roles.

Logistics technology innovations are equally critical in ensuring the seamless movement of goods and services within and outside these Cities of Hope. The use of sophisticated logistics software can optimize supply chain operations, from inventory management to distribution networks. Smart warehouses equipped with automated sorting and inventory management systems can drastically cut down on waste and inefficiencies, ensuring that resources are stored and utilized as optimally as possible.

In addition, the advent of autonomous vehicles holds promise for revolutionizing transportation within these towns. Self-driving trucks and delivery drones can ensure timely, cost-effective transportation of goods, reducing the dependency on human drivers and the associated logistical challenges. Automated public transit solutions can also enhance mobility for residents, ensuring they have access to employment opportunities, education, and community services without the need for personal vehicles.

Data analytics and artificial intelligence can play a crucial role in continuous improvement processes. By leveraging AI to analyze data collected from various automated systems, towns can gain insights into operational efficiencies, resource utilization, and areas that require improvement. Predictive analytics can help in proactively addressing potential issues before they become critical, ensuring smooth operations at all times.

Moreover, the implementation of Internet of Things (IoT) devices can facilitate smart monitoring and management of infrastructure. IoT sensors can monitor everything from air quality and energy usage to maintenance needs of public facilities. This real-time data collection enables proactive management of the towns, ensuring resources are used efficiently and that any issues are addressed promptly.

Finally, **the use of blockchain technology** can offer significant advantages in transparency and security, particularly in supply chain management and transactional processes. Blockchain can ensure that transactions, whether they involve goods, services, or finances, are secure and transparent, reducing the risk of fraud and ensuring trust among all stakeholders.

To sum up, the role of technology, especially in automation and logistics, is indispensable in scaling the concept of Cities of Hope. By embracing and integrating these innovations, we can create efficient, sustainable, and economically viable communities that address homelessness and contribute to the broader goal of societal well-being. The key is to not just adopt these technologies, but to effectively integrate them into the fabric of these towns, ensuring they work in harmony to drive continuous improvement and long-term success.

Legal and Ethical Considerations

Building Cities of Hope to eradicate homelessness and create profitable communities is not just a logistical challenge but also a legal and ethical one. Ensuring that these towns are developed and managed with fairness, transparency, and respect for all residents' rights is paramount. Let's delve into the critical legal and ethical considerations that must be addressed to make this vision a reality.

Ensuring Fair Labor Practices

One of the principal considerations is the employment practices within these Cities of Hope. Given that these communities aim to provide job opportunities for the homeless, we must ensure that these individuals are not exploited. Fair labor practices, including equitable wages, safe working conditions, and reasonable working hours, are essential. This means adhering to both state and federal labor laws without compromise.

Moreover, it is crucial to guarantee that workers are given clear contracts outlining their job roles, responsibilities, and rights. This can help prevent misunderstandings and protect both the employees and the employers. Regular audits and inspections should be conducted to maintain compliance and address any labor issues promptly.

Protecting Resident Rights

Protecting the rights of residents goes beyond their employment. It encompasses their civil liberties and access to essential services. Residents must have access to adequate healthcare, education, and social services without discrimination.

Furthermore, it is essential to set up a robust legal framework that protects residents from any form of abuse, be it physical, emotional, or financial. This includes creating accessible avenues for residents to report grievances and ensuring that issues are addressed swiftly and justly.

Environmental and Zoning Regulations

Cities of Hope must comply with all environmental and zoning laws to ensure they are sustainable and do not adversely affect the surrounding areas. This involves adhering to regulations on land use, emissions, waste management, and resource consumption.

It is also vital to engage with local communities and government bodies to ensure that the development of Cities of Hope aligns with broader regional planning goals. This collaboration can help mitigate any potential conflicts or legal challenges that could arise from the town's establishment and growth.

Data Privacy and Ethical Use of Technology

Given the integration of smart city technologies in Cities of Hope, there are significant concerns about data privacy and the ethical use of technology. Residents' data, including their personal information and daily activities, must be collected, stored, and utilized responsibly. Robust cybersecurity measures should be in place to protect data from breaches.

Transparency about what data is collected and how it is used can help build trust among residents. Policies ensuring that data is used solely to improve living conditions and services rather than for surveillance or exploitation are fundamental.

Community Representation and Participation

Finally, residents must have a say in how their community is run. This can be achieved by establishing local governance structures that allow residents to participate in decision-making processes. Creating forums and councils where residents can voice their opinions and concerns ensures that the town evolves in a way that benefits everyone.

Ensuring legal and ethical standards in the development and management of Cities of Hope is not merely about compliance; it's about fostering a community environment where every individual feels valued and protected. By addressing these considerations right from the planning stages, we pave the way for Cities of Hope that are economically viable and just and compassionate places to live.

Ensuring Fair Labor Practices

As we forge ahead with the creation of Cities of Hope to address the homeless crisis, it is crucial that we uphold fair labor practices to ensure ethical treatment and protection of workers. At the core of this initiative is the idea that equitable employment conditions will not only provide immediate economic benefits but will also foster long-term community stability and individual well-being.

Adhering to fair labor practices means ensuring that all labor laws are strictly followed, from minimum wage regulations to safe working conditions. This starts with compliance with federal, state, and local labor laws that govern wages, hours, and occupational safety. By enforcing these regulations within our Cities of Hope, we protect worker rights while also creating an environment that attracts and retains talent.

Additionally, fair labor practices involve eliminating discriminatory practices in hiring, promotion, and termination. It's essential that our Cities of Hope establish clear, transparent policies that promote equal opportunity for all residents, regardless of race, gender, age, religion, or disability. This commitment to non-discriminatory practices will not only enhance workplace morale but also pave the way for a more inclusive and dynamic workforce.

Moreover, establishing a grievance redressal system where employees can report issues without fear of retribution is crucial. This system should be robust and well-publicized, ensuring that workers know their rights and have the means to voice any concerns. Independent oversight bodies can be incorporated to audit these practices regularly, providing an additional layer of transparency and accountability.

In addition to legal compliance, ethical considerations extend to providing contracts that clearly outline job responsibilities, wages, benefits, and conditions of employment. Ambiguity in agreements can lead to exploitation and dissatisfaction, so clear, written contracts must be a standard practice. This also means ensuring that employees receive fair compensation, including overtime pay, benefits, and paid leave, aligned with prevailing standards and laws.

Finally, fostering a culture of continuous improvement and worker development is integral to maintaining fair labor practices. This includes offering ongoing training programs, opportunities for skill upgrades, and paths for career advancement. By investing in the workforce, we empower individuals, contributing to their personal growth and enhancing the overall productivity of the town's economy.

In conclusion, ensuring fair labor practices is not simply a legal obligation but a foundational pillar for the sustainable development of our Cities of Hope. By committing to ethical labor standards, we can create environments where residents thrive both economically and socially, ultimately leading to the eradication of homelessness and the creation of vibrant, profitable communities.

Protecting Resident Rights

One of the foundational pillars of creating sustainable and ethical Cities of Hope lies in prioritizing the rights of their residents. Given that these communities aim to address homelessness and improve the socio-economic standing of individuals, safeguarding resident rights is not just a legal mandate but an ethical imperative.

Informed Consent and Transparency

Transparency must be embedded in all aspects of town governance and management. Community members need comprehensive information about housing contracts, employment terms, and community regulations. Ensuring informed consent means that residents fully understand and agree to the conditions under which they live and work, allowing them to make decisions based on clear and accessible information.

Affordable and Quality Housing

Quality of housing is another critical area where resident rights need protection. Affordable housing should not equate to substandard living conditions. Construction materials, building standards, and maintenance practices must ensure that homes are safe, comfortable, and durable..

Labor Rights and Fair Wages

Cities of Hope will be hubs of economic activity, making it essential to uphold labor rights. Ensuring fair wages and safe working conditions must be non-negotiable. Collaborations with labor unions and ongoing compliance checks can help uphold these standards. Moreover, there should be avenues for workers to report grievances without fear of retribution.

Access to Essential Services

Equitable access to healthcare, education, and other essential services is a fundamental right that needs protecting. Residents must have reliable access to medical facilities, educational institutions, and social services. Policies should be implemented to ensure that these services are of high quality, guaranteeing that all residents receive the necessary support.

Privacy and Data Protection

As technological integration and data collection become increasingly prevalent, protecting the privacy of residents is paramount. Clear guidelines must be in place regarding how data is collected, stored, and used. Residents should have the right to opt out of non-essential data collection and should be informed about how their information will be used to improve community services.

Participation and Representation

Residents should have a voice in the governance and administration of their communities. Mechanisms for civic participation, such as town hall meetings, advisory councils, and surveys, should be established to ensure that resident input is regularly solicited and acted upon. This participatory approach not only empowers residents but also fosters a sense of community and shared responsibility.

Non-Discrimination and Inclusivity

A commitment to non-discrimination and inclusivity is vital. Cities of Hope should be open to individuals from diverse backgrounds, ensuring that opportunities for housing and employment are accessible to all, regardless of race, gender, age, or socioeconomic status. Policies should be in place to prevent any form of discrimination and to promote equitable treatment.

In conclusion, protecting resident rights involves a multifaceted approach that encompasses transparent governance, quality housing, fair labor practices, access to essential services, data privacy, civic participation, and inclusivity. By embedding these principles into the fabric of Cities of Hope, we can create communities where residents thrive and feel valued and respected, ultimately contributing to the broader goal of eradicating homelessness and ensuring long-term sustainability.

NOW LET US TALK ABOUT CONSTRUCTION SYSTEMS, LOW-COST BUILDING SYSTEMS AND MORE

Introduction- Construction & Low-Cost Building Systems

The issue of homelessness is a pressing global concern demanding innovative and practical solutions. Addressing it requires the convergence of efficient housing and building systems, supportive funding models, and sustainable development practices.

Homelessness is often perceived as an insurmountable problem due to the complex web of economic, social, and political factors involved. However, history has shown that significant advancements usually stem from the synthesis of interdisciplinary knowledge and a commitment to innovation. By focusing on the principles of low-cost construction, modular and prefabricated building systems, and the implementation of cutting-edge technologies like 3D printing, this book will demonstrate pathways to creating sustainable and economically viable housing projects.

One key objective is to introduce the concept of building low-cost towns equipped with not just housing but also industrial facilities designed to generate revenue. Integration of workspaces within residential areas not only provides employment opportunities but also enhances the economic vibrancy of these communities. Such an approach calls for a comprehensive understanding of construction techniques, financial strategies, and legal frameworks that support the development of these integrated towns.

Moreover, public-private partnerships (PPPs) play an essential role in the sustainable development of housing systems. Collaborations between public agencies and the private sector can stimulate investment and innovation, ensuring that housing projects meet current needs and are scalable and adaptable for future challenges.

This section of the book will guide you through various technological advancements and methodologies that have been successfully implemented in low-cost housing projects worldwide. It will also present case studies that highlight best practices and lessons learned, providing valuable insights into overcoming common obstacles in town-building projects. By examining these elements, readers will gain a deeper understanding of how to create sustainable, low-cost, economically beneficial housing solutions.

As we delve into each sub-section, it is essential to keep in mind the overarching goal: demonstrating how low-cost, efficient housing systems can be a pivotal solution in addressing homelessness. The implications of such an endeavor extend beyond immediate shelter needs, encompassing economic stability, social cohesion, and sustainable development. The collaborative effort of academics, policymakers, professionals, and community members can turn this vision into reality.

Key Principles of Low-Cost Construction

The economic viability of low-cost construction solutions presents a monumental opportunity to address the multifaceted issue of homelessness. At its core, low-cost construction focuses on providing affordable, durable, and efficient housing options without sacrificing quality or safety. This chapter explores the fundamental principles that support such construction methodologies aimed at creating practical and sustainable housing solutions.

Defining Low-Cost Construction

In its simplest terms, low-cost construction refers to building methods and materials that reduce initial and long-term expenses while maintaining structural integrity and meeting regulatory standards. The goal is to optimize resources, labor, and materials to achieve cost-effective construction. A key component involves utilizing locally available resources to minimize transportation costs and supporting labor from within the community, contributing to local economic growth.

Essential Materials and Techniques

Central to low-cost construction is the selection of materials that are not only affordable but also sustainable and durable. Common materials include:

- **Recycled materials:** Incorporating materials like recycled steel and reclaimed wood can significantly lower construction costs while promoting sustainability.

- **Locally sourced materials:** Utilizing locally available resources, such as adobe in arid regions or bamboo in tropical areas, reduces transportation costs and supports local economies.

- **Prefabricated components:** These components can streamline the construction process, reduce labor costs, and ensure quality control.

Several construction techniques are particularly advantageous for low-cost housing:

- **Modular Construction:** This involves assembling pre-built sections (modules) on-site. It's a method that speeds up construction time and reduces costs significantly.

- **Prefabricated Building Systems:** Like modular construction, this involves using pre-made sections but specifically focuses on large panels or entire rooms being constructed off-site and assembled on-location.

- **3D Printing:** An emerging technology where building components or even entire structures are printed layer by layer. This approach has shown promise in reducing both time and material waste in construction.

Adoption of labor practices that enhance productivity and skill utilization is key to efficiently implementing these techniques. Training local labor in these methodologies ensures sustainability and contributes to community development.

Another pivotal principle is the emphasis on planning and design efficiency. Design choices, such as optimizing space utilization and ensuring energy efficiency through passive solar design or superior insulation, can greatly reduce both construction and operational costs.

Moreover, the integration of renewable energy sources and smart home technologies into these low-cost housing solutions can further enhance their efficiency and sustainability. Employing solar panels, wind turbines, and advanced energy management systems not only mitigates environmental impact but also reduces long-term operational costs.

Overall, the principles of low-cost construction are built on a foundation of pragmatism, sustainability, and community-oriented practices. By adhering to these principles, effective, affordable housing solutions can be provided that address the dire issue of homelessness and contribute to the overall socio-economic development of communities.

Defining Low-Cost Construction

Low-cost construction serves as a cornerstone in the effort to address homelessness effectively and sustainably. Fundamentally, it refers to the methods and materials used to create affordable and efficient housing without compromising safety and habitability. The aim is to balance cost savings with the necessity for quality, thereby providing a practical solution to the housing crisis.

In the context of low-cost construction, it's important to consider the broader economic and social framework. As housing costs escalate, the implementation of cost-effective building practices becomes increasingly critical. We will delve into the principles behind these practices, offering a robust framework for understanding how low-cost construction can be both economically viable and socially beneficial.

Cost savings can be achieved through various avenues, including the careful selection of materials, innovative construction methods, and economies of scale. For instance, the use of locally sourced and recycled materials significantly reduces transportation costs and environmental impact. Similarly, labor costs can be minimized by employing modular and prefabricated construction techniques, which streamline the building process and decrease the need for skilled labor on-site.

Another crucial aspect of low-cost construction is the planning and design phase. Efficient design principles, such as optimizing spatial layouts and using standardized building components, contribute to reducing overall costs. Moreover, incorporating energy-efficient technologies and sustainable practices from the outset can lead to long-term financial savings and improved living conditions.

Ultimately, defining low-cost construction is about more than just cutting expenses. It entails a strategic approach to resource allocation, innovative problem-solving, and a commitment to creating resilient and inclusive communities. By understanding and applying these principles, stakeholders can develop housing solutions that are not only affordable but also durable and conducive to a higher quality of life.

Essential Materials and Techniques

Low-cost construction emphasizes affordability, functionality, and sustainability. The selection of appropriate materials and the adoption of efficient construction techniques are paramount to achieving these objectives. This section delves into the essential materials and techniques that form the backbone of low-cost construction, particularly in the context of addressing the widespread homelessness problem.

Materials:

- *Concrete:* Concrete remains a cornerstone of low-cost construction due to its availability, durability, and versatility. Innovations like precast concrete and concrete blocks streamline the building process, reducing labor costs and time.

- *Recycled Materials:* Utilizing recycled materials, such as reclaimed wood, metal, and plastic, not only lowers costs but also promotes sustainability. Recycling reduces the environmental footprint of construction while maintaining material quality.

- *Earth-Based Materials:* Adobe and rammed earth are traditional materials experiencing a resurgence due to their low cost and thermal efficiency. These materials are locally sourced and require minimal processing, making them economically and environmentally viable options for low-cost housing.

- *Light-Gauge Steel:* For structural integrity with the benefit of being lightweight, light-gauge steel frames are a preferred choice. They offer both strength and ease of installation, leading to reduced construction time and labor expenses.

Techniques:

- *Prefabrication:* Prefabrication involves manufacturing building components off-site under controlled conditions, which enhances quality while reducing construction time on-site. Techniques such as modular construction, where entire rooms or sections are prefabricated and assembled on-site, exemplify the efficiency and cost-effectiveness of this approach.

- *Local Skill Utilization:* Training and employing local labor for construction activities harnesses community involvement and reduces costs. By investing in skill development, communities can become self-reliant, ensuring future maintenance and construction needs are sustainably met. Some of our homeless citizens can start working with basic training, bringing an additional sense of pride and embracing the Cities of Hope.

- *Innovative Roofing Solutions:* Roofing can be a significant cost factor. Techniques such as the use of corrugated metal sheets or fiber-cement panels provide durable and cost-effective alternatives. Additionally, incorporating green roofs can offer thermal benefits and environmental advantages.

- *Efficient Design Principles:* Design plays a crucial role in reducing construction costs. Implementing simple, modular designs that maximize space usage and minimize waste can significantly cut down on expenses. Design solutions should also focus on maximizing natural light and ventilation, which can reduce energy costs in the long term.

Integrating these materials and techniques makes construction more affordable and paves the way for sustainable, community-driven development. Focusing on local resources and innovative practices makes it feasible to create low-cost yet high-quality housing solutions that can fundamentally address homelessness.

Financial Implications and Budgeting

A critical component in addressing the homelessness crisis through low-cost and efficient housing systems lies in understanding and managing the financial implications and budgeting requirements of such projects.

Cost-Effective Budgeting Techniques

Effective budgeting is essential to maximize resource utilization and ensure financial sustainability. Cost-effective budgeting techniques involve meticulous planning, continuous monitoring, and adaptive management to respond to unforeseen challenges.

Initial Cost Assessment: Begin by conducting a comprehensive cost assessment, including land acquisition, construction materials, labor, and operational expenses. This initial assessment provides a clear baseline for financial planning.

Value Engineering: Implement value engineering to optimize costs without compromising quality. This technique involves evaluating alternative construction methods and materials to identify cost savings, ensuring that the project remains within budget while maintaining its integrity and functionality.

Phased Development: Consider a phased development approach to spread costs over time. Starting with essential infrastructure and core housing units allows the project to demonstrate viability and deploy additional funding for subsequent phases. This approach also minimizes initial financial risk.

Continuous Financial Monitoring: Establish a robust financial monitoring system to track expenses and revenues continuously. Regular financial reviews enable early identification of cost overruns and facilitate timely adjustments to the budget.

Contingency Planning: Allocate a portion of the budget to contingency funds to address unexpected expenses. Unforeseen challenges, such as construction delays or price fluctuations in materials, can significantly impact project finances. Having contingency funds in place ensures that the project can proceed without financial disruptions.

In conclusion, managing the financial implications and budgeting effectively is fundamental to the success of low-cost housing projects. By diversifying funding sources and employing cost-effective budgeting techniques, stakeholders can ensure the financial viability and sustainability of such initiatives. The following sections will delve deeper into specific construction methods and technologies, further exploring their cost implications and practical applications.

Cost-Effective Budgeting Techniques

Effective financial management is crucial to the success of any low-cost housing initiative aimed at alleviating the homelessness crisis. Cost-effective budgeting techniques can play a fundamental role in ensuring that resources are utilized efficiently, allowing for the creation of sustainable and affordable housing solutions while maintaining financial viability.

Meticulous planning and forecasting are paramount. This involves comprehensive cost estimation at various project stages—from land acquisition to construction, maintenance, and long-term operations. Detailed cost estimation allows for better allocation of funds and minimizes the risk of budget overruns. It also helps identify potential areas where cost savings can be achieved without compromising on quality or efficiency.

Another significant aspect of cost-effective budgeting is the efficiency maximization of funding sources. A blend of public funding, private investments, and philanthropic contributions can provide a diversified financial base. Public funding often comes with stipulations that encourage efficient resource use, while private investments can introduce innovative financial instruments, such as social impact bonds, which link financial returns to measurable improvements in social outcomes. My proposed financial architecture involves both public and private sector partnerships.

Moreover, value engineering practices can substantially reduce costs. This process involves critically analyzing the functions of building materials and systems to ensure that they deliver the required performance at the lowest possible cost. For instance, substituting high-cost materials with equally durable but less expensive alternatives can result in significant savings. Similarly, optimizing labor efficiency, perhaps through the use of modular or prefabricated construction methods, can cut labor costs dramatically.

Monitoring and controlling project costs through robust financial oversight mechanisms is also essential. Regular financial audits and the use of advanced project management tools that offer real-time tracking of expenses against the budget can help identify and rectify financial discrepancies immediately. This proactive approach ensures adherence to the budget and fosters a culture of transparency and accountability.

Furthermore, adopting a long-term perspective on costs, including maintenance and operational expenditures, is critical. <u>Initial cost savings should not lead to higher lifecycle costs.</u> Sustainable design practices, such as using energy-efficient systems and materials with longer lifespans, might involve higher upfront costs but will prove cost-effective over the building's lifecycle by reducing maintenance and utility expenses.

In conclusion, cost-effective budgeting techniques encompass a wide array of strategies focused on ensuring financial efficiency and sustainability. Through meticulous planning, value engineering, diverse funding, rigorous financial oversight, and a comprehensive understanding of long-term costs, it is possible to create practical, affordable housing solutions that significantly address the issue of homelessness.

Modular Construction Systems

In addressing the multifaceted homelessness crisis, exploring innovative and cost-effective housing solutions is essential. One such promising approach involves modular construction systems. Modular construction, often confused with prefabricated buildings, involves creating modules or sections of a structure in a factory setting and then assembling these components on-site. This method holds immense potential for providing rapid, durable, and low-cost housing, which can be a game-changer in the fight against homelessness.

Overview of Modular Homes

Modular homes are built in standardized sections known as modules, which are produced off-site in controlled factory environments. These modules are then transported to the construction site and assembled to form a complete building. The benefits of this approach are manifold, including time efficiency, cost savings, and high-quality construction due to the controlled environment of the factory setting.

Another key advantage of modular construction is its flexibility in design. Modules can be customized and combined in various configurations to meet diverse housing needs, whether for single-family homes, multi-family units, or even larger residential complexes. This adaptability is valuable for creating varied housing solutions in different geographic and socio-economic contexts.

Cost Analysis and Implementation

One of the chief advantages of modular construction is cost reduction. Traditional construction can be plagued by delays, weather-related disruptions, and higher labor costs. By contrast, modular construction can reduce overall project timelines by up to 50%, leading to significant savings. Moreover, since labor is primarily concentrated in a factory setting, it results in higher labor productivity and a reduction in on-site labor needs.

However, Implementing modular construction systems comes with its own challenges and considerations. Initial costs for factory setup and transportation of modules can be significant. Additionally, local building codes and zoning laws can sometimes complicate the use of modular systems. Despite these challenges, many cities and countries are increasingly investing in modular construction as part of their housing strategy. For example, several projects in the U.K. and the U.S. have successfully utilized modular construction to create affordable and rapid housing units for vulnerable populations.

Given the potential of modular construction systems, governments, policymakers, and housing developers should consider integrating these methods into their housing strategies. By leveraging the efficiency and cost-effectiveness of modular building techniques, it is possible to make significant inroads into alleviating the homelessness crisis.

Overview of Modular Homes

Modular homes represent a significant advancement in the field of housing construction, especially pertinent to the goal of addressing homelessness through efficient, low-cost solutions. By definition, modular construction involves the creation of building sections or "modules" in a controlled factory setting before they are transported to the site and assembled to create a cohesive structure. This process offers substantial benefits in terms of speed, cost-efficiency, and quality.

The modular construction system leverages a high degree of standardization, which translates to reduced construction timeframes and labor costs. Unlike traditional construction methods, where building processes are sequential and often hampered by weather-related delays, modular homes are fabricated concurrently with site preparation. This parallelism allows for a rapid assembly on-site, drastically cutting down the overall project timeline.

From a financial perspective, producing modular homes in a factory setting allows for bulk purchasing of materials, streamlined labor, and minimized waste. Factories optimize every step, from cutting materials to assembling modules, which significantly reduces the cost per unit. Furthermore, the controlled environment of factories ensures a higher level of quality control and adherence to building codes and standards, which in turn reduces potential defects and future maintenance costs.

Modular homes also offer flexibility in design. Using an array of pre-designed modules, these homes can be customized to meet various aesthetic and functional requirements. This modulatory nature does not compromise quality; rather, it enhances the durability and energy efficiency of the homes. Studies have shown that modular homes can be as robust as—or even more so than—conventionally built homes.

Given the advantages of modular homes, they become a practical solution for creating low-cost, efficient towns integrated with industrial facilities. These structures can be rapidly deployed to build residential areas that not only provide shelter but also workspaces, thus addressing multiple facets of the homelessness problem. Modular construction aligns well with contemporary needs for sustainable, efficient, and economical housing solutions.

Cost Analysis and Implementation

Modular construction systems present a viable solution for addressing the critical need for low-cost and efficient housing, particularly for tackling homelessness. The cost analysis and implementation of these systems involve several key factors that collectively demonstrate their potential advantages.

First and foremost, modular construction significantly reduces construction costs compared to traditional building methods. This reduction stems from standardized production processes and economies of scale achieved by manufacturing modules in factory settings. Factory-based construction benefits from streamlined workflows, reduced labor costs, and minimized material wastage, contributing to an overall decrease in spending.

Another notable financial advantage lies in the accelerated construction timeline associated with modular systems. Modular projects often see a 20-50% faster completion rate compared to conventional construction. This speed not only curtails labor costs but also allows for quicker occupancy, translating into faster revenue generation and reduced interest payments on construction loans.

Implementation involves several crucial steps. Initially, an in-depth cost-benefit analysis is essential to ascertain the feasibility of modular construction for a specific project. This analysis should evaluate land costs, module transportation expenses, and on-site assembly costs alongside potential savings in labor and time.

Next, it is critical to secure reliable suppliers and manufacturers who adhere to industry standards and deliver high-quality modules. Establishing strong partnerships with manufacturers ensures consistency, reliability, and adherence to project timelines and budgets.

Despite the advantages, there are implementation challenges to consider. Transporting modules from factories to construction sites requires meticulous logistical planning. Additionally, local zoning laws and building codes may necessitate modifications to standard module designs, potentially impacting cost and efficiency.

In conclusion, modular construction systems' cost analysis and implementation highlight their potential to revolutionize low-cost housing solutions. With significant cost savings, faster project completion, and effective use of public and private funding, these systems offer practical and scalable solutions to the homelessness crisis.

Prefabricated Building Systems

In recent years, prefabricated building systems (PBS) have emerged as a promising solution to address the growing need for affordable housing. These systems offer several advantages, such as reduced construction time, lower costs, and improved quality control. This section delves into the types of prefabricated systems available, their cost parameters, and the benefits they offer.

Types of Prefabricated Systems

Prefabricated building systems can be broadly categorized into several types depending on their construction and assembly processes. The most common types include:

1. **Panelized Systems:** These consist of pre-constructed panels for walls, floors, and roofs, which are assembled on-site. Panelized systems are versatile and allow for customization, making them a popular choice for residential buildings.

2. **Modular Systems:** In modular construction, whole sections or "modules" of a building are constructed off-site and then transported to the site for assembly. Each module is often fully finished, with plumbing, electrical, and interior finishes already installed. This type is ideal for multi-story buildings and can significantly reduce construction time.

3. **Component Systems:** This type involves prefabricating distinct components like beams, columns, and floor slabs, which are then assembled on-site. Component systems are particularly beneficial for complex architectural designs that require precise engineering.

4. **Steel Frame Systems:** These involve prefabricating structural steel frames and joining them on-site. Steel frame systems provide high strength and durability, making them suitable for high-rise buildings and industrial facilities.

Cost Parameters and Benefits

One key advantage of prefabricated building systems (PBS) is their potential for cost savings. By standardizing and streamlining the construction process, PBS can lower both direct and indirect costs associated with traditional building methods.

- **Reduced Labor Costs:** Since much of the fabrication occurs in a controlled factory environment, the labor required on-site is significantly reduced. This leads to lower labor costs and less dependency on skilled workers who are in short supply.

- **Material Efficiency:** Prefabrication allows for optimized material use, reducing waste. Additionally, bulk purchasing of materials for factory assembly often results in cost savings.

- **Time Savings:** Faster construction timelines mean reduced financing costs for developers and quicker occupancy for users. This translates to faster revenue generation, which is particularly beneficial for projects aiming to address homelessness rapidly.

- **Quality Control:** Factory settings offer more control over the construction process, leading to better quality and fewer defects. This can reduce long-term maintenance costs and increase the building's lifespan.

Additionally, prefabricated systems align well with sustainability goals. The controlled environment minimizes waste and energy usage during construction, contributing to more eco-friendly building practices. The benefits of PBS extend beyond just cost saving; they contribute to creating a more efficient, sustainable, and scalable solution for affordable housing.

In summary, prefabricated building systems present a compelling case for addressing the diverse needs of affordable housing projects. Their adaptability, efficiency, and economic benefits make them a vital component in the broader strategy to combat homelessness. As we proceed to explore 3D-printed housing solutions in the next section, the focus will remain on driving innovation and efficiency in affordable housing.

Types of Prefabricated Systems

Prefabricated building systems represent a crucial advancement in addressing the need for low-cost, efficient housing solutions. The several types of prefabricated systems each offer unique advantages and can be tailored to meet the varying requirements of different projects. These systems facilitate rapid construction and ensure quality control, cost efficiency, and minimal environmental impact.

1. Panelized Systems

Panelized systems involve the factory production of flat panels that are then transported to the construction site for assembly. These panels can include wall sections, floor panels, and roof trusses. By leveraging advanced manufacturing techniques, panelized systems achieve a high level of precision, which minimizes waste and reduces on-site labor costs.. Among the primary benefits are the speed of assembly and the potential for customization to suit specific project requirements.

2. Modular Systems

Modular systems take prefabrication a step further by producing complete modules or "boxes" that are assembled with pre-installed utilities, finishes, and fixtures. Each module is designed to fit together seamlessly with others, forming complete structures such as homes, offices, or apartment units. This approach offers exceptional time savings and ensures consistent quality because much of the construction occurs in a controlled factory environment. Modular systems also have the advantage of being relocatable, providing versatility in urban planning and development.

3. Volumetric Construction

Volumetric construction, akin to modular systems, involves the assembly of three-dimensional units in a factory setting. The difference lies in the complexity and size of the units produced. Volumetric construction often includes fully finished rooms or larger residential sections that are transported to the site and connected with minimal on-site adjustments. This method results in significant reductions in construction time and improved quality control. It's particularly beneficial for large-scale developments where repetitive modularity can achieve economies of scale.

4. Hybrid Systems

Hybrid systems combine different prefabrication methods to optimize the construction process. For instance, a project might use panelized walls in conjunction with volumetric modules for kitchens and bathrooms. This hybrid approach allows for the benefits of each system to be utilized where they are most advantageous, resulting in a highly efficient and cost-effective construction process. By integrating various prefabrication techniques, hybrid systems can better meet specific site challenges or design preferences.

5. Component (Kit-of-Parts) Systems

Component systems, often referred to as "kit-of-parts" systems, involve the prefabrication of individual building components that are then assembled on-site. This method allows for a high degree of flexibility and customization. Each component, such as beams, columns, and panels, is produced to exact specifications, facilitating quick and accurate assembly. This style of prefabrication supports complex architectural designs and can be particularly useful in retrofit projects or areas with logistical constraints.

In summary, the variety of prefabricated systems available today offers numerous pathways to developing low-cost, efficient housing solutions. Each system presents distinct advantages and can be strategically selected based on the project's specific needs and constraints. The principles of prefabrication ensure quicker project timelines and promote sustainable building practices, making them an essential component of the effort to address homelessness through practical and affordable housing solutions.

Cost Parameters and Benefits

Prefabricated building systems present a range of cost parameters and benefits that make them a viable solution for low-cost and efficient housing, addressing the significant challenge of homelessness. These systems capitalize on advanced manufacturing techniques and economies of scale, offering robust, scalable solutions that traditional construction methods often can't match.

One of the primary cost parameters in prefabricated building systems is the initial investment in production facilities and technology. These upfront costs can be substantial, but several factors offset them. Increased production efficiency, reduced material waste, and lower labor costs contribute to the overall affordability of prefabricated buildings. For instance, prefabricated construction can reduce overall project costs by 20% to 50% compared to traditional methods.

Additionally, the speed of construction is a significant benefit. Prefabricated systems allow for simultaneous site preparation and building fabrication, drastically reducing construction timelines. This dual approach can cut construction time by up to 60%. This rapid deployment is particularly beneficial in emergency housing situations and can play a crucial role in quickly providing shelter for homeless populations.

Transportation and assembly are other critical cost factors. The modular nature of prefabricated systems means that parts are designed for easy transport and assembly, minimizing on-site labor, which is often one of the costliest components of construction projects. Transportation costs can be managed effectively with proper logistical planning, further reducing the economic burden.

From a long-term perspective, the benefits of prefabricated building systems extend beyond the immediate cost savings. The durability and sustainability of these systems lead to lower maintenance costs and a longer lifespan for the buildings. The use of high-quality, precision-manufactured components ensures better performance and less frequent need for repairs. Environmentally, reduced waste and higher energy efficiency align with sustainable development goals, enhancing the overall value proposition for public and private investors involved in housing projects.

Moreover, the adaptability of prefabricated systems to various designs and functions means they can be effectively integrated into multifunctional town plans, incorporating both residential and industrial spaces. This flexibility supports the development of communities that are not only affordable but also economically sustainable, generating revenue through embedded industrial parks and other commercial ventures. This holistic approach can mitigate the costs and promote a self-sustaining economic model for future housing solutions.

The combined effect of these cost parameters and benefits underscores the potential of prefabricated building systems in addressing the complex challenge of homelessness through low-cost, efficient, and sustainable housing solutions.

3D-Printed Housing Solutions

As challenges in affordable housing intensify, the advent of 3D-printed housing offers transformative potential. By harnessing the power of technology, 3D printing represents a leap forward in achieving the goals of low-cost, rapid, and efficient housing solutions. This chapter delves into the technological process of 3D printing, its practical implementation, and its financial viability.

Technology and Process

3D printing, or additive manufacturing, involves creating three-dimensional objects through layer-by-layer deposition of materials. In housing, this typically involves using a large-scale 3D printer to build up walls and other structural elements from materials like concrete, earth, or recycled plastics. The process starts with a digital model designed using CAD software, which the printer follows to construct the desired structure.

The core advantage of 3D printing lies in its efficiency and precision. Traditional construction methods can be labor-intensive and prone to human error. In contrast, a 3D printer operates with high precision, significantly reducing material waste and ensuring uniform quality.

Additionally, 3D printing allows for greater design flexibility. Complex architectural features, previously challenging and costly to create, can be easily printed, expanding the possibilities for both aesthetic and functional designs. Moreover, the automation of this process considerably reduces manual labor, mitigating labor shortages and lowering construction costs.

Budget and Efficiency Considerations

One of the primary attractions of 3D-printed housing is its potential for cost efficiency. According to research, the cost savings primarily come from reduced labor and material waste. Conventional construction techniques often result in significant material wastage, which the precise nature of 3D printing can minimize. Furthermore, the speed of construction can dramatically lower labor costs. For example, while traditional construction may take months, basic 3D-printed homes can be erected in mere days.

However, there are initial setup costs to consider. The price of a large-scale 3D printer and the associated software can be substantial. Yet, these costs are often offset over time by the savings achieved through reduced labor, quicker turnaround, and less waste.

Another critical financial consideration is the potential for scalable production. Once a 3D printer is set up, it can produce multiple homes with relatively minor incremental costs. This scalability could be instrumental in addressing housing shortages swiftly and affordably.

The durability and sustainability of 3D-printed homes also contribute to their attractiveness. The use of locally sourced materials or recycled aggregates can reduce costs and environmental impact, aligning with sustainable construction practices.

Challenges and Future Prospects

Despite its promise, the adoption of 3D-printed housing is not without challenges. Regulatory hurdles, including building codes and zoning laws, can slow down the implementation of 3D-printed structures. Furthermore, there is a learning curve associated with new technological processes that require skilled operators and ongoing maintenance of the equipment.

Nevertheless, technological advancements are addressing many of these issues. As the industry matures, we can expect improvements in print speeds, material range, and overall cost-effectiveness. Additionally, increased collaboration between technology developers, construction firms, and regulatory bodies will pave the way for broader acceptance and integration of 3D printing in mainstream construction.

In conclusion, 3D-printed housing represents a compelling solution to the global housing crisis. It offers a path to efficient, cost-effective, and sustainable construction, aligning with the broader goals of creating practical housing solutions for the homeless. As technology advances and barriers diminish, we anticipate that 3D-printed housing will play an increasingly vital role in future urban planning and development.

Technology and Process

The advent of 3D-printed housing solutions marks a pivotal innovation in construction technology, promising to revolutionize how we approach affordable housing. This section delves into the specific technologies and processes that make 3D-printed homes feasible and highly beneficial in addressing the homelessness crisis.

At the core of 3D printing in construction is additive manufacturing, a technique that builds structures by layering materials based on digital models. This method contrasts starkly with traditional subtractive approaches, where materials are cut away from large blocks. In the realm of housing, the primary material used is typically a concrete or mortar mix, tailored to ensure optimal viscosity and setting time to support the layered construction process.

The process begins with designing a digital model of the home using Computer-Aided Design (CAD) software. These models include precise specifications for electrical, plumbing, and ventilation systems. After design, the digital file is transferred to a 3D printer, usually a large-scale robotic arm equipped with nozzles that extrude the concrete mix layer by layer. Each layer is carefully laid down, often with automated systems that can adjust for varying speeds and pressures to ensure uniformity and structural integrity.

A significant advantage of 3D printing technology is its ability to reduce waste. Traditional construction methods often involve a high level of material wastage due to cutting and fitting, whereas additive manufacturing employs only the exact amount of material needed for each layer. This not only lowers costs but also minimizes the environmental footprint. Furthermore, the use of locally sourced materials can further reduce transportation costs and build times.

Another notable aspect is the speed of construction. Traditional homes can take several months to build, whereas a 3D-printed house can be erected in a matter of days. This rapid assembly is partly due to the automation of labor-intensive tasks and the reduction of dependencies on weather conditions, which often delay conventional builds. This speed is crucial for addressing urgent housing shortages effectively.

The integration of smart technology is another area in which 3D-printed homes excel. During the design phase, homes can be pre-fitted with cavities and conduits for electrical wiring and plumbing, facilitating easier installation of smart home systems. This preemptive integration paves the way for future enhancements in energy efficiency and home automation, directly linking to broader sustainable development goals.

Budget and Efficiency Considerations

The application of 3D-printed housing solutions heralds a transformative approach to tackling the homelessness crisis. However, budget and efficiency considerations are fundamental to realizing their potential. To ensure these innovative construction methods translate into practical, affordable housing options, a detailed analysis of cost factors and operational efficiencies is crucial.

A primary consideration in the budgeting phase is the initial capital investment in 3D printing technology. Although the cost of 3D printers has decreased over time, the initial expenditure remains significant. Large-scale industrial 3D printers, capable of producing structural components, require substantial financial outlays. However, these upfront costs can be offset by longer-term savings in labor and materials. For instance, traditional construction methods are labor-intensive, often accounting for up to 30% of total project costs. In contrast, automated 3D printers minimize labor requirements, significantly reducing overall expenditure. However, considering the fact that homeless citizens may well start working for Cities of Hope in the construction phase, the 3D-printed housing option may be utilized for a small portion of the overall construction of these industrial towns. However, I recommend exploring this option as well.

Another pivotal factor is material efficiency. 3D printing allows for precise material usage, minimizing waste compared to conventional methods. This precision in material use cuts costs and contributes to sustainable construction practices, aligning with broader environmental, social, and governance (ESG) goals. Moreover, materials such as concrete and bio-based composites can be optimized for 3D printing to ensure cost-effectiveness and structural integrity.

Labor costs, while reduced, still warrant attention. Specialized training is required for operators of 3D printing machinery, which can introduce additional expenses. However, these costs are typically outweighed by the reduced need for a large workforce. The transition toward automated systems could result in net savings over time, especially as the technology and workforce become more proficient.

Efficiency in the speed of construction is another significant benefit. 3D printing can expedite the building process, reducing completion times from months or years to mere weeks. This acceleration translates into lower costs for project management and site maintenance. Furthermore, faster construction times enable quicker turnover and occupancy, facilitating quicker ROI (Return on Investment) for developers and stakeholders.

Additionally, the modular nature of 3D-printed components allows for easier scalability and adaptability. This means that large volumes of housing can be produced quickly to meet urgent demands, such as those posed by homelessness. The adaptability of design also permits customization without significant cost implications, catering to diverse housing needs and preferences.

In sum, the convergence of reduced labor costs, material efficiency, rapid construction times, and scalable solutions positions 3D-printed housing as a financially viable and efficient option. Thus, for legislators, planners, and developers, integrating 3D-printed housing solutions could significantly contribute to the broader goal of developing low-cost, efficient towns that not only provide shelter but also stimulate economic growth through embedded industrial facilities.

Energy-Efficient Building Practices

As the world faces escalating environmental challenges and energy costs, integrating energy-efficient building practices into low-cost housing solutions becomes not just advantageous but essential. This section explores various strategies and technologies aimed at achieving energy efficiency in housing, which can significantly reduce operational costs and environmental impact. These practices are crucial for creating affordable and sustainable towns that not only provide shelter but also contribute to a healthier planet.

Renewable Energy Sources

One of the primary strategies for achieving energy efficiency in housing is the incorporation of renewable energy sources. Solar power, wind energy, and geothermal systems offer sustainable alternatives to traditional fossil fuels. Solar panels, for example, can be installed on rooftops to harness solar energy, converting sunlight into electricity through photovoltaic cells. This method not only reduces dependency on non-renewable energy sources but also lowers electricity costs.

Wind turbines, though less common in individual residential projects, can be a viable option for community-level energy production in low-cost towns. Placing wind turbines in strategically windy areas, coupled with battery storage systems, can provide a continuous and stable energy supply. Similarly, geothermal energy harnesses the Earth's natural heat to provide heating and cooling solutions, which can be particularly effective in regions with significant temperature variations.

Smart Home Technology and Its Application

The integration of smart home technologies can further enhance energy efficiency in low-cost housing. Smart thermostats, for instance, allow residents to control heating and cooling systems remotely via smartphones or other devices, optimizing energy consumption based on usage patterns and reducing waste. These systems often feature machine learning capabilities that learn residents' habits and adjust accordingly, ensuring maximum efficiency.

Moreover, smart lighting systems employing LED bulbs and sensors can significantly reduce energy use. These systems can automatically adjust lighting based on the time of day or occupancy, ensuring lights are only on when necessary. Studies show that smart lighting can reduce energy consumption by up to 80% compared to traditional incandescent bulbs.

Lastly, the implementation of energy management systems (EMS) in community housing projects offers a broader scope of control. These systems monitor and manage energy usage across multiple houses or entire neighborhoods, providing data and insights that can be used to further optimize energy efficiency.

Such systems are particularly beneficial in larger low-cost housing communities as they can detect inefficiencies and suggest corrective actions.

Integrating both renewable energy sources and smart home technologies creates a multifaceted approach to energy-efficient building practices. These strategies not only align with the goal of affordable and sustainable housing but also contribute to broader environmental sustainability efforts. Through thoughtful application and ongoing innovation, energy efficiency can play a pivotal role in addressing the homelessness crisis by making housing solutions both affordable and environmentally responsible.

By focusing on these strategic practices, we can pave the way for low-cost towns that are not just shelters but exemplars of sustainable living. The subsequent sections will delve into other facets of this integrated approach, such as sustainable development and embedded industrial parks, rounding off our holistic view of creating viable solutions to homelessness.

Renewable Energy Sources

In the context of energy-efficient building practices, utilizing renewable energy sources is integral to creating sustainable and cost-effective housing solutions. Renewable energy sources, such as solar, wind, and geothermal power, provide numerous benefits that align with the goals of low-cost and efficient housing systems. These benefits include reducing energy costs, decreasing environmental impact, and enhancing the long-term sustainability of housing developments.

Solar energy is one of the most accessible and cost-effective renewable energy options. Photovoltaic (PV) panels can be installed on rooftops or integrated into building materials to convert sunlight directly into electricity. This technology not only reduces reliance on traditional power grids but also decreases operational costs for residential and industrial facilities. Additionally, passive solar design principles, which involve orienting buildings to maximize natural light and heat from the sun, can further enhance energy efficiency.

Wind energy is another viable option, particularly for areas with consistent wind patterns. Small-scale wind turbines can be installed within community spaces to generate electricity, contributing to the overall energy mix. While the initial investment may be higher compared to solar energy, wind power can offer significant energy outputs, especially in regions with high wind speeds. Community wind projects can also foster local ownership and economic benefits.

Geothermal energy harnesses the Earth's internal heat for heating and cooling applications. Geothermal heat pumps, for instance, can be used to regulate indoor temperatures through a system of buried pipes that transfer heat between the building and the ground. This method is highly efficient and can significantly reduce energy costs associated with traditional HVAC systems. Moreover, geothermal energy systems have a relatively small land footprint, making them suitable for urban and high-density areas.

In addition to these primary renewable sources, integrating energy storage systems such as batteries can enhance the reliability and flexibility of renewable energy solutions. These systems ensure a steady energy supply by storing excess energy generated during peak production times even when renewable resources are not actively producing. This is particularly valuable for maintaining a consistent energy flow in housing developments and industrial facilities.

Implementing renewable energy sources in the design and construction of low-cost, energy-efficient housing addresses immediate energy needs and contributes to long-term sustainability goals. These practices reduce the carbon footprint of housing projects, lessen dependence on non-renewable energy sources, and can lead to significant cost savings over time. As we continue to explore and adopt innovative energy solutions, renewable energy remains a cornerstone of future-focused, efficient housing development.

Smart Home Technology and Its Application

Incorporating smart home technology within energy-efficient building practices offers substantial benefits, particularly when considering developing low-cost and efficient housing systems to address homelessness. With advancements in technology, smart homes provide convenience and significant energy savings, making them a vital component in the construction of affordable, eco-friendly housing.

The integration of smart home technology allows for the optimization of energy consumption through the automation and control of various systems. Smart thermostats, for instance, can regulate heating and cooling with precision, learning the patterns of occupants to adjust temperatures accordingly. This not only ensures comfort but also reduces energy usage by avoiding unnecessary heating or cooling when the home is unoccupied.

Another critical application is in lighting systems. Smart lighting can be programmed to turn off when rooms are not in use or adjust the brightness based on natural light availability. These systems often include motion sensors and timers, significantly cutting down on electricity consumption. Studies have shown that smart lighting can reduce energy usage by up to 40% compared to traditional lighting systems.

Smart technology can also enhance the efficiency of household appliances. Smart power strips and outlets can monitor and control device power usage, effectively reducing "phantom loads"—energy consumed by electronics while they are switched off but still plugged in. This small yet constant drain can add up, and smart appliances can help alleviate this waste.

Moreover, the application of smart water systems ensures efficient water usage within homes. Smart irrigation controllers, leak detectors, and water-efficient fixtures can significantly reduce water wastage. These technologies are particularly beneficial in areas facing water scarcity, ensuring that every drop is utilized optimally.

Adopting smart home technology is not only about individual home efficiency but also contributes to the broader energy-efficient ecosystem within a community. When homes are interconnected through a smart grid, the collective management of resources can lead to enhanced energy savings and a more resilient energy infrastructure. This interconnectedness allows for better management of renewable energy sources such as solar panels and wind turbines, making them more effective and reliable.

In conclusion, the integration of smart home technology within energy-efficient building practices is essential for creating sustainable, cost-effective housing solutions. By optimizing energy and resource usage, smart homes play a critical role in reducing the environmental footprint and operational costs of housing projects aimed at alleviating homelessness. As we continue to innovate in this field, the potential for smart home technology to enhance the quality and affordability of housing solutions will only grow, making it a key component in the development of future low-cost, energy-efficient towns.

Sustainable Development and ESG

Sustainable development and the integration of Environmental, Social, and Governance (ESG) criteria are pivotal for achieving long-term solutions to the homelessness crisis through low-cost, efficient housing systems. When we talk about sustainability in the context of housing, it goes beyond just the environmental aspects; it encompasses economic and social dimensions, ensuring that development meets the needs of the present without compromising the ability of future generations to meet their own needs.

Understanding ESG Criteria

The ESG criteria provide a framework for assessing the sustainability and societal impact of an investment in a given company or business. ESG has three main components:

1. *Environmental*: This focuses on the conservation of the natural world. It includes initiatives related to energy efficiency, waste management, pollution reduction, resource conservation, and sustainable building practices.

2. *Social*: The social aspect of ESG aims at promoting social equity and community involvement. It encompasses human rights, labor practices, community engagement, and initiatives to combat homelessness and social exclusion.

3. *Governance*: Governance pertains to the organization's or project's management structure. It includes the board's composition, stakeholder rights, transparency, and ethical business conduct.

When it comes to low-cost and efficient housing systems designed to alleviate homelessness, embedding ESG criteria can ensure the development is sustainable and socially responsible. For instance, eco-friendly building materials like recycled plastic or bamboo, coupled with socially inclusive practices such as hiring local labor, can make a substantial impact.

Impact Investing in Housing Projects

Impact investing is an investment strategy that aims to generate specific beneficial social or environmental effects alongside financial returns. Housing projects focusing on homelessness can attract impact investors by showing the economic viability and social benefits of these projects. Here are key components:

- **Economic Performance:** Low-cost housing projects need to demonstrate potential economic returns, including cost savings from energy efficiency and production gains from industrial integration within housing areas.

- **Measurable Social Impact:** Track metrics such as the reduction in homelessness rates, employment rates from integrated industrial facilities, and improved living standards. Using these metrics, projects can gain credibility with impact investors.

- **Environmental Benefits:** Highlight the reduced carbon footprint due to energy-efficient building practices and the use of sustainable materials, which align with the environmental aspect of ESG.

By aligning project goals with ESG criteria, developers and investors can ensure that housing projects not only provide shelter but also contribute to broader societal and environmental objectives. This approach fosters community resilience, reduces long-term costs, and positions housing projects favorably in the eyes of stakeholders, including governments and non-profits aiming to address homelessness.

Integrating sustainable development and ESG principles into low-cost housing projects is not just a theoretical exercise but a strategic necessity. It aligns with global priorities like the United Nations' Sustainable Development Goals (SDGs), specifically Goal 11, which focuses on making cities inclusive, safe, resilient, and sustainable. As we move forward, these frameworks will be crucial in ensuring that the solutions to homelessness are not only effective and efficient but also sustainable in the long run.

Understanding ESG Criteria

Environmental, Social, and Governance (ESG) criteria play a crucial role in shaping sustainable development practices, especially when it comes to addressing pressing issues such as homelessness through low-cost and efficient housing systems. Understanding ESG criteria helps stakeholders—including policymakers, investors, and developers—ensure that housing projects are not only economically viable but also socially equitable and environmentally sound.

Environmental Criteria

Environmental criteria focus on how housing projects impact the natural world. This includes the efficient use of resources, reduction of carbon footprints, and implementation of renewable energy systems. For instance, incorporating energy-efficient building practices (renewable energy sources and smart home technology) can minimize environmental harm while enhancing sustainability. By prioritizing eco-friendly materials and construction methods, developers contribute to a lower environmental impact, which is in line with broader sustainability goals.

Social Criteria

Social criteria examine the project's impact on people and communities. This encompasses a diverse range of factors, such as health and safety standards, community engagement, and the provision of essential services. Ensuring that socially inclusive housing projects can lead to better community outcomes and holistic development. Social criteria emphasize the importance of integrating social support systems and essential community facilities such as healthcare, education, and recreational spaces. These aspects are crucial for the well-being of residents and the sustainable growth of communities.

Governance Criteria

Governance criteria pertain to the policies, practices, and procedures that ensure a project is managed responsibly. This covers ethical business practices, transparency, and adherence to both local and international regulations. Good governance is critical for attracting investment and maintaining public trust. Projects that adhere to high governance standards are more likely to be successful and sustainable in the long term.

The integration of ESG criteria in housing projects aimed at solving homelessness is not merely an option but a necessity. It ensures that these projects are aligned with broader societal goals of sustainability and ethical responsibility, making them more attractive to diverse stakeholders, including investors, policymakers, and the communities they serve.

Impact Investing in Housing Projects

Impact investing represents a critical convergence point between financial returns and positive social and environmental outcomes. Within the realm of sustainable development and ESG (Environmental, Social, and Governance) criteria, impact investing in housing projects has emerged as a powerful tool to address the pressing issue of homelessness while promoting economic stability and environmental stewardship.

Impact investors seek to generate not only a financial return but also social or environmental benefits. This dual objective is particularly resonant in the housing sector, where the need for affordable, sustainable housing is acute. Housing projects that incorporate low-cost construction techniques and sustainable practices can attract impact investors looking to make a measurable difference. These projects are evaluated not just on their financial viability but also on their contribution to societal well-being and environmental sustainability, aligning perfectly with ESG criteria.

Investment in low-cost, efficient housing projects can create transformative impacts. For one, it directly addresses the issue of housing affordability, enabling governments and organizations to provide housing solutions at scale. With the adoption of innovative construction methods such as modular homes, prefabricated systems, and 3D-printed structures, these projects can significantly reduce construction time and costs, making it feasible to develop large-scale housing within a shorter timeframe and lower budget.

Moreover, by embedding energy-efficient practices and renewable energy sources into these housing projects, the environmental impact is minimized. Implementing smart home technology further contributes to the energy efficiency of these homes, reducing the overall carbon footprint and aligning with broader sustainability goals.

Impact investing in housing projects also stimulates local economies by creating jobs and promoting economic activities. The construction phase itself provides employment opportunities, and once the housing is operational, the integration of industrial facilities within these housing projects can generate continuous revenue streams. This model of mixed-use development fosters economic resilience and self-sufficiency among communities, reducing reliance on external funding and subsidies.

In conclusion, impact investing in housing projects aligns the objectives of sustainable development with financial returns, making it a compelling approach to solving homelessness. By focusing on low-cost and efficient housing systems, and integrating ESG criteria, these investments not only provide immediate shelter but also build the foundation for sustainable, economically viable communities.

Cities of Hope fully qualifies for ESG and Impact Investing, which creates multiple other financing options besides the financial architecture I am proposing.

Additional Case Studies of Successful Town Projects

Examining real-world applications reveals that a multifaceted approach to developing low-cost housing and industrial integration can yield successful outcomes. The following case studies demonstrate how thoughtful planning, innovative construction methods, and strategic economic integration have translated into cost-effective, sustainable, and revenue-generating towns.

Project A: Sunnyvale Estates

Sunnyvale Estates in Arizona provides another compelling example. Launched in 2017, the project focused on leveraging 3D-printed housing technologies and renewable energy sources to create a low-cost, sustainable living environment.

Construction Techniques:

The use of 3D-printed homes significantly reduced construction costs and waste. Each house was printed using locally sourced materials, further minimizing transportation expenses and carbon footprint. The cost per unit was reduced by 30% compared to traditional building methods without compromising structural integrity or aesthetical appeal.

Energy Efficiency:

Sunnyvale Estates was designed with energy efficiency as a core principle. Homes were equipped with solar panels and advanced insulation materials, cutting down on energy consumption. The neighborhood offset its energy costs by selling excess power back to the grid, creating an additional revenue stream for the town.

Community Engagement:

Community engagement played a vital role in Sunnyvale Estates' success. Residents participated in planning and decision-making processes, ensuring that the community's needs were met. Social services, including vocational training and wellness programs, were integrated into the community, contributing to higher employment rates and better health outcomes.

The key takeaway from Sunnyvale Estates is the advantage of embracing innovative construction technologies and renewable energy to create cost-effective and sustainable housing solutions.

Project B: Greenfield Town

Greenfield Town in Oregon represents a case where prefabricated building systems and sustainable development principles came together to address homelessness and economic stagnation.

Construction Techniques:

The project relied heavily on prefabricated building systems. These systems allowed for rapid assembly and kept construction costs low. The prefabricated units were designed to be both functional and aesthetically pleasing, offering dignified living spaces for residents.

Sustainable Development:

Greenfield Town adhered to stringent Environmental, Social, and Governance (ESG) criteria, prioritizing sustainability in every aspect. Green spaces, renewable energy systems, and resource-efficient water management practices were integral to the town's design. These sustainable practices not only reduced the environmental footprint but also lowered long-term operational costs.

Economic Model:

To bolster economic self-sufficiency, Greenfield Town included commercial areas and co-working spaces within its design. These areas provided residents with the means to start small businesses or work remotely, ensuring that the community-generated revenue and attracted investment.

Greenfield Town illustrates that prefabricated building systems, combined with a focus on sustainability and economic diversity, can create thriving, low-cost communities.

Detailed Analysis of Previous Projects

Various town projects have served as benchmarks in addressing homelessness through low-cost, efficient housing. The analysis of these projects offers invaluable insights into the practical application of theoretical frameworks and construction techniques. This section details several successful initiatives that have combined residential housing with industrial facilities, presenting a feasible model for sustainable and revenue-generating communities.

One notable example is the Aranya Community Housing Project in Indore, India. Initiated in the mid-1980s by the architect Balkrishna Doshi, the project is a paradigm of how well-planned, low-cost housing can be both functional and aesthetically pleasing. Comprising around 6,500 housing units, Aranya was designed to accommodate diverse economic groups, which facilitated a natural integration of workspaces, public utilities, and residential areas. With the use of locally available materials and labor, the construction costs were kept to a minimum while still providing durable living conditions. The employment landscape was also diversified by embedding small-scale industries within residential zones, effectively turning the community into a self-sustained ecosystem.

Another project worthy of attention is the Iquique, Chile initiative, known as the "Half a House" project by the architectural firm ELEMENTAL. This project tackled the challenge of providing low-cost housing while allowing for future expansion by its occupants. ELEMENTAL constructed a series of half-built homes designed with essential living features but left enough room and structural integrity for residents to complete or expand the homes as their resources allowed. This incremental building strategy significantly reduced initial costs and empowered residents to invest gradually in their property. The success of this model lies in its flexibility and the sense of ownership it fosters among residents, facilitating not just housing but long-term community stability.

In the United States, Austin's Community First! Village offers a robust example of integrating those experiencing chronic homelessness into a supportive and revenue-generating community. The project consists of micro-homes, RVs, and canvas-sided cottages that leverage low-cost building techniques. What sets this initiative apart is the inclusion of industries such as an art studio and a community market, providing residents with employment opportunities and avenues for skill development. This integrated approach has proven not only to house the homeless but also to upkeep their dignity and purpose, creating a sustainable cycle of social and economic benefits.

These projects underscore the feasibility of constructing efficient, low-cost housing solutions that address homelessness while also fostering community integration and economic self-reliance. By examining the specific elements that contributed to their success—such as the wise choice of construction materials, incremental building strategies, and the inclusion of revenue-generating activities—we can distill essential lessons for future implementations.

Lessons Learned and Best Practices

Several critical lessons have emerged from analyzing successful town projects that address homelessness through low-cost and efficient housing systems. These insights are invaluable for future endeavors and provide a roadmap for policymakers, urban planners, and stakeholders involved in similar initiatives.

- **Incorporate Comprehensive Planning:** One consistent theme across successful projects is the importance of comprehensive planning. This involves thorough feasibility studies, community consultations, and detailed project timelines. Effective planning ensures that all potential challenges are identified and addressed early, reducing the likelihood of costly setbacks.

- **Leverage Modular and Prefabricated Construction:** The use of modular and prefabricated systems has proven to be a game-changer in many projects. These techniques not only reduce costs but also significantly cut down on construction time. Projects that adopted these methods reported higher efficiency and faster occupancy rates.

- **Prioritize Sustainability and Energy Efficiency:** Successful projects consistently integrate sustainable practices and renewable energy solutions. This aligns with environmental, social, and governance (ESG) criteria and reduces long-term operational costs. Utilizing smart home technology and renewable energy sources, such as solar panels, has proven to be economically and environmentally beneficial.

- **Economic Integration through Embedded Industrial Parks:** Embedding industrial parks within residential areas can generate needed revenue streams and provide employment opportunities for residents. This dual approach to housing and economic development has created more resilient and self-sustaining communities.

- **Engage in Public-Private Partnerships:** Collaborations between public agencies and the private sector have been essential for securing funding, expertise, and resources. Such partnerships enable projects to leverage strengths from both sectors, ensuring higher success rates.

- **Ensure Community Development and Support Services:** Integrating essential community facilities and social support systems, such as healthcare, education, and vocational training, has been crucial. Projects that provided these services reported better social outcomes and higher rates of resident satisfaction and stability.

- **Navigate Zoning and Legal Challenges:** Understanding and navigating zoning laws and legal requirements is critical. Successful projects often involve proactive engagement with local authorities to ensure compliance and mitigate any legal hurdles that might arise.

These best practices, drawn from various successful town projects, provide a blueprint for future initiatives to create low-cost and efficient housing solutions. Applying these lessons can significantly enhance the effectiveness and sustainability of efforts to combat homelessness.

Public-Private Partnerships

Solving the homelessness crisis through efficient, low-cost housing solutions necessitates robust collaborations between public agencies and the private sector. This section delves into Public-Private Partnerships (PPPs) dynamics and their significance in developing sustainable, profitable towns designed to address housing shortages.

The Role of Public Agencies

Public agencies, primarily local, state, and federal governments, play a crucial role in the execution of affordable housing projects. They provide essential support through funding, policy frameworks, and regulatory approvals. These agencies are often responsible for allocating public land, offering tax incentives, and establishing policy guidelines that ensure the feasibility and sustainability of housing projects. For instance, the U.S. Department of Housing and Urban Development (HUD) provides crucial grants and funding opportunities aimed at housing the homeless population.

Public agencies also help streamline the legal and zoning requirements, eliminating bureaucratic red tape that can delay or inhibit development projects. Streamlined approval processes and clear guidelines can significantly reduce the time and financial burdens associated with project initiation and completion.

Collaborations with Private Sector

The involvement of private sector entities brings in essential business acumen, efficiency, and innovation, which are indispensable for the success of large-scale housing projects. Private developers, construction companies, and financial institutions contribute not just through investment but also by offering novel solutions in construction technologies, project management, and sustainability practices.

For example, collaborations with companies specializing in modular construction, prefabricated building systems, and 3D-printed housing allow for cost-effective and rapid housing unit development. The private sector's ability to incorporate cutting-edge technological advancements can ensure that housing developments are both sustainable and energy-efficient, aligning with broader ESG (Environmental, Social, and Governance) criteria.

Moreover, private entities can help in generating revenues for these housing projects through the integration of industrial parks and commercial spaces. Such mixed-use developments not only provide housing but also create employment opportunities, thereby fostering economic growth within the community. Businesses occupying these industrial parks benefit from tax incentives and reduced rental costs, creating a symbiotic relationship between housing and economic activities.

- **Economic Incentives:** Tax reliefs, grants, and subsidies can make projects financially viable.

- **Land Acquisition:** Public agencies can provide land at reduced or no cost, which significantly lowers project costs.

- **Innovation and Technology:** Private sector entities bring modern construction techniques, which ensure cost efficiency and speed.

- **Regulatory Support:** Streamlined processes and favorable zoning laws can expedite project timelines.

- **Employment Generation:** Industrial parks and commercial spaces within these towns generate local employment.

In conclusion, Public-Private Partnerships stand as a cornerstone in creating effective, low-cost housing solutions. Governments set the stage by providing the necessary regulatory and financial environment, while the private sector contributes expertise, innovation, and investment. This synergistic approach ensures that housing projects not only meet immediate shelter needs but also contribute to long-term economic and social sustainability.

The Role of Public Agencies

Public agencies play a crucial role in developing and sustaining public-private partnerships (PPPs) in the housing sector, particularly when seeking low-cost and efficient solutions for homelessness. These agencies often serve as facilitators, regulators, and enablers of projects, ensuring that the partnership meets the public interest while harnessing the efficiencies and innovations from the private sector.

First and foremost, public agencies provide the essential regulatory framework that governs PPP projects. This includes setting the legal and operational guidelines for project implementation. Well-defined regulations ensure that both public and private entities understand their roles, responsibilities, and limitations. The regulatory framework facilitates clearer communication and coordination between the different stakeholders involved in PPPs.

Moreover, public agencies are often responsible for providing the initial funding or securing financing for these projects. They might leverage public funds or issue municipal bonds to gather capital. By doing so, they reduce the financial risk for private investors, making the projects more attractive. This initial financial commitment from public agencies can be particularly significant in low-cost housing initiatives, where returns on investment might be lower than other real estate ventures.

I am proposing that HUD issue bonds for the debt side and that the Department of State undertake a novel visa program that will generate substantial fees from applications, serving as the equity portion for the overall funding of Cities of Hope. My financial architecture has flexibility, and the equity piece can also be raised locally in the US as Cities of Hope qualifies for ESG and Impact Investing and will prove to be very profitable in attracting institutional capital sources for Equity.

Additionally, public agencies serve as oversight bodies, ensuring that the project adheres to its outlined objectives and remains accountable to the public. They monitor the project's progress, compliance with regulations, and overall impact on the community. Oversight by public agencies is critical in maintaining the integrity of PPP projects, as it provides a check against potential mismanagement or focus on profit over public good.

Public agencies are also instrumental in land acquisition and zoning, which can be significant hurdles in creating new housing developments. By streamlining zoning laws and facilitating land acquisition processes, public agencies can lower barriers for the private sector to enter into PPP projects. This can expedite the development timeline significantly, thus addressing housing crises more promptly.

Furthermore, public agencies often play a role in community engagement and ensuring that community concerns are addressed within the project plan. Effective PPPs require strong community support and alignment with local needs. Public agencies can use their platforms to gather community input, organize public consultations, and ensure that the housing solutions proposed are inclusive and beneficial to the intended populations.

In conclusion, public agencies are instrumental in creating the foundation and environment necessary for successful PPPs in the housing sector. By providing the regulatory framework, initial funding, oversight, land acquisition assistance, and community engagement, they help ensure that projects not only meet the needs of the homeless population but also do so efficiently and sustainably.

Collaborations with Private Sector

Collaborations with the private sector play a pivotal role in the development of low-cost, efficient housing systems designed to address homelessness effectively. Private sector involvement brings innovation, efficiency, and a wealth of resources that are often beyond the reach of public entities alone. These collaborations can take various forms, including joint ventures, public-private partnerships (PPPs), and strategic alliances with construction companies, financial institutions, and technology providers.

One of the primary advantages of private-sector collaboration is access to advanced technologies and construction methods. For example, construction companies specializing in modular and prefabricated building systems bring valuable expertise in quick, cost-effective construction techniques. These methods not only reduce the time and cost required to build housing units but also improve the quality and sustainability of the buildings.

Moreover, financial institutions and investors play a critical part in funding housing projects. Private financing can supplement public funds, allowing for larger-scale projects and more comprehensive development plans. Innovative financial models, such as social impact bonds, have proven effective in securing private investment while ensuring social outcomes. This approach aligns the interests of private investors with the public good, fostering sustainable development.

Technology providers also offer crucial support through smart home innovations and renewable energy solutions. Smart home technologies can enhance the efficiency and livability of housing units, providing residents with modern amenities while reducing utility costs. Renewable energy solutions, like solar panels and energy-efficient appliances, contribute to sustainable living environments and lower long-term operating costs.

Furthermore, the private sector's role in economic development within these housing projects cannot be underestimated. By integrating industrial parks and workspaces within residential areas, private companies can create job opportunities and stimulate local economies. This integration fosters a self-sustaining community model where residents have access to employment, reducing dependency on external job markets and support systems.

Effective collaboration with the private sector requires clear communication, mutual trust, and shared goals between public agencies and private entities. Setting up transparent governance structures and ensuring accountability through performance metrics and regular audits can help sustain these partnerships. Additionally, leveraging the strengths of each sector—innovation and efficiency from the private sector and regulatory and social oversight from the public sector—maximizes the impact of housing projects.

Overall, engaging the private sector in the effort to develop low-cost, efficient housing systems is indispensable for addressing homelessness. These collaborations bring innovative solutions, financial muscle, and operational expertise that can lead to the successful realization of sustainable housing projects that are both economically viable and socially beneficial.

Overcoming Common Challenges

Implementing strategies for town building, particularly with the objective of addressing homelessness through low-cost and efficient housing systems, presents a variety of challenges. These challenges span financial limitations, regulatory hurdles, community resistance, and technical constraints, all of which must be strategically navigated to ensure project success.

Financial Limitations

One of the primary challenges in town building is securing adequate funding. Limited financial resources can impede the construction of both residential and industrial facilities essential for the sustainability of low-cost towns. Innovative financial models such as micro-financing, community investments, and public-private partnerships can provide viable solutions. Developing a diversified funding portfolio helps mitigate risk and ensures continuous financial inflows. **My proposed financial architecture is one viable option that can be pursued.**

Regulatory Hurdles

Navigating the legal landscape and adhering to zoning laws and building codes can be complex. Regulatory restrictions often cause significant delays and can escalate project costs. A proactive approach involves early and ongoing engagement with local authorities to streamline approvals and negotiate flexible regulatory frameworks that support innovative construction methods such as modular and prefab systems.

Community Resistance

Community resistance is another crucial barrier. Local residents may oppose new developments due to misconceptions about their potential impact on property values and community dynamics. Initiating community engagement programs and transparent communication strategies can address these concerns. Demonstrating the socio-economic benefits, such as job creation through embedded industrial parks and enhanced community facilities, can help garner local support.

Technical Constraints

Technical constraints related to the integration of advanced building technologies, such as 3D printing and energy-efficient systems, can pose significant obstacles. These technologies require substantial upfront investment and skilled labor, which might not be readily available. Training programs and partnerships with technological firms can help build local expertise and facilitate the adoption of these innovative solutions.

Coordination and Project Management

Coordinating multiple stakeholders, including government agencies, private investors, contractors, and community members, demands robust project management frameworks. Effective project management ensures that the project progresses on schedule and within budget while maintaining quality standards. Adopting Agile or Lean construction principles can enhance flexibility and responsiveness to unforeseen challenges.

Ultimately, addressing these challenges requires a multifaceted approach that combines financial ingenuity, regulatory flexibility, community engagement, technical expertise, and efficient project management. Successfully overcoming these hurdles not only advances the goal of creating sustainable, low-cost townships but also contributes to resolving the overarching issue of homelessness.

Future Prospects and Innovations

The future of low-cost, efficient housing systems is teeming with potential. As we forge ahead in our quest to tackle homelessness, emerging technologies and innovative approaches will play pivotal roles. This section examines the advances on the horizon that promise to revolutionize how we conceptualize and build affordable housing.

Emerging Technologies in Construction

The construction industry is experiencing a technological renaissance. Innovations such as augmented reality (AR) and virtual reality (VR) are transforming the way architects and builders approach design and construction. By enabling real-time visualization, AR and VR can significantly reduce errors and streamline the construction process.

Furthermore, the integration of artificial intelligence (AI) into construction is proving to be a game-changer. AI can optimize project management by predicting potential delays and resource shortages. This can lead to cost savings and more efficient project timelines. Machine learning algorithms are also being applied to improve the precision of prefabricated and modular construction systems, making these methods even more viable for large-scale housing projects.

Projections for Future Housing Solutions

Looking forward, we see a concerted effort towards creating self-sufficient communities that address housing needs and provide employment opportunities. One promising concept is the development of smart, integrated townships with embedded industrial parks. These townships aim to create a symbiotic relationship between residential and industrial zones, fostering economic activity and community welfare simultaneously.

Moreover, advances in sustainable building materials are set to redefine the construction landscape. The development of carbon-negative materials, like bioconcrete and engineered timber, will reduce the environmental footprint of housing projects. Additionally, the circular economy approach - where building materials are reused and recycled - will become more prevalent, furthering sustainability goals.

On the energy front, advancements in renewable energy technologies will enable new housing projects to be energy-independent. Solar panels, wind turbines, and energy storage solutions are continually becoming more efficient and cost-effective. Smart grid technology will also enhance the management and distribution of energy within these communities, ensuring a reliable and sustainable power supply.

Emerging Technologies in Construction

Emerging technologies in construction are critically shaping the future of housing, providing avenues for cost reduction, efficiency, and sustainability. These advancements are particularly pertinent in addressing the housing needs of homeless populations through the creation of low-cost, efficient towns that include both residential and industrial facilities. This section delves into some of the most promising technological innovations in the construction industry.

One of the pioneering technologies in construction is Building Information Modeling (BIM). BIM is a digital representation of the physical and functional characteristics of a facility, facilitating improved planning, design, and management across the building's lifecycle. Through its use, architects and engineers can anticipate potential issues early in the design phase, thereby saving costs and reducing delays. This technology is advantageous for low-cost housing as it enhances the precision of construction, ensuring resources are used as efficiently as possible.

Another game-changing technology is the application of advanced robotics and drones in construction activities. Robots can perform repetitive tasks with high accuracy, reducing labor costs and increasing productivity. Drones, on the other hand, offer unprecedented capabilities in surveying and monitoring construction sites, providing real-time data that can improve decision-making processes. These innovations can significantly lower the cost and time required to develop housing for the homeless.

Additionally, new materials such as graphene and self-healing concrete are setting the stage for durable and sustainable constructions. Graphene, known for its strength and conductivity, is being integrated into building materials to improve their resilience and efficiency. Self-healing concrete, embedded with bacteria that produce limestone to fill cracks, can greatly extend the lifespan of buildings while reducing maintenance costs. Incorporating these materials into construction can make housing developments long-lasting and less expensive to maintain.

Another critical innovation is the integration of the Internet of Things (IoT) in construction. IoT facilitates smart homes equipped with sensors and devices that monitor and optimize energy use, enhancing the sustainability and efficiency of residential areas. For instance, smart thermostats and lighting systems can significantly reduce utility costs, making housing more affordable for low-income residents.

Moreover, advancements in 3D printing technology are revolutionizing the way homes are built. 3D-printed houses can be constructed quickly and at a fraction of the cost of traditional methods, making it a viable solution for low-cost housing. These structures can be designed to incorporate energy-efficient features, further reducing long-term costs for residents.

These emerging technologies in construction promise to make housing more affordable and efficient and contribute to the overall goal of creating self-sustaining communities. By employing these innovations, policymakers, developers, and community planners can effectively address the homelessness crisis, providing a dignified and sustainable living environment for all.

Projections for Future Housing Solutions

In an era marked by rapid technological advancements and growing socio-economic challenges, projecting future housing solutions necessitates a multi-faceted approach that integrates innovative construction methodologies, flexible policy frameworks, and sustainable economic models.

One of the most promising avenues for future housing solutions lies in the continued evolution of modular and prefabricated construction technologies. These methods have already demonstrated significant reductions in construction time and costs. Future projections suggest that as these technologies mature, the integration of AI-driven design and robotic assembly will further streamline production. This shift is anticipated to reduce labor costs and minimize material waste, making affordable housing more accessible.

A critical component of future housing solutions will be the adoption of sustainable building practices, particularly those utilizing renewable energy sources and smart home technologies. Innovation in renewable energy systems, such as advanced solar panels and energy-efficient geothermal heating, will likely become standard in new housing developments. Smart home technologies, which optimize energy use and improve home management, will contribute significantly to reducing overall living costs.

In terms of social and economic integration, future housing solutions will emphasize the development of mixed-use spaces that combine residential, commercial, and industrial areas. By embedding industrial parks within residential zones, new towns can create self-sustaining ecosystems where residents have access to employment opportunities within close proximity to their homes. This model not only supports economic stability but also fosters a strong sense of community. In essence, Cities of Hope is a concept of the past and the future at the same time.

Policy innovation will also play a pivotal role in shaping future housing solutions. Progressive zoning laws and supportive regulatory frameworks are essential to encourage the development of new housing models. Governments at various levels must consider long-term benefits and adopt policies that facilitate public-private partnerships and incentivize sustainable development practices.

In summary, the future of housing solutions is intricately tied to advancements in construction technologies, sustainable practices, and supportive policies. By embracing these innovations, we can create efficient, low-cost housing systems that address homelessness effectively while fostering stable and thriving communities.

Conclusion

The journey to eradicate homelessness through low-cost, efficient housing is complex, but the future holds considerable promise. Emerging technologies, sustainable practices, and innovative policies will collectively drive the evolution of housing solutions. By harnessing these advancements, we can build resilient communities that offer not just shelter but also pathways to economic and social well-being.

If embraced and accepted, the Cities of Hope could stand as a prime example of this approach.

NOW LET US TALK ABOUT FINANCE , SOURCE OF FUNDS , NOVEL VISA PROGRAMME AND OTHER FINANCIAL ASPECTS OF THE PROJECT

The Novel Visa Program.

The homelessness crisis in the United States has persisted for decades despite the numerous programs and initiatives aimed at alleviating it. Innovative solutions are required to tackle the root causes of homelessness and offer sustainable pathways for reintegration. One such innovative approach is my proposed **Special Visa Program for Foreign Workers**, a unique global initiative designed to support the development of self-sustaining communities—referred to as the **Cities of Hope**—while providing economic opportunities for skilled and semi-skilled workers from around the world.

This chapter delves into the structure, benefits, challenges, and broader implications of the Special Visa Program. It examines how this program can be instrumental in creating and sustaining the Cities of Hope, offering a comprehensive solution that addresses homelessness on multiple fronts.

Program Overview: A Global Lottery for Hope

At the heart of the Special Visa Program is a global lottery system, which is projected to attract over 110 million applicants from around the world. This lottery is not just a chance for participants to secure a visa but an opportunity to build a new life in the United States while contributing to the vital cause of eradicating homelessness. The lottery system ensures a fair and inclusive selection process, drawing from a diverse pool of applicants with a wide range of skills and backgrounds.

Once selected, the lottery winners will undergo a rigorous vetting process to ensure they meet the specific job requirements needed in the Cities of Hope. These requirements will be aligned with the needs of the community, focusing on sectors such as construction, healthcare, agriculture, and various trades critical to the development and operation of these self-sustaining towns.

Multiple strategies might be pursued for the lottery and the selection process after the lottery. One strategy I can propose is that the lottery can be arranged in accordance with each job classification, which might be as many as 60-70 different job descriptions, and each lottery might be based on a certain job description. Post the lottery, a shortlist can be selected, such as 200.000 winners versus the 50.000 to be selected. This will allow for qualification-based selection based on the CV's accomplishments, language proficiency, skillsets, and other criteria that can be applied. Artificial intelligence can be utilized to support the workload of USCIS for the initial screening, which will be followed by interviews at the consulates and embassies.

The Special Visa Program is designed with dual objectives: to fill labor shortages in critical sectors that directly support the Cities of Hope and to offer foreign workers a meaningful opportunity to contribute to society while building a secure future for themselves and their families.

The Package for Special Visa Lottery Winners

The Special Visa Program offers an enticing and life-changing package for the lottery winners who will be selected to work in the Cities of Hope. This comprehensive package provides significant economic benefits and facilitates a smooth transition into life in the United States, making it a highly attractive opportunity for millions of applicants worldwide.

Financial and Material Benefits

Each lottery winner will receive an average **net monthly salary of $3,000**, which is a substantial income, especially when considering the additional benefits included in the package. This income is designed to ensure that workers can support themselves and their families while building a stable future in the U.S.

In addition to the competitive salary, winners will be provided with **free housing** in the Cities of Hope. These accommodations will be modern, comfortable, and designed to foster a sense of community among the workers and local residents. This benefit not only eliminates the significant cost of housing but also ensures that workers are living in proximity to their place of work, reducing commute times and enhancing work-life balance.

Moreover, each worker will receive a **free car**, allowing them the freedom to travel within and outside the city. This benefit is crucial for integrating into American society, where personal transportation is often essential for daily life. The provision of a car also symbolizes the mobility and independence that the program aims to provide to its participants.

Pathway to Permanent Residency

One of the most compelling aspects of the package is the pathway to permanent residency. After completing five years of work within the Cities of Hope, participants will be eligible to apply for a **Green Card**, granting them permanent residency in the United States. This opportunity is a significant motivator for many applicants, as it offers not just a job, but a potential future in one of the world's most sought-after countries for immigrants.

Cultural and Social Integration

While the material benefits are substantial, the Special Visa Program also offers invaluable cultural and social experiences. Participants will have the chance to immerse themselves in American life, interacting daily with individuals from diverse backgrounds, including U.S. citizens, fellow foreign workers, and the homeless residents they are helping to support. This exposure will provide a deep understanding of American culture, work ethics, and social systems, equipping participants with the knowledge and experience necessary to thrive in the U.S.

The holistic package offered by the Special Visa Program is designed to attract a large number of applicants, with estimates suggesting over 110 million people might participate in the lottery. (22 million people applied for the Green Card Lottery in 2023, and it does not include any package, although there is no application fee as the downside in comparison) Given the application fee of $200, the program is also poised to generate significant revenue, contributing billions of dollars to the funding of the Cities of Hope as equity.

Financial Architecture: Application Fees and CAPEX Contributions

A significant financial component of the Special Visa Program is the application fee. With an estimated 110 million applicants worldwide, the program could generate substantial revenue even before the lottery process begins. For instance, if each applicant is charged an average fee of $200, this would yield **$22 billion** in initial revenue. This substantial inflow of funds would be pivotal in covering a significant portion of the estimated capital expenditure (CAPEX) required to develop the Cities of Hope.

This revenue can be allocated to various phases of the project, including land acquisition, infrastructure development, housing construction, and community services. By using these funds as the equity portion of the financial architecture, the initiative can reduce its reliance on traditional financing methods, such as loans and bonds, thereby lowering overall project costs. Additionally, the application fees could be tiered based on various factors, allowing for a flexible and scalable financial model that can adjust to the project's needs.

The financial strategy behind the Special Visa Program ensures that the economic burden is not placed solely on federal or state budgets. Instead, it leverages global interest and participation to create a self-sustaining funding model that can support the ambitious goals of the Cities of Hope.

The Economic and Social Framework of the Program

Economic Impact: Driving Growth and Sustainability

The Special Visa Program is expected to have a profound economic impact on the Cities of Hope. By attracting skilled labor, the program will expedite the construction and operational phases of these towns, ensuring that infrastructure projects are completed on time and within budget. This labor influx will also support ongoing community services, from healthcare and education to food production and waste management.

Foreign workers will play a crucial role in bridging the skill gaps that currently exist within the homeless population. Many homeless individuals may lack the specific training or experience required for certain jobs, which can delay the development of these communities. By filling these gaps, the Special Visa Program ensures that the Cities of Hope can quickly become functional and self-sustaining, reducing reliance on external support.

Moreover, the economic activities generated by the presence of foreign workers will contribute to local economies. Their labor and consumer activities will create a multiplier effect, generating additional revenue that can be reinvested into the Cities of Hope. This economic growth will benefit not only the new residents of these towns but also the broader regions in which they are located.

Social Integration and Cultural Exchange

Beyond the economic benefits, the Special Visa Program is designed to foster social integration and cultural exchange. The presence of foreign workers in the Cities of Hope introduces a diverse range of perspectives, skills, and cultural practices that can enrich the community as a whole. These workers, motivated by the opportunity to start anew, will likely exhibit a strong work ethic and a deep commitment to the success of the Cities of Hope.

Comprehensive orientation programs, including cultural competency training, language classes, and community-building activities, will support the integration process. These initiatives ensure that foreign workers and local residents, including the formerly homeless, can coexist harmoniously and work together towards common goals.

This cultural exchange is not a one-way street; it also benefits the U.S. by fostering a deeper understanding and appreciation of different cultures. Such exchanges can break down social barriers and contribute to the creation of a more inclusive and cohesive society, both within the Cities of Hope and in the broader national context.

Challenges and Mitigation Strategies

Regulatory and Legal Complexities

Implementing the Special Visa Program involves navigating a complex web of immigration laws and policies. These regulatory hurdles must be carefully managed to avoid delays and ensure that the program operates smoothly. This requires close coordination between various government agencies, including the Department of State, the Department of Labor, and the U.S. Citizenship and Immigration Services (USCIS).

To address these challenges, the program will include robust oversight mechanisms and regular audits to ensure compliance with all relevant laws and regulations. These measures will help mitigate the risk of legal complications and ensure that the program remains transparent, fair, and effective.

Preventing Exploitation and Ensuring Fair Treatment

One of the primary concerns with any large-scale visa program is the potential for exploitation of foreign workers. To prevent this, the Special Visa Program will include stringent protections for workers' rights. Regular monitoring and inspections will enshrine these protections in the program's guidelines and enforce these protections.

Foreign workers will have access to legal recourse and support services to address any issues related to unfair labor practices, discrimination, or other forms of exploitation. Ensuring that these workers receive fair wages, safe working conditions, and adequate social support is critical to the program's success and its long-term sustainability.

Community Integration and Social Cohesion

Integrating foreign workers into the Cities of Hope presents its own challenges, particularly in overcoming cultural and language barriers. These challenges can be addressed through targeted cultural competency training, language classes, and ongoing community-building initiatives.

Moreover, the program will emphasize the importance of mutual respect and understanding between foreign workers and local residents. By fostering an environment of collaboration and inclusivity, the program can help build strong, resilient communities that are capable of addressing the complex social dynamics of homelessness.

Leveraging Global Interest: A Positive Perception of the United States

The Special Visa Program has the potential to generate global interest and goodwill toward the United States. The program's emphasis on humanitarian goals—helping to eradicate homelessness while offering economic opportunities—can enhance the U.S.'s image as a leader in innovative social solutions. By attracting millions of applicants from around the world, the program also creates a valuable database of skilled individuals eager to contribute to the U.S. economy. This database could be leveraged to address other labor shortages or recruit talent for specific industries, further enhancing the program's long-term value.

Why Foreign Workers Will Be Dedicated and Vigilant

A Second Chance for a New Life

One of the Special Visa Program's unique strengths is the profound motivation foreign workers bring to the table. For many of these individuals, this program represents a rare opportunity to start anew in the United States—a land synonymous with freedom, opportunity, and the pursuit of happiness. This context cannot be understated; it is not just a job for these workers but a genuine second chance at life.

The participants in this program are acutely aware that their selection is both a privilege and a responsibility. With this opportunity comes the understanding that their success within the Cities of Hope is directly tied to their future prospects, including the chance to secure permanent residency in the United States. This profound connection to their own life goals ensures that these workers will approach their roles with unparalleled dedication and vigilance.

Incentives for Success: Pathway to Permanent Residency

The promise of a **Green Card** after five years of dedicated service in the Cities of Hope is a powerful motivator. This incentive is not just a reward but a life-changing opportunity that many around the world aspire to achieve. Knowing that their hard work and commitment can lead to a permanent life in the U.S., these workers are likely to exhibit a level of focus, determination, and perseverance that aligns perfectly with the objectives of the Cities of Hope.

This incentive structure ensures that the foreign workers will not only perform their duties diligently but will also actively engage in the success of the overall community. Their vested interest in the outcome of these cities naturally leads to a strong work ethic and a collaborative spirit, both of which are essential for the development of sustainable communities.

Resilience and Adaptability

Foreign workers participating in the Special Visa Program are often individuals who have faced significant challenges in their lives. These individuals possess a resilience that makes them particularly well-suited for the demands of building and sustaining new communities, whether due to economic hardship, political instability, or other adversities in their home countries.

This resilience is coupled with strong adaptability—a trait essential for anyone moving to a new country and adjusting to a new culture. These workers will bring this adaptability to the Cities of Hope, where their ability to navigate new environments and overcome obstacles will be invaluable in ensuring the success and stability of these towns.

A Shared Mission with the Homeless Residents

Interestingly, the foreign workers' experience mirrors that of the homeless residents they will work alongside. Both groups are seeking stability, security, and a chance to rebuild their lives. This shared sense of purpose fosters a natural alliance between the foreign workers and the homeless citizens, creating a strong community bond.

Foreign workers, understanding the gravity of their second chance, will be naturally inclined to support and uplift the homeless residents. This dynamic will not only contribute to the social cohesion within the Cities of Hope but will also enhance the overall success of the initiative by fostering an environment of mutual respect, cooperation, and shared growth.

A Motivated Workforce for a Noble Cause

The foreign workers participating in the Special Visa Program will be more than just employees—they will be dedicated partners in the mission to eradicate homelessness and build sustainable communities. Their personal investment in the success of the Cities of Hope, driven by the promise of a better life, ensures that they will approach their roles with the utmost dedication and vigilance. This motivation, combined with their resilience and shared mission with the homeless residents, makes them an invaluable asset to this bold initiative.

Conclusion: A Bold Vision for the Future

The Special Visa Program for Foreign Workers is more than just a solution to labor shortages; it is a bold vision for addressing homelessness in a sustainable and innovative way. By combining the strengths of a global workforce with the needs of self-sustaining communities, the Cities of Hope initiative offers a comprehensive strategy that can transform lives and revitalize underutilized areas across the United States.

The financial architecture of this program, including the significant revenue generated from application fees, ensures that the initiative is not only economically viable but also capable of driving substantial social impact. While challenges exist, they are surmountable with careful planning, robust oversight, and a commitment to fair and ethical practices. If implemented effectively, this program has the potential to create a model that can be replicated in other contexts, both within the U.S. and globally, as a means of addressing homelessness and fostering economic and social integration.

In essence, the Special Visa Program for Foreign Workers represents a powerful convergence of humanitarian goals and economic strategy, offering a new pathway to prosperity for both foreign workers and the homeless individuals they will work alongside in the Cities of Hope. **This comprehensive approach alleviates homelessness and reinforces the United States" role as a beacon of hope and opportunity on the global stage.**

Funding -Cost Estimation - Budgeting

This comprehensive plan envisions the creation of 100 Cities of Hope across the country, each designed to house 5,000 homeless individuals. These towns will be equipped with essential amenities, retail spaces, educational and medical facilities, robust infrastructure, and employment opportunities to ensure all residents' high quality of life.

Housing Solutions

Each industrial town will feature modular apartments, offering a cost-effective and efficient way to provide housing. The apartments will each be 500 square feet, ensuring ample space for comfort and privacy.

- **Total Apartments:** 550,000 (including 50,000 for foreign workers)
- **Average Apartment Size:** 500 square feet
- **Total Residential Space Required:** 275,000,000 square feet

To accommodate a total workforce of 500,000 individuals, including homeless citizens and additional American workers, the Cities of Hope will require 550,000 modular apartments. This update also includes the integration of Belief Centers as key community infrastructure components.

Housing Development:

- **Total Apartments:** 550,000 units, each 500 square feet.
- **Total Residential Space Required:** 275 million square feet.
- **Building Configuration:**
  - Stories per Building: 5
  - Apartments per Floor: 6
  - Total Buildings Required: 18,334.
- Cost Analysis:
  - **Cost per Modular Apartment:** $60 per square foot.
  - **Total Construction Cost per Apartment:** $30,000.
  - **Total Construction Cost for Apartments: $16.5 billion.**

Expanded Common Areas, Facilities, and Belief Centers

The increased population and integration of Belief Centers require an expansion of common areas and essential services.

Common Areas:

- **Retail Boulevards and Theatres:**
  - **Total Retail Space per Town:** 300,000 square feet.
  - **Theatre Space:** 35,000 square feet.
- **Essential Services:**
  - 2 Police Stations (20,000 sq ft total).
  - 1 Hospital (100,000 sq ft).
  - 5 Clinics (5,000 sq ft each).
  - 2 Schools (50,000 sq ft each).
  - 2 Community Centers (40,000 sq ft total).
  - Parks and Recreational Areas (300,000 sq ft).
- **Belief Centers:**
  - **Space per Town:** 50,000 square feet.
  - **Total Space for 100 Towns:** 5 million square feet.
- Total Common Area Space per Town: 895,000 square feet.

Cost Estimates for Common Areas:

- **Average Cost per Square Foot: $200.**
- **Total Cost for Common Areas per Town: $179 million.**

Expanded Infrastructure Investment

Each town will require substantial infrastructure investments to support the expanded population and ensure sustainability.

Breakdown of Infrastructure Costs:

1. **Roads:**
   - **Length of Roads per** Town: 55 miles.
   - **Cost per Mile of Road:** $1 million.
   - **Total Road Cost per** Town: $55 million.
2. **Sewage Systems:** $22 million.

3. **Power Connections:** $11 million.

4. **Water Supply Systems:** $17 million.

5. **Telecommunication Networks:** $6 million.

- **Total Infrastructure Cost per Town: $111 million.**

Total Updated Construction Costs

- **Residential Apartments:** $16.5 billion.

- **Common Areas :** $17.9 billion (for 100 towns).

- **Infrastructure:** $11.1 billion (for 100 towns).

- **Total Construction Cost for Housing, Common Areas, and Infrastructure: $45.5 billion.**

Employment and Economic Development

With 500,000 workers, the Cities of Hope will include a mix of homeless individuals and additional foreign workers, supporting a diverse range of industries.

1. Call Centers:

- **Total Employment:** 25,000 employees.

- **Revenue:** $1.25 billion annually.

2. Greenhouses and Agriculture:

- **Total Employment:** 30,000 employees.

- **Revenue:** $1.2 billion annually.

3. Renewable Energy & Recycling Projects:

- **Total Employment:** 13,000 employees.

- **Revenue:** $2.6 billion annually.

4. Basic Manufacturing Industries:

- **Total Employment:** 432,000 employees.

- **Revenue:** $64.8 billion annually.

Analysis of the Actual Workforce from 500,000 Homeless Individuals

To determine the potential workforce of the 500,000 homeless individuals, we need to account for several factors, including the effectiveness of rehabilitation, medical treatment, training programs, and the health and readiness of the individuals. Based on industry statistics and average conditions, we can make a reasoned estimate.

Factors Influencing Workforce Readiness

1. **Rehabilitation and Medical Treatment Success Rates**

   - **Mental Health and Substance Abuse Rehabilitation:** Approximately 60% of individuals undergoing these programs show significant improvement, allowing them to return to work (The Medical Care Blog) (National Alliance to End Homelessness).

   - **Chronic Medical Conditions Management:** With proper treatment, around 70% of individuals with chronic conditions can manage their health well enough to maintain employment (National Alliance to End Homelessness).

2. **Training Program Effectiveness**

   - **Vocational Training and Job Placement:** These programs typically have a success rate of 70-80% in preparing individuals for the workforce (The Medical Care Blog) (National Alliance to End Homelessness).

Estimated Workforce Readiness

Based on these factors, we can estimate the workforce readiness as follows:

1. **Rehabilitation and Medical Treatment**

   - **Total Individuals Receiving Treatment:** 500,000

   - **Successful Rehabilitation (60%):** 300,000 individuals

   - **Effective Medical Treatment (70%):** 350,000 individuals

Assuming that individuals who benefit from rehabilitation and medical treatment overlap significantly, we estimate that around 70% of the treated population will be ready for work.

500,000×0.70=350,000 individuals

2. **Training Program Success**

   - **Workforce-Ready Individuals Post-Treatment:** 350,000

   - **Effective Training (75%):** 262,500 individuals

Thus, around 75% of the workforce-ready individuals will successfully transition to employment through vocational training and job placement programs.

Estimated Actual Workforce

Actual Workforce Estimate:

- **Initial Workforce-Ready Population:** 500,000 individuals

- **Post-Treatment Workforce-Ready Population (70%):** 350,000 individuals

- **Successfully Trained Workforce (75% of 350,000):** 262,500 individuals

Summary

Based on the estimated success rates of rehabilitation, medical treatment, and training programs, the potential actual workforce out of the 500,000 homeless individuals is approximately:

262,500 individuals
This analysis takes into account the average effectiveness of various support programs and the health and readiness of the homeless population. It provides a realistic estimate of the number of individuals who can be integrated into the workforce through the proposed comprehensive support and development plan.

Additional Workers: To ensure full employment, 237,500 American workers will be recruited. These workers will be distributed across the various sectors, helping to drive economic growth.

Updated Cost Analysis for Business Establishment and Operation

1. Call Centers:

- **Number of Call Centers:** 500.
- **Cost to Establish Each Call Center:** $10 million.
- **Total Cost for Call Centers:** $5 billion.

2. Greenhouses and Agriculture:

- **Number of Greenhouses:** 1,000.
- **Cost to Establish Each Greenhouse:** $2 million.
- **Total Cost for Greenhouses:** $2 billion.

3. Renewable Energy Projects:

- **Number of Projects:** 500 Solar Farms + 200 Wind Turbine Projects.
- **Cost to Establish Each Solar Farm:** $20 million.
- **Cost to Establish Each Wind Turbine Project:** $15 million.
- **Total Cost for Renewable Energy Projects: $13 billion.**

4. Basic Manufacturing Industries:

- **Number of Plants:** 2,160.
- **Cost to Establish Each Plant:** $15 million.
- **Total Cost for Manufacturing Plants: $32.4 billion.**

Total Business Establishment Costs

- **Total Cost for Call Centers, Greenhouses, Renewable Energy Projects, and Manufacturing Industries: $52.4 billion.**

Comprehensive Annual Revenue and Cost Analysis

Revenue Forecast:

- **Call Centers:** $1.25 billion.

- **Greenhouses:** $1.2 billion.

- **Renewable Energy Projects:** $2.6 billion.

- **Manufacturing Industries:** $64.8 billion.

- **Combined Annual Revenue: $69.85 billion.**

Annual Costs:

- **Food and Healthcare for 237,500 Non-Working Individuals:** $4,275 billion.

- **Running Costs for 100 Towns:** $700 million.

- **Debt Servicing Costs:** $5,287 billion

- **Total Annual Costs:** $10.26 billion.

EBITDA Forecast:

- **EBITDA (20% Margin): $13.97 billion.**

Financing Structure

Total CAPEX: $45.5 billion (housing, common areas, infrastructure) + $52.4 billion (business establishment) = **$97.9 billion**.

Equity Financing:

- **Total Equity:** $22 billion.

- **Source:** Application fees from the Special Visa Program. (or other alternatives)

Debt Financing (Bond Issuance by HUD):

- **Total Debt:** $75.9 billion.

- **Bond Terms:** 25 years, 5% interest rate, annual amortization.

- **Annual Debt Service (Principal + Interest): $5.28 billion.**

Conclusion

The Cities of Hope initiative, encompassing 550,000 modular apartments, including Belief Centers, presents a comprehensive financial model with robust employment and revenue projections. Including additional American workers, the project is fully staffed, ensuring economic and social sustainability.

The financial structure, combining $22 billion in equity from global interest in the Special Visa Program and $75.9 billion in debt financing, ensures the initiative's feasibility. Even with the substantial investment, the project's projected EBITDA and long-term economic benefits make it a transformative solution for addressing homelessness and revitalizing underutilized areas in the United States.

Tax Exempt Designated Economic Zones (TEZ)

These Cities of Hope will be designated as Tax Exempt Designated Economic Zones (TEZ) with the following advantages:

1. **No Taxation:** For-profit businesses within these zones will benefit from no corporate taxes, encouraging investment and economic growth.

2. **Additional Workforce:** The TEZs will attract skilled foreign workers, enhancing the talent pool and increasing productivity.

3. **Value Added to the Economy:** By producing goods and services domestically, the TEZs will reduce the reliance on imports, leading to a stronger economy.

4. **Economic Impact:** The TEZs will generate significant economic activity, boosting local economies and creating a positive ripple effect across the nation.

Advantages of TEZs

1. **Increased Employment:** By creating 500,000 jobs, the TEZs will significantly reduce unemployment.

2. **Economic Diversification:** The diverse industries within the TEZs will contribute to a more resilient and varied economy.

3. **Reduced Import Dependency:** Producing goods and services domestically will decrease import needs, improving the trade balance.

4. **Enhanced Innovation:** The influx of skilled foreign workers will foster innovation and technological advancements.

Financial Architecture and Structure

Financing the development and sustainability of Cities of Hope requires innovative and multi-faceted funding strategies. This chapter outlines a robust financial plan leveraging federal bond issuances and an innovative visa program designed to generate substantial funds through application fees. These approaches aim to provide the necessary capital for constructing and maintaining Cities of Hope while fostering economic growth and stability within these communities.

Federal Funding: HUD Bond Issuances

The primary source of funding for the initial development of Cities of Hope will come from the issuance of bonds by the Department of Housing and Urban Development (HUD). These bonds are a reliable and effective means of raising capital for large-scale housing projects and community development initiatives.

1. **Purpose and Utilization of HUD Bonds:**

   o The funds raised through HUD bond issuances will be allocated to the construction of housing units, community centers, healthcare facilities, and other essential infrastructure within the Cities of Hope.

   o Additionally, these funds will support the establishment of educational and vocational training programs, recreational facilities, and sustainable industrial projects.

   o A significant portion of the proceeds from HUD bonds will also be used to finance the development of manufacturing plants and other revenue-generating units within the towns. These facilities will create employment opportunities and contribute to the economic self-sufficiency of the community.

2. **Benefits of HUD Bonds:**

   o **Long-Term Investment**: HUD bonds offer a stable and long-term investment opportunity, attracting institutional investors and ensuring a steady flow of capital.

   o **Low-Interest Rates**: Government-backed bonds typically have lower interest rates, reducing the cost of borrowing and enabling more funds to be directed towards community development.

   o **Community Impact**: By investing in HUD bonds, stakeholders contribute to a significant social cause, helping to alleviate homelessness and revitalize communities.

Innovative Visa Program: Special Visa Lottery

Complementing the HUD bond issuances, a special visa program will be introduced by the Department of State to attract qualified foreign professionals to work in these towns. This program not only addresses workforce needs but also generates substantial funds through application fees.

1. **Special Visa Lottery Program:**

   o The program will issue a total of 50,000 visas, specifically targeting professionals with skills suitable for the needs of Cities of Hope, such as healthcare workers, educators, engineers, and tradespeople.

   o The visas will be distributed through a lottery system, ensuring a fair and transparent selection process.

2. **Application Fees and Revenue Generation:**

   o Each applicant will be required to pay a $200 fee to enter the lottery. Given the high demand for such visas, this fee structure is expected to generate significant revenue.

   o Considering the lucrative benefit package, we estimate the number of applicants could increase by a factor of five from the 22.3 million applications received for the Green Card Lottery in 2023. This results in an estimated 111.5 million applicants.

   o With 110 million applicants, the total application fees would generate $22 billion.

3. **Allocation of Funds:**

   o Funds generated from the application fees ($22 billion) will be allocated as equity for the revenue-generating units within the towns, such as manufacturing plants, and other development and operational costs, including housing construction, infrastructure development, and community services. (Equity can also be raised in the US without having to depend on the success of lottery fees as this overall investment qualifies for ESG and Impact Investing as Cities of Hope will prove to be profitable)

   o Additional funds required for revenue-generating units will be raised as debt, with experienced American sponsor firms managing and operating these units. These firms will own equity in the units and receive a portion of the revenue generated.

4. **Benefit Package for Foreign Workers:**

   o Every worker selected through the visa lottery will receive a comprehensive benefits package that includes:

     - **Free Housing**: Comfortable and eco-friendly housing units within the community.

     - **Free Car**: Access to a vehicle for commuting and personal use.

     - **Average $3,000 Monthly Salary**: A competitive salary to ensure financial stability.

     - **Path to Green Card**: Eligibility to apply for a Green Card after five years of continuous employment in the town.

     - This benefits package is designed to attract highly qualified professionals and ensure their well-being and satisfaction while working in these challenging yet rewarding roles.

5. **Supervision and Employment Opportunities for Americans:**

   o Foreign workers will work under the supervision of American professionals, creating additional employment opportunities for U.S. citizens.

   o Supervisory roles will be filled by Americans, enhancing job creation and fostering collaboration between local and foreign workers.

6. **Economic and Social Benefits:**

   o **Workforce Enhancement**: The special visa program will bring in skilled professionals, filling critical roles within the Cities of Hope and contributing to their economic and social development.

   o **Cultural Diversity**: The influx of foreign professionals will enrich the community, fostering cultural exchange and global perspectives.

   o **Long-Term Residency**: Professionals granted these visas will have the opportunity to apply for long-term residency, promoting stability and continuity within the workforce.

Financial Sustainability and Accountability

Ensuring the financial sustainability and accountability of the funding mechanisms is crucial for the long-term success of Cities of Hope.

1. **Transparent Financial Management:**

   o Regular audits and transparent financial reporting will be implemented to maintain accountability and build trust among stakeholders.

   o A dedicated financial management team will oversee the allocation and utilization of funds, ensuring that all expenditures align with the goals of community development and sustainability.

2. **Public-Private Partnerships:**

   o In addition to HUD bonds and the special visa program, partnerships with private sector entities will be pursued to secure additional funding and resources.

   o Corporate sponsors and philanthropic organizations will be encouraged to contribute through donations, grants, and in-kind support.

3. **Tax Incentives and Offtake Agreements:**

   o Federal and state tax exemptions will be provided to the revenue-generating units, incentivizing corporate investment and participation.

   o U.S. corporations can enter into offtake agreements to purchase products and services produced in these units, ensuring steady demand and revenue.

4. **Continuous Evaluation and Improvement:**

   o Ongoing evaluation of the funding mechanisms and their impact on the community will be conducted to identify areas for improvement and optimize resource allocation.

   o Feedback from residents, stakeholders, and financial experts will inform adjustments to the funding strategies, ensuring they remain effective and responsive to the community's needs.

In Summary

Total Initial Investment: USD 97.9 bn

Equity from Visa Program: USD 22 bn (or other sources of equity)

Remaining Amount to be Financed through Bonds:

97.9 bn USD −22 bn USD =75.9 bn USD

Bond Offering

A 25-year bond offering with a government guarantee will be issued to cover the remaining initial investment. The bonds will be repaid using the EBITDA generated from the towns.

Annual Debt Service Calculation

Assuming an interest rate of 5% and equal annual payments:

Annual Debt Service 5.28 bn USD

Estimated Annual EBITDA

Based on the previous calculation:

13,970,000,000 USD

Advanced Capital Market Practices

To enhance financial sustainability and accelerate debt repayment scenarios, advanced capital market practices will be employed for interim asset management as well as the accumulation of accelerated debt service reserves:

1. **Zero Coupon Bonds**: These bonds will be issued at a discount and mature at face value, providing long-term capital without immediate interest payments, facilitating more cash flow for community development.

2. **Senior Life Settlements**: Purchasing senior life settlements can provide a high return on investment, offering an innovative way to generate funds.

3. **Sinking Funds**: Establishing sinking funds will ensure there are dedicated resources for repaying bonds over time, reducing the financial burden on the community.

Conclusion

The innovative combination of HUD bond issuances and the special visa lottery program provides a solid financial foundation for the development and sustainability of Cities of Hope. By leveraging federal support and generating substantial revenue through visa application fees, this comprehensive funding strategy ensures the availability of necessary resources to build thriving, self-sustaining communities. The proceeds from these funding mechanisms will be used to finance essential infrastructure, manufacturing plants, and other revenue-generating units, fostering economic growth and stability. Through transparent management, continuous improvement, and strategic partnerships, these funding mechanisms will address the homeless population's immediate needs and pave the way for long-term stability and growth. The collaboration between foreign workers and American supervisors will further enhance job creation and foster a collaborative and diverse community environment. The participation of the private sector and the implementation of advanced financial practices will provide additional financing options, ensuring the sustainability and success of these towns while offering a second chance for our homeless population.

Additional Notes:

This plan is an exercise in developing a comprehensive solution to the homelessness crisis. It is open to improvements and optimization with input from society and individuals concerned with homelessness. The financial model and operational framework can be further refined with collaborative efforts and innovative ideas, ensuring a robust and effective solution for the future.

I have approached the cost estimates for both the initial investments and the ongoing operational expenses with a conservative outlook. Drawing from my extensive experience in capital markets, cost optimization, offshoring strategies for machinery and equipment, construction, real estate development, and C-Suite leadership, I am confident these costs could potentially be reduced by at least 30-35%, offering substantial room for further savings.

The industry composition for revenue generation in the Cities of Hope can be adjusted to achieve lower costs and provide more extensive employment opportunities. For instance, industries like Animal Food Manufacturing or Catering Services, which I have included under Basic Industries, are unlikely to require an average investment of $15 million per plant. Instead, my analysis has utilized average figures to provide a high-level overview. However, according to my research into SBA and USDA financing programs, the average loan for manufacturing industries nationwide is approximately $4.2 million, reflecting a more accurate cost estimate.

Adding corporate sponsorships, current funding channels to be diverted to Cities of Hope, and other potential initial financing and annual contributions have the potential to bring down the costs even further, making Cities of Hope a very profitable initiative.

As homeless citizens gain upward mobility and transition to other cities, the annual operating costs of these towns could be reduced. Once the initial models have established a solid learning curve, there is significant potential to enhance cost efficiency and develop more revenue-generating models. These improvements will further optimize the overall financial framework.

NOW LET US TALK ABOUT THE SOCIAL ASPECTS AND NON-FINANCIAL METRICS OF THE PROJECT

Identifying the Needs of Homeless Populations

Understanding the needs of homeless populations is critical for the successful establishment and sustainability of Cities of Hope. These needs can be broadly categorized into physical, psychological, and sociological considerations. This section delves into the multifaceted requirements of homeless individuals to ensure that our Cities of Hope are equipped to provide comprehensive support.

Physical Needs

The first aspect to consider is the physical needs of the homeless. This encompasses basic necessities such as shelter, food, water, clothing, and healthcare. Without these essentials, addressing any other aspect of their well-being becomes nearly impossible. Adequate housing solutions must be provided, offering not just a roof over their heads but also safety and dignity.

- **Shelter:** Secure and stable housing is paramount. This means not just temporary shelters but long-term living solutions that offer privacy and safety.

- **Food and Water:** Access to nutritious food and clean drinking water is indispensable. Nutritional services should be comprehensive, ensuring balanced meals to cater to various dietary needs.

- **Healthcare:** Many homeless individuals suffer from chronic health issues that require ongoing medical attention. Establishing accessible healthcare facilities within these towns is crucial.

- **Clothing:** Providing appropriate clothing for different seasons and ensuring access to hygienic facilities for washing and storing clothes is essential.

Psychological and Emotional Needs

Beyond physical requirements, the psychological and emotional needs of the homeless must be comprehensively addressed. Homelessness often results in significant emotional distress, including feelings of isolation, hopelessness, and trauma.

- **Mental Health Services:** Access to mental health services, including counseling and psychiatric care, is vital. These services can help individuals cope with past traumas and rebuild their lives.

- **Emotional Support:** Providing spaces for community engagement and peer support can foster a sense of belonging and alleviate feelings of isolation.

- **Substance Abuse Programs:** Many homeless individuals struggle with substance abuse. Integrated substance abuse programs that offer both medical treatment and counseling are essential.

Sociological Considerations

Sociological needs often impact both the individual and the community. Addressing these needs helps create a cohesive and supportive community within Cities of Hope.

- **Social Integration:** Community spaces and activities can encourage social interactions and foster a sense of community. This helps individuals feel accepted and part of a social structure.

- **Education and Employment:** Access to education and job training programs can empower individuals to become self-sufficient. These programs should focus on marketable skills relevant to the industries established within the towns.

- **Legal Support:** Many homeless individuals face legal issues that complicate their ability to find stable housing and employment. Legal aid services can assist them in resolving these issues.

In summary, understanding and addressing the physical, psychological, and sociological needs of homeless populations is foundational to the success of Cities of Hope. By focusing on these areas, we can create environments that provide temporary relief and pave the way for long-term stability and growth.

Physical Needs

When establishing the concept of Cities of Hope, it's crucial to address the physical needs of homeless populations at the foundational level. Without focusing on these basic necessities, building a sustainable community where individuals can thrive and eventually reintegrate into mainstream society is impossible. The primary factors to consider include shelter, hygiene, nutrition, and healthcare.

Shelter: Adequate housing is the cornerstone of any initiative aimed at providing for the homeless. These houses need to offer not just structural integrity but also a sense of security and privacy. Additionally, incorporating energy-efficient designs will reduce operational costs and promote environmental responsibility.

Hygiene: Ensuring access to clean water and sanitation facilities is another critical aspect. Public restrooms, bathing areas, and laundry facilities should be readily available and well-maintained. These amenities are essential to the individuals' sense of dignity and well-being and have a direct impact on health outcomes.

Nutrition: A balanced diet is vital for both physical and mental health. Establishing food services that provide nutritious meals can significantly impact the community's well-being. Integrating community kitchens and food banks can also encourage communal activities and social interactions, further strengthening the community fabric.

Healthcare: Access to healthcare services cannot be overlooked. Establishing clinics within these towns can facilitate regular health check-ups, immediate medical interventions, and ongoing treatment for chronic conditions. Additionally, mental health services should be integrated to address the psychological needs that often accompany physical ailments.

By addressing these physical needs, Cities of Hope can provide a solid foundation for individuals to build their lives. These infrastructures will enable the residents to focus on skill-building, employment, and eventually gaining independence, aligning with the broader objectives of creating sustainable, thriving communities.

Psychological and Emotional Needs

Addressing homeless individuals' psychological and emotional needs is pivotal to fostering a sustainable and thriving community in Cities of Hope. These needs, often overshadowed by the urgency of providing physical necessities, are critical for ensuring long-term stability and well-being. Understanding and addressing these aspects can help residents rebuild their lives with dignity and hope.

Homelessness can result in a profound sense of isolation, trauma, and helplessness. Ensuring that homeless populations receive adequate psychological and emotional support involves creating an environment where they feel safe, valued, and connected. This begins with welcoming individuals into a community that recognizes their inherent worth and offers support structures tailored to their unique experiences.

The trauma associated with homelessness often includes a history of abuse, neglect, and loss. This necessitates access to comprehensive mental health services, including counseling and therapy. Affordable and accessible mental health care must be integrated into the fabric of Cities of Hope. Establishing partnerships with mental health professionals and organizations ensures that residents receive the care they need without stigma or barriers.

Emotional support extends beyond professional counseling. It is crucial to build a community where individuals can form trusting relationships. Community-building activities, such as support groups, peer counseling, and communal gatherings, foster an environment of mutual support. These activities help residents develop social connections, reduce feelings of isolation, and improve overall emotional health.

Resilience and self-worth are essential components of emotional well-being. Empowering residents through skill-building workshops, educational opportunities, and employment training can significantly boost their self-esteem and confidence. When individuals are given the tools to succeed and contribute meaningfully to their community, they find a renewed sense of purpose and identity.

Moreover, the design and atmosphere of the homeless town play a significant role in addressing psychological needs. Spaces should be designed to promote peace, security, and community interaction. Green spaces, communal areas, and recreational facilities provide opportunities for relaxation and socialization, which are essential for emotional health.

Hope and motivation are vital for overcoming the challenges associated with homelessness. Programs that celebrate achievements, recognize progress, and provide future-oriented goals can instill a sense of optimism. Celebrity involvement, sponsorships, and public support can amplify these efforts, showing residents that society values their recovery and success.

Ultimately, addressing the psychological and emotional needs of homeless populations is not just about providing mental health services. It's about creating a compassionate, inclusive community where individuals can heal, grow, and flourish. Cities of Hope can pave the way for a holistic approach to rehabilitation and sustainable living by prioritizing these needs alongside physical necessities.

Sociological Considerations

Understanding the sociological considerations of homeless populations is a multifaceted task demanding a nuanced approach. These considerations encompass the complex interplay of social dynamics, cultural backgrounds, and community interactions that shape the daily lives of individuals experiencing homelessness. Therefore, the establishment of Cities of Hope must focus on physical and psychological needs and address the broader social structures and relationships within these communities.

A significant aspect of sociological considerations is the sense of community among homeless populations. Many individuals experiencing homelessness form tight-knit groups for mutual support and protection. Though forged under challenging conditions, this sense of community can be a critical asset in designing Cities of Hope. It highlights the need for communal spaces where residents can gather, share experiences, and build supportive networks. These spaces must be thoughtfully designed to encourage positive social interactions and foster a strong sense of belonging.

Another crucial factor is the stigmatization often faced by homeless individuals. This stigma can create barriers to accessing essential services and integrating into broader society. By addressing sociological considerations, Cities of Hope can actively combat this stigmatization. This involves creating environments that promote dignity and respect, where residents are seen as active contributors rather than passive recipients. Educational and training programs can also play a role, equipping individuals with skills and knowledge that enhance their social status and self-esteem.

Understanding the diverse backgrounds of homeless populations is essential. Individuals experiencing homelessness come from various ethnic, cultural, and socioeconomic backgrounds, each bringing different needs and perspectives. Cities of Hope must be inclusive, accommodating these diverse backgrounds through culturally sensitive practices and policies. This inclusivity can be reflected in providing culturally appropriate services, celebrating various cultural events, and incorporating diverse voices in community decision-making processes.

The role of social networks cannot be overlooked. Many homeless individuals rely on informal support networks, such as friends and family, even when these connections are strained. Strengthening these social networks within Cities of Hope is crucial. Initiatives like family reunification programs, peer mentorship schemes, and community-building activities can help reinforce these bonds, providing a stable support system for residents. This can lead to improved mental health outcomes and better overall well-being.

Cities of Hope must also address the issue of power dynamics within communities. Homeless individuals often experience powerlessness and a lack of agency in their lives. To counteract this, it is vital to foster a sense of empowerment and self-determination among residents. This can be achieved through participatory governance models where residents have a say in decision-making processes. Creating platforms for residents to voice their concerns and contribute to community development can help build a sense of ownership and responsibility.

Moreover, the intersection of homelessness with other social issues, such as substance abuse, mental health, and domestic violence, cannot be ignored. These issues often compound the challenges faced by homeless individuals. Addressing these interconnected issues requires a holistic approach integrating social, psychological, and medical services. Providing comprehensive support services within Cities of Hope ensures that residents have access to the resources they need to address these multifaceted challenges.

Incorporating recreational and cultural activities is another important sociological consideration. These activities provide an outlet for self-expression and creativity, which are essential for mental and emotional well-being. Community theaters, art workshops, and music programs can offer residents the opportunity to explore their talents and passions. Moreover, these activities can strengthen community bonds as residents come together to create and enjoy shared experiences.

Economic empowerment is a critical aspect of sociological considerations. Providing employment opportunities within or near Cities of Hope can significantly improve the quality of life for residents. Job training programs, partnerships with local businesses, and establishing social enterprises can create pathways to financial independence. This not only enhances individual well-being but also contributes to the overall economic sustainability of the community.

Education is another cornerstone of sociological considerations. Access to education and skills training is crucial for breaking the cycle of homelessness. Cities of Hope should prioritize educational initiatives for all age groups, from early childhood education to adult literacy programs. Education empowers individuals to pursue their goals and aspirations, fostering a culture of lifelong learning and personal development.

Volunteerism and community engagement can also play a significant role. Encouraging residents to participate in volunteer activities within the town can foster a sense of purpose and community spirit. These activities can range from neighborhood clean-ups to mentoring programs, allowing residents to contribute to the betterment of their community while developing valuable skills and connections.

Finally, the role of external perceptions and societal attitudes towards Cities of Hope must be considered. Public campaigns to raise awareness about the realities of homelessness and the efforts being undertaken within these towns can help shift negative perceptions. Engaging with media, influential figures, and broader society to build a narrative of empathy and solidarity can create a more supportive and inclusive environment for homeless individuals.

In conclusion, addressing the sociological considerations in designing and implementing Cities of Hope is essential for creating a supportive, inclusive, and sustainable community. By fostering a sense of community, combating stigmatization, celebrating diversity, strengthening social networks, empowering residents, and addressing the intersection of related social issues, Cities of Hope can provide a foundation for individuals to rebuild their lives. Incorporating recreational, educational, and economic opportunities ensures that residents have the resources and support they need to thrive. Ultimately, the success of **Cities of Hope hinges on our ability to understand and address these complex sociological factors, creating environments where all individuals have the opportunity to live with dignity and purpose.**

Amenities and Services

Creating a robust support system in Cities of Hope necessitates offering a variety of amenities and services that cater to the diverse needs of residents. The integrity of these communities depends on their ability to provide shelter and substantive quality of life through comprehensive service infrastructures. This chapter discusses key aspects such as food and nutrition services, education and training programs, and recreational activities—each pivotal to the well-being and integration of residents.

Food and Nutrition Services

Food security is one of the foundational pillars of any stable community. In Cities of Hope, reliable access to nutritious meals is paramount. Community kitchens and dining halls will be established to ensure that no one goes hungry. These facilities will be strategically located to serve all neighborhoods within the town effectively. Additionally, partnerships with local farms, grocery stores, and food banks will help maintain a steady supply of fresh produce and essentials. (aimed at non-working citizens)

Programs that emphasize nutritional education will also be implemented. These include cooking classes and workshops that teach residents how to prepare balanced meals. The goal is to empower people with the knowledge and skills they need to sustain their health independently. Special dietary needs such as allergies, diabetes, and other medical conditions will be meticulously considered in meal planning and distribution.

Education and Training Programs

Empowerment through education is a philosophy that guides the establishment of various learning opportunities in the Cities of Hope. Educational initiatives will be aimed at all age groups, offering everything from early childhood education to adult literacy programs. Modern, well-equipped classrooms and learning centers will be integrated into the community infrastructure, fostering an environment conducive to academic excellence.

Vocational training and skill development are equally critical. Tailored programs focusing on trades, technological skills, and professional certifications will help bridge the employment gap. Collaborations with local industries and educational institutions will facilitate internships, apprenticeships, and job placements. Education and training not only pave the way for economic self-sufficiency but also instill a sense of purpose and self-worth.

Recreational Activities

A well-rounded lifestyle is incomplete without opportunities for leisure and recreation. Recreational activities offer residents a chance to relax, socialize, and engage in healthy physical activities. Multipurpose sports complexes, community parks, and arts and crafts centers will be readily accessible. These venues are essential for community engagement and improve both physical and mental health.

Organized activities will range from team sports such as soccer and basketball to individual pursuits like yoga and running clubs. A calendar of events, including movie nights, cultural festivals, and talent shows, will encourage participation and foster a sense of community. Recreational activities are not just about fun—they help build social bonds, reduce stress, and promote overall well-being.

In conclusion, the provision of well-thought-out amenities and services is at the heart of creating thriving Cities of Hope. By addressing basic needs, fostering education and vocational skills, and facilitating recreational activities, these communities can provide their residents with a dignified and sustainable way of life. The success of Cities of Hope hinges on the holistic development and care of individuals, empowering them to reach their full potential both personally and professionally.

Belief Centers

Belief Centers in the Cities of Hope will be key to fostering spiritual growth, reflection, and community support. These inclusive spaces welcome people of all faiths and backgrounds, offering areas for worship, meditation, and spiritual counseling. Regular interfaith dialogues and workshops will promote mutual respect and understanding, while spiritual counseling services will provide emotional and mental support to residents. Beyond spiritual guidance, Belief Centers will engage in community service initiatives and celebrate religious and cultural holidays, enriching the community's cultural diversity and strengthening social bonds. These centers will be instrumental in nurturing the overall well-being of residents, contributing to a resilient and compassionate society.

Food and Nutrition Services

Food and nutrition services are foundational to the well-being of residents in Cities of Hope. In these communities, ensuring access to nutritious, balanced meals isn't just about meeting basic needs—it's a cornerstone for fostering stability, improving health, and enhancing the quality of life. A comprehensive food and nutrition program can bridge gaps in food security and contribute to the holistic development of individuals and the community as a whole.

Central to this effort is the implementation of community kitchens and dining facilities. These kitchens will serve meals prepared with locally sourced ingredients from nearby greenhouses and urban farms, integrating with the wider goal of industrial sustainability. This not only reduces costs but also offers fresher, healthier food options and provides vocational opportunities in culinary arts and agriculture. Residents can participate in meal preparation, creating a sense of ownership and community. (non-working citizens would be ideal)

The importance of dietary diversity and nutritional education can't be overstated. Programs designed to educate residents on the benefits of a balanced diet, proper food handling, and cooking techniques will empower individuals to make healthier choices. These initiatives can include workshops, cooking classes, and seminars conducted by nutrition experts and healthcare professionals. Providing this knowledge equips residents with skills that are beneficial both within and outside the community.

Moreover, partnerships with non-profits and local businesses will be crucial. Surplus food redistribution from local supermarkets and donations from partner organizations can help supplement daily meals, ensuring a steady supply while tackling food wastage. Strategic alliances with restaurants and food service companies can also offer additional diversity and quality in meal planning.

Special considerations will be made for vulnerable groups within the Cities of Hope, such as children, the elderly, and those with specific dietary requirements. Tailored meal plans and dedicated support services can address these unique needs, ensuring everyone receives appropriate nutritional care. Regular health assessments conducted by on-site healthcare facilities will help in tracking the nutritional status of residents, allowing for timely adjustments to meal programs as needed.

Lastly, fostering an environment where food brings people together is paramount. Shared meals and communal dining experiences can significantly strengthen social bonds and build a sense of community. Festivals, themed dinners, and cultural cuisine nights can instill a sense of normalcy and celebration, promoting psychological well-being alongside physical health.

In conclusion, the food and nutrition services in Cities of Hope are not just about sustenance; they're about building a resilient, informed, and interconnected community. By addressing nutritional needs comprehensively, we create a foundation for healthier, happier lives, facilitating smoother transitions into sustainable, long-term stability.

Education and Training Programs

Integral to the success of the Cities of Hope is the comprehensive education and training programs designed to empower residents with the skills necessary to achieve self-sufficiency and personal growth. Recognizing that education is a cornerstone of sustainable communities, these programs focus on both academic and vocational training to ensure a well-rounded developmental approach.

Academic education in Cities of Hope aims to provide residents with the foundational knowledge required for various life and career paths. From basic literacy and numeracy skills to more advanced subjects, the curriculum is tailored to meet the diverse needs of the community members. Young children have access to quality early childhood education, while adults can participate in continuing education opportunities that cater to their unique life circumstances and aspirations.

Vocational training is particularly emphasized, reflecting the need for practical skills that directly translate to employment opportunities. Programs are designed in collaboration with the adjacent industrial facilities to ensure alignment with labor market demands. Residents can engage in a wide range of training options, including but not limited to manufacturing, agriculture, and IT services. These initiatives enhance employability and foster a sense of purpose and confidence among participants.

Specialized training programs are also available to address specific community needs and individual interests. For example, entrepreneurship training empowers residents to develop their own business ventures, potentially leading to further economic growth within the towns. Additionally, partnerships with local universities and colleges provide pathways for higher education, offering scholarships and support services to ensure accessibility.

Ongoing support and mentorship are integral components of these programs. Trained educators and volunteers, including experts from various industries, provide guidance and support to ensure successful outcomes. Moreover, community learning centers serve as hubs for continuous education and social interaction, fostering a culture of lifelong learning and collaboration.

By prioritizing education and vocational training, Cities of Hope equips residents with the skills necessary for individual success and strengthens the overall community, paving the way for a sustainable and thriving society. The holistic approach to education and training in these towns embodies the belief that every individual, regardless of their starting point, has the potential to contribute to and benefit from a vibrant, self-sustaining community.

Recreational Activities

The inclusion of recreational activities within the amenities and services of Cities of Hope is imperative, given the holistic approach to well-being these communities aim to foster. Recreational activities serve as a critical facet of this initiative, providing physical, mental, and social benefits that contribute significantly to residents' overall quality of life.

An array of recreational options will be available, strategically designed to cater to diverse interests and capabilities. These activities will be both structured and unstructured, ensuring that every resident has the opportunity to engage in fulfilling and enjoyable pursuits. The variety offered will accommodate various preferences and skill levels, from sports and outdoor games to arts and crafts.

Sports and Physical Fitness

Sports and physical fitness activities are essential for physical health and fostering a sense of community. Facilities such as basketball courts, soccer fields, and running tracks will be integral parts of the town's layout. Organized sports leagues and fitness classes will encourage regular participation and promote teamwork and discipline. Additionally, partnerships with local sports clubs and fitness trainers will enhance the quality and accessibility of these programs.

Arts and Cultural Programs

For those inclined towards creative pursuits, arts and cultural programs will offer a broad spectrum of activities, including painting, music, dance, and theater. Workshops and classes led by professional artists and instructors will provide skill development and serve as therapeutic outlets. Community theaters and galleries will host regular exhibitions and performances, giving residents platforms to showcase their talents.

Outdoor Recreation

The importance of connecting with nature cannot be overstressed. Therefore, parks, gardens, and green spaces will be interspersed throughout the town. Hiking trails, picnic areas, and communal gardens will offer residents opportunities to relax and enjoy the outdoors. These spaces will also support environmental sustainability objectives by integrating green practices such as community farming and eco-friendly landscaping.

Social and Community Activities

Recreational activities also encompass events and gatherings that strengthen the social fabric of the towns. Weekly community events like movie nights, holiday celebrations, and social clubs will provide venues for residents to interact and bond. These events will be supported by local volunteers and organizations, fostering a sense of belonging and community pride.

The overarching aim of these recreational programs is to enrich the lives of residents, offering them not only a respite from daily stresses but also a path toward personal growth and community integration. By providing a well-rounded array of recreational activities, Cities of Hope demonstrates a commitment to the comprehensive well-being of every resident, ensuring that their journey toward stability and fulfillment is as enriching as possible.

Belief Centers

Belief Centers will serve as a cornerstone for spiritual growth, reflection, and community support within the Cities of Hope. These centers will be inclusive spaces that welcome people from all faiths and spiritual backgrounds, fostering an environment of mutual respect and understanding. By providing a dedicated space for worship, meditation, and spiritual counseling, Belief Centers will cater to the diverse spiritual needs of the community, contributing to the overall well-being of its residents.

Worship and Meditation Spaces

Each Belief Center will house various worship and meditation spaces designed to accommodate different religious practices and spiritual traditions. These spaces will include chapels, meditation rooms, and prayer halls, all thoughtfully designed to provide a serene and respectful environment. Residents will have the opportunity to engage in daily or weekly religious services, meditation sessions, and spiritual practices guided by community leaders and faith-based volunteers.

Interfaith Dialogues and Community Engagement

Belief Centers will regularly host interfaith dialogues, workshops, and seminars to promote unity and understanding among residents of different faiths. These events will encourage open discussions on spirituality, ethics, and social justice, helping bridge cultural and religious divides. By fostering a culture of mutual respect and shared values, these dialogues will strengthen the social fabric of the Cities of Hope.

Spiritual Counseling and Support

Recognizing the role of spirituality in mental and emotional well-being, Belief Centers will also offer spiritual counseling services. Trained counselors and clergy members from various faiths will be available to provide guidance, support, and comfort to residents facing personal challenges. Whether dealing with grief, addiction, or the stress of rebuilding one's life, residents will find solace and support within these centers.

Community Services and Outreach

Belief Centers will extend their mission beyond spiritual support by organizing community service initiatives and outreach programs. These initiatives might include food drives, clothing donations, and volunteer services aimed at helping the most vulnerable members of the community. By participating in these activities, residents will not only receive support but also contribute to the well-being of others, fostering a sense of purpose and belonging.

Celebration of Religious and Cultural Holidays

The Belief Centers will also serve as venues for the celebration of religious and cultural holidays. These celebrations will provide an opportunity for residents to share their traditions and customs, enriching the community's cultural diversity, whether it's a Christmas service, Diwali celebration, Hanukkah observance, or Ramadan iftar, these events will be inclusive and open to all, promoting unity through shared experiences.

In summary, Belief Centers will play a vital role in nurturing the spiritual, emotional, and social well-being of residents in the Cities of Hope. By offering spaces for worship, facilitating interfaith dialogues, and providing spiritual support, these centers will contribute to the holistic development of the community, helping to create a resilient and compassionate society.

Psychological and Social Support

The establishment of Cities of Hope requires a multifaceted approach to ensure the wellbeing of their inhabitants. Among the most crucial aspects are the psychological and social support systems. These systems not only provide essential services but also foster a sense of belonging and community, which is essential for long-term rehabilitation and integration.

Counseling and Mental Health Services

Mental health is a significant concern among homeless populations. Many individuals have experienced trauma, loss, and chronic stress. Addressing these needs necessitates a robust framework of counseling and mental health services. Qualified mental health professionals should be available to offer both individual and group therapy sessions. These services would tackle a range of issues, from anxiety and depression to post-traumatic stress disorder (PTSD).

It's also important to provide crisis intervention services. Immediate support can greatly mitigate the long-term impact of acute mental health episodes. Integration with local healthcare providers will ensure continuity of care, facilitating a comprehensive approach to each resident's mental health.

Community Building Activities

Creating a sense of community is a powerful tool in helping individuals regain stability and purpose. Community-building activities serve this purpose by bringing people together, fostering relationships, and building trust. Activities such as community meetings, social events, and cooperative projects are vital. These not only alleviate feelings of isolation but also promote personal and communal growth.

Resident-led initiatives can be particularly effective. When the community members themselves propose and organize activities, it encourages a sense of ownership and responsibility. Such initiatives can range from neighborhood clean-ups and gardening projects to art and music workshops. The key is to provide a variety of opportunities for engagement, catering to the diverse interests and talents of the residents.

Substance Abuse Programs

For many homeless individuals, substance abuse is both a cause and a consequence of their predicament. Therefore, targeted substance abuse programs are essential. These should include a combination of detoxification services, rehabilitation programs, and ongoing support groups. The goal is to offer pathways to recovery that are accessible and tailored to individual needs.

Successful substance abuse programs often integrate counseling and vocational training. By addressing both the psychological aspects and the socioeconomic factors that contribute to substance abuse, these programs can offer a holistic solution. Additionally, community support plays a pivotal role. Peer mentoring and support groups provide essential encouragement and accountability, significantly enhancing the recovery process.

Creating a supportive environment in Cities of Hope involves more than just providing services; it involves cultivating an ecosystem that promotes mental health, community, and recovery. By integrating these elements, Cities of Hope can offer a place to live and a pathway to a better life. A comprehensive psychological and social support approach is indispensable for achieving the vision of sustainable, thriving communities.

As we move forward in this initiative, collaboration with mental health professionals, social workers, and community organizers will be key. It's an endeavor that requires dedication, empathy, and an unwavering commitment to the betterment of our fellow human beings.

Counseling and Mental Health Services

When addressing the well-being of individuals in Cities of Hope, counseling and mental health services are foundational components of Psychological and Social Support. These services aim to provide residents with the emotional resilience and psychological stability needed to rebuild their lives. In our vision, every City of Hope will have integrated mental health facilities, underscoring the importance of addressing both the mind and body in holistic care.

Accessible and comprehensive mental health services can be life-changing for homeless populations that often face a myriad of stressors. Chronic exposure to trauma, instability, and disempowerment takes a toll on mental health, necessitating a multifaceted approach to care. Licensed psychologists, therapists, and social workers will offer individual and group counseling, targeting a spectrum of issues from anxiety and depression to post-traumatic stress disorder (PTSD) and substance abuse disorders.

Effective mental health support goes beyond traditional therapy. Staffed by trained community members with lived experiences, peer support groups will cultivate a sense of belonging and understanding. These groups provide emotional support and empower residents through shared experiences and mutual aid.

In addition to counseling and peer support, on-site workshops will be available to enhance coping strategies, emotional regulation, and stress management. These educational sessions will focus on practical skills, such as relaxation techniques, mindfulness practices, and resilience-building activities. Additionally, emergency mental health crisis intervention services will be integral, providing immediate support in acute situations.

Importantly, the creation of trust and safety within the community is paramount. Confidentiality in counseling services, cultural sensitivity, and non-judgmental attitudes will be central tenets in the delivery of care. Residents will be assured that their dignity and privacy are respected, encouraging them to seek and continue treatment.

Recognizing the interconnectedness of various aspects of well-being, mental health services will be integrated with other support systems like housing, employment, and healthcare to create a cohesive safety net. This integration ensures that mental health is not treated in isolation but as a part of a comprehensive support system that contributes to overall stability and growth.

Fostering mental health in Cities of Hope isn't solely about providing services; it's about building a community where individuals feel valued and understood. The goal is to establish environments where every resident can find the strength and support to navigate their challenges, knowing they're not alone on their journey to recovery and stability.

Community Building Activities

Community building activities are instrumental in creating a sense of belonging, purpose, and stability within Cities of Hope. The importance of such activities cannot be understated as they serve as the backbone for social cohesion and psychological well-being.

One approach is to organize regular group events such as communal meals, town hall meetings, and local festivals. These events can help residents feel more invested in their community and provide opportunities for social interaction. Communal meals, in particular, offer a chance to share experiences and develop mutual understanding. Town hall meetings allow residents to have a voice and a role in the decision-making processes that affect their daily lives, fostering a sense of ownership and responsibility.

Additionally, skill-sharing workshops and hobby groups can be an excellent way to both build up individual capabilities and create bonds between residents. Workshops could include everything from carpentry and gardening to cooking and art classes. Offering these activities not only helps residents to develop new skills that can be useful in both personal and employment contexts but also acts as a platform through which relationships can be formed.

Mentorship programs can play a key role in the integration process for new residents. Matching newcomers with long-term residents who can act as guides and support systems ensures that new residents feel welcomed and supported as they acclimate to their new environment.

Sports and physical activities should also be incorporated. Regular sports events, outdoor exercise classes, and team games can significantly contribute to the physical and mental health of the residents. These activities also encourage team spirit and provide another avenue for social interaction and stress relief.

Community gardens are another powerful tool for community building. Not only do they provide a source of fresh food, but they also offer residents a joint project that promotes cooperation and a sense of accomplishment. Working together in a garden can instill a sense of pride and responsibility in residents while also beautifying communal spaces and contributing to the town's sustainability efforts.

Lastly, cultural activities, including music performances, theater, and art exhibitions, serve to enrich the communal life of the residents. These events provide a platform for expression and celebration of various backgrounds and experiences, fostering an inclusive and vibrant community culture.

Altogether, these community-building activities are essential for developing a cohesive, supportive, and dynamic community within Cities of Hope. They help break down social barriers, reduce isolation, and create a supportive network that significantly improves the residents' overall quality of life.

Substance Abuse Programs

Substance abuse is often both a cause and a consequence of homelessness, creating a vicious cycle that's tough to break. Addressing substance abuse effectively becomes critical in the framework of Cities of Hope, which aims to integrate industrial facilities nearby to foster economic sustainability. This section outlines the key components of substance abuse programs designed to support residents in their journey to recovery and reintegration into society.

The substance abuse programs within Cities of Hope are multifaceted, combining immediate intervention with long-term support. The approach is compassionate and pragmatic, ensuring that individuals receive the help they need while also contributing to the town's broader sustainability and community-building objectives.

Firstly, immediate intervention services are crucial. These include detoxification centers that provide medical supervision in a safe and controlled environment. Rapid access to such services can prevent the escalation of health crises and offer a stepping stone toward recovery. However, detoxification is just the beginning.

Long-term recovery requires comprehensive treatment plans tailored to the individual's needs. These plans often incorporate counseling and mental health services—a topic detailed earlier in this chapter. Effective substance abuse programs integrate individual and group therapy sessions, cognitive-behavioral therapy (CBT), and other evidence-based practices. Peer support groups play a significant role here, fostering a sense of community and mutual support among individuals facing similar challenges.

Another critical component is the inclusion of vocational training and employment opportunities, as outlined in later chapters. Providing job training, particularly in the sustainable industries situated near the Cities of Hope, contributes to both psychological well-being and financial independence. Employment can be a powerful motivator for overcoming substance abuse, offering a sense of purpose and belonging while also helping to break the cycle of poverty and addiction.

Integration with broader community activities can't be overlooked. Programs designed to build community, including recreational and cultural activities, are essential. Engaging in these activities helps residents form healthy connections and discover interests that can serve as alternatives to substance use. Community-building efforts create a supportive environment where residents feel valued and included.

Effective substance abuse programs also recognize the importance of continuity of care. Upon completion of initial treatment phases, ongoing support, including outpatient services and regular check-ins, helps prevent relapse. Creating a network of support that persists even after residents leave structured programs reinforces the stability needed for lasting recovery.

In sum, the substance abuse programs within Cities of Hope are crafted to address both the immediate needs and long-term goals of individuals struggling with addiction. These programs are intertwined with the towns' industrial facilities and broader community activities, ensuring a holistic approach that promotes overall well-being and economic self-sufficiency. This integrated model not only helps individuals regain control over their lives but also contributes to the vitality and sustainability of the Cities of Hope themselves.

Role of Celebrities in Cities of Hope

The role of celebrities in the development and sustainability of Cities of Hope cannot be understated. Their influence extends beyond mere financial contributions, touching on awareness, fundraising, and holistic community support. In this chapter, we will delve into the multifaceted roles that celebrities play in these unique communities.

Awareness Campaigns

One of the most significant contributions celebrities can make is raising public awareness. With their massive reach, celebrities can spotlight issues faced by homeless populations, which might otherwise be overlooked by mainstream society. Awareness campaigns initiated by celebrities can break through societal apathy and bring critical issues to the forefront.

Celebrities often leverage their social media platforms, public appearances, and other media engagements to share compelling stories, statistics, and calls to action. These initiatives can mobilize vast numbers of people and galvanize support from a broader audience, fostering a more empathetic and informed public.

Fundraising Events

Beyond awareness, celebrities are instrumental in fundraising efforts for Cities of Hope. Star-studded events such as charity galas, benefit concerts, and televised fundraisers can generate substantial funds, ensuring that these communities have the additional resources they need to thrive. The visibility and glamour associated with celebrity involvement attract attendees and sponsors who might not otherwise contribute to such causes.

These events provide a dual benefit: they bring in necessary financial support while also serving as pivotal awareness tools. The more high-profile the event, the greater its potential to reach broader audiences and secure media coverage, thereby expanding the impact on public perception and involvement.

Celebrity Endorsements and Sponsorships

Another crucial role celebrities play is through endorsements and sponsorships. High-profile endorsements can lend credibility to the initiatives aimed at building and sustaining Cities of Hope. When celebrities publicly support a cause, it often encourages their fan base to follow suit, creating a ripple effect of support.

Moreover, celebrities bring in corporate sponsorships and partnerships that might not be easily accessible otherwise. Endorsement deals can translate into long-term commitments from brands, providing steady revenue streams to fund essential services such as healthcare, education, and vocational training programs within these towns.

To sum up, celebrities play a pivotal role that goes beyond monetary contributions. Their involvement elevates the conversation around homelessness, garners essential funding, and catalyzes broader societal support. This multifaceted engagement is crucial for the success and sustainability of Cities of Hope, ensuring that they are not just temporary shelters but thriving, self-sustaining communities.

As we move forward, understanding and leveraging these roles effectively will be key to the ongoing development of Cities of Hope. By continuing to engage celebrities in these initiatives, we can foster an environment where these communities not only survive but flourish.

Awareness Campaigns

When it comes to creating meaningful change in Cities of Hope, awareness campaigns spearheaded by celebrities can be incredibly impactful. These campaigns serve to shine a spotlight on the issues and rally public support, making significant contributions to both funding and policy changes.

First and foremost, celebrities have the unique ability to capture attention. Their involvement can help to bring media coverage, social media attention, and public interest to the plight of homeless populations. A well-executed awareness campaign can make the general population more empathetic and motivated to contribute to solutions.

Moreover, celebrities can utilize their platforms to educate the public about the complex issues surrounding homelessness. By sharing personal stories and highlighting the needs of these communities, they can break down stereotypes and misconceptions. Education leads to better understanding, which in turn encourages more effective public policy and community support.

Additionally, awareness campaigns can also create a ripple effect by motivating other influential figures and organizations to get involved. When a celebrity takes a stand, it often inspires others to follow suit, creating a cascading impact that can amplify the message and the resources directed toward the cause. This collective action can be instrumental in driving long-term, sustainable solutions.

In contemporary society, digital platforms play a crucial role in awareness campaigns. Social media, podcasts, and online video channels provide celebrities with direct access to millions of followers. By leveraging these tools, they can effectively promote awareness campaigns, reaching a diverse global audience instantaneously.

In summary, the strategic use of awareness campaigns involving celebrities can significantly boost public understanding and support for Cities of Hope. By capturing attention, educating the public, and inspiring collective action, these campaigns can play a pivotal role in driving meaningful change and ensuring the success of the projects aimed at uplifting homeless populations.

Fundraising Events

Fundraising events play a crucial role in the success and sustenance of Cities of Hope, especially when celebrity involvement is in the mix. These events are not mere social gatherings but are meticulously planned occasions aimed at drawing attention to the cause and generating substantial financial support. The dual objectives are to raise funds and build a community of supporters, creating an ongoing source of goodwill and resources.

When celebrities participate in fundraising events, their star power can significantly influence the turnout and the amount of money raised. Celebrities bring their fan base with them, extending the event's reach far beyond the immediate community. This is more than just star-studded galas; it includes concerts, sports events, art auctions, and even virtual gatherings. Their involvement lends credibility and visibility to the cause, helping to bridge the gap between awareness and action.

Concerts and Performances Concerts and performances are especially effective in raising funds and awareness. A live concert by a renowned artist can attract thousands of attendees, each contributing financially through ticket sales, merchandise, and donations. The emotional connection that music and performance create between the artist and the audience can translate into a deeper commitment to supporting Cities of Hope.

Auction Events Auction events featuring memorabilia, experiences, and items donated by celebrities can also generate significant funds. Fans are often willing to pay premium prices for a piece of their favorite celebrity's history or for unique, exclusive experiences. These auctions often include both live and silent bidding, increasing participation and driving up the amount raised.

Sports Events Sports events, such as charity matches or tournaments with celebrity participants, also garner extensive public interest. These events not only attract fans of the sport but also followers of the celebrities involved. The competitive yet friendly nature of these events makes them enjoyable to attend and participate in, ensuring a successful turnout and significant proceeds.

Virtual Gatherings With the advent of digital platforms, virtual fundraising events have become increasingly popular. Online concerts, virtual meet-and-greets, and live-streamed auctions provide an opportunity for global participation. Such events can transcend geographical boundaries, enabling a broader audience to contribute financially and emotionally to the cause.

Each fundraising event is a well-orchestrated effort to highlight the ongoing needs of Cities of Hope and garner financial support. The funds raised are directly channeled into essential services, infrastructure, and sustainable initiatives, making a tangible difference in the lives of the residents.

The involvement of celebrities in these events not only amplifies their success but also keeps the conversation about homelessness in the public eye. Their support can inspire others, from average citizens to influential figures, to contribute and engage. Through these collective efforts, fundraising events become more than just ways to gather money; they become vital components in creating a sustainable, supportive environment for Cities of Hope.

Celebrity Endorsements and Sponsorships

Celebrity endorsements and sponsorships' role in creating sustainable and thriving Cities of Hope can't be understated. Celebrities possess the reach and influence necessary to bring attention to critical social issues, including homelessness. By leveraging their platforms, celebrities can galvanize public interest and generate substantial support for homeless initiatives.

Visibility and Awareness

When celebrities endorse a cause, they lend their fame and visibility to it. This can significantly boost public awareness. For example, a well-known actor or musician might attend events, post on social media, and participate in interviews discussing the Cities of Hope. This heightened visibility can lead to increased media coverage, bringing the issues and solutions into mainstream discussions.

Fundraising and Donations

Additionally, celebrity-backed fundraising events can draw significant donations from both individuals and corporations. High-profile events, such as charity concerts, galas, and auctions, can raise considerable funds that directly benefit the development and maintenance of Cities of Hope. Celebrities often have personal, business, and social networks that will contribute to these causes when they see a trusted figure actively supporting them.

Sponsorships and Partnerships

Corporate sponsorships often follow celebrity endorsements. When a celebrity throws their support behind Cities of Hope, companies are more likely to align their brands with these initiatives. This can lead to valuable partnerships, providing necessary resources, services, and financial backing for the towns. Companies might donate goods, fund programs, or even sponsor entire community projects.

Inspiration and Hope

On a more personal level, celebrities can serve as role models and sources of inspiration for the homeless population. When individuals see someone they admire advocating for their well-being, it can instill a sense of hope and motivation. Realizing that notable figures care about their situation can foster a renewed sense of self-worth and community spirit among the residents of the Cities of Hope.

In summary, celebrity endorsements and sponsorships play a multifaceted role in the success of Cities of Hope. By bringing awareness, generating funds, encouraging corporate sponsorships, and offering hope, celebrities can make a significant impact on these communities. This collaboration between public figures, businesses, and the general public ensures a robust support system, helping to transform the vision of Cities of Hope into a sustainable reality.

Partnerships with Major Companies

Collaborating with major companies is pivotal in the creation and success of Cities of Hope. These partnerships bring not only financial resources but also professional expertise and a commitment to Corporate Social Responsibility (CSR). This chapter explores how corporations can and should become integral partners in this transformative endeavor.

Corporate Social Responsibility (CSR) Initiatives

Companies with established CSR programs are in a unique position to support Cities of Hope. By aligning their values with these communities' missions, they can contribute significantly to social welfare. CSR initiatives can take various forms, from providing financial assistance for infrastructure to donating products and services that address immediate needs.

Moreover, corporations can engage their employees in volunteer programs, fostering a sense of community and shared responsibility. For instance, tech companies can offer digital literacy programs, while construction firms can help build and maintain housing units. Such initiatives not only enhance the quality of life for residents but also offer companies an opportunity to make a tangible impact on society.

Employment and Job Training Programs

One of the most substantial contributions a company can make is through employment and job training programs. These programs can be tailored to meet the specific needs of the residents, providing them with the skills and opportunities required to re-enter the workforce. Companies can offer on-the-job training, internships, and mentorship programs that empower individuals to gain meaningful employment.

By incorporating job training centers within Cities of Hope, companies can offer continuous skill development and career advancement opportunities. For instance, a partnership with a technology firm could lead to coding boot camps or IT training sessions, while a collaboration with a manufacturing company might result in apprenticeships or certification programs. Such initiatives not only benefit the residents but also help companies cultivate a diverse and skilled workforce.

Sponsorship Programs

Sponsorship programs provide another layer of support wherein companies can underwrite various initiatives within the Cities of Hope. These can include educational programs, healthcare services, and recreational activities. By sponsoring these essential services, companies ensure that residents have access to a holistic support system.

Corporations can also sponsor community events and activities, fostering a vibrant and cohesive environment. Educational workshops, health fairs, and cultural festivals are examples of programs that can be sponsored. Such sponsorships promote social interaction and a sense of belonging among residents. Such sponsorships create a win-win scenario, where companies enhance their public image while contributing to the community's well-being.

In conclusion, establishing partnerships with major companies is a cornerstone for the success and sustainability of Cities of Hope. These collaborations bring invaluable resources, expertise, and support, ensuring that the communities not only survive but thrive. By engaging in CSR initiatives, providing employment and job training programs, and supporting sponsorship opportunities, corporations can make a difference that transcends the bottom line. It's a powerful reminder that when businesses and communities work together, remarkable transformations are possible.

Corporate Social Responsibility (CSR) Initiatives

Corporate Social Responsibility (CSR) initiatives play a pivotal role in the symbiotic relationship between Cities of Hope and the major companies that partner with them. By leveraging their resources, expertise, and influence, these companies aim to create meaningful social impact while also fostering a sense of communal and economic sustainability within the Cities of Hope.

First and foremost, CSR initiatives often start with identifying the specific needs of the community. This can range from providing essential goods and services to investing in long-term development projects. Companies engage in initiatives such as building housing units, healthcare centers, and educational facilities that directly benefit the residents. By contributing to the infrastructure, they ensure that the Cities of Hope are well-equipped to offer a dignified living experience for all inhabitants.

Another significant aspect of CSR is the focus on creating job opportunities and vocational training. Partnering companies often establish employment and job training programs designed to empower residents with practical skills and sustainable livelihoods. These initiatives not only enhance the employability of the individuals but also contribute to the overall economic health of the community. For instance, collaborations might include internships, apprenticeships, and even full-time positions in the companies' operational sectors.

Moreover, companies can support Cities of Hope through sponsorship programs. These programs can take various forms, from financial grants to in-kind contributions such as donating technology, clothing, or food supplies. By ensuring consistent and reliable support, these sponsorships build a robust foundation that helps the towns thrive amidst challenges.

Engagement in CSR initiatives is not solely about financial and material support; it also includes promoting social well-being. Companies often volunteer in community-building activities, organize welfare programs, and encourage their employees to participate in local events. Such activities build a sense of solidarity and inclusion, which are crucial for psychological well-being and social cohesion within the Cities of Hope.

Furthermore, CSR initiatives often extend to environmental sustainability projects, aligning with the broader goals of the Cities of Hope. Companies can contribute to green building practices, renewable energy projects, and effective waste management systems. By integrating sustainable practices, they ensure that the development within these communities is environmentally responsible and forward-looking.

In conclusion, Corporate Social Responsibility initiatives are indispensable to the development and sustainability of Cities of Hope. By aligning their resources and goals with the needs of these communities, major companies play a transformative role. Their contributions help build not only the physical and economic infrastructure but also foster a strong, resilient, and supportive environment for everyone.

Employment and Job Training Programs

Strategic partnerships with major companies play a crucial role in the development and sustainability of employment and job training programs within the Cities of Hope. These collaborations aim to provide residents with meaningful work opportunities and the skills necessary to secure long-term employment. By aligning with partner companies' corporate social responsibility (CSR) initiatives, Cities of Hope can offer a holistic approach to employment that includes on-the-job training, mentorship, and a pathway to career advancement.

Companies involved in these partnerships typically offer a variety of job training programs tailored to the unique skills and aspirations of the residents. From entry-level positions in manufacturing and service industries to specialized roles in technology and healthcare, the range of opportunities is broad and designed to accommodate diverse backgrounds. Regular workshops, seminars, and training sessions are organized to ensure that residents stay updated with the latest industry trends and technological advancements.

Key components of these training programs include:

- **Skills Assessment:** Each resident undergoes a thorough assessment to identify their strengths, weaknesses, and areas of interest. This helps in tailoring the training programs to individual needs, maximizing their potential for success.

- **Soft Skills Training:** Emphasis is placed on developing essential soft skills such as communication, teamwork, problem-solving, and time management. These skills are crucial for personal and professional growth and are highly valued by employers.

- **Technical Training:** Residents have access to hands-on training in various technical fields. This can include anything from computer programming and digital marketing to advanced manufacturing techniques and healthcare support services.

- **Certification Programs:** To enhance employability, residents can pursue certification programs that are recognized by industry leaders. These certifications serve as a testament to their skills and commitment, making them more attractive to potential employers.

- **Mentorship and Internships:** Partner companies often provide mentorship programs where experienced professionals guide residents. Internships offer practical experience, allowing residents to apply their knowledge in real-world settings.

By leveraging partnerships with major companies, Cities of Hope creates a bridge between unemployment and meaningful, sustainable employment. This approach not only empowers residents by providing financial independence but also instills a sense of purpose and community belonging. It builds a resilient workforce capable of contributing to both the local economy and society at large.

These employment and job training programs are not static; they continuously evolve to meet the changing needs of industries and the job market. Feedback loops and regular evaluations ensure that the programs remain relevant and effective, offering residents the best possible chances for success. Ultimately, these initiatives pave the way for a brighter future, where residents can reclaim their dignity and live fulfilling lives.

Sponsorship Programs

Partnering with major companies through sponsorship programs is an essential strategy for advancing the development and sustainability of Cities of Hope. These programs not only provide much-needed funds but also foster a sense of community responsibility and corporate citizenship. Sponsorships can range from financial contributions to in-kind donations, ensuring that residents' various needs are met effectively and efficiently.

First and foremost, financial sponsorships are often directed towards critical infrastructure development, such as constructing housing units, healthcare facilities, and community centers. Companies might also fund specific amenities like libraries, recreational parks, or fitness centers, adding invaluable assets that improve quality of life.

Beyond financial contributions, in-kind donations also play a crucial role. Companies can provide products and services that are essential for day-to-day operations. This can include everything from basic necessities like clothing and hygiene products to more specialized needs such as educational materials and job training equipment.

An effective sponsorship program should also involve the active participation of sponsoring companies in the community. Volunteering initiatives where company employees dedicate their time and expertise can create strong bonds and offer real, hands-on support. For example, tech companies might offer coding workshops, while healthcare firms could run health clinics and wellness programs.

It's important to craft sponsorship agreements that align with the mission and values of both the Cities of Hope project and the sponsoring companies. Clear communication and shared goals ensure that these partnerships are mutually beneficial and sustainable over the long term.

Moreover, recognition of corporate sponsors through various channels, such as community events, newsletters, and social media, can further strengthen these relationships. Celebrating these partnerships not only highlights the company's corporate social responsibility but also inspires other businesses to get involved.

- **Long-term Commitments:** Encouraging long-term sponsorships can secure ongoing support, making it possible to plan and execute ambitious projects without constant concern for funding.

- **Multi-tiered Sponsorships:** Creating various levels of sponsorship options can allow companies of different sizes to participate, fostering inclusivity and broader community support.

- **Performance Metrics:** Establishing clear metrics and regular reporting can help sponsors see the tangible impact of their contributions, reinforcing their commitment.

Lastly, successful sponsorship programs can serve as a model for other communities and initiatives, demonstrating the possible outcomes when businesses step up to make a difference. To ensure the long-term success of Cities of Hope, it's vital to seek innovative sponsorship opportunities and nurture existing partnerships continually.

Way of Life in Cities of Hope

The establishment of Cities of Hope introduces a new paradigm in community living, characterized by a thoughtfully designed structure, robust support systems, and a strong focus on sustainability. This chapter delves into the everyday experiences, governance, and cultural activities that define life in these uniquely purposed communities.

Daily Routines

Daily life in Cities of Hope is designed to be stable and enriching, providing a structured environment that supports personal growth and well-being. Residents typically begin their day with a nutritious breakfast provided through community kitchens. Those engaged in employment or training programs proceed to their respective roles, often within nearby industrial facilities or community services.

Education and skill development sessions are scheduled regularly, ensuring residents have ample opportunities to enhance their capabilities. Recreational and wellness activities, such as yoga classes, art workshops, and group therapy sessions, complement these. The goal is to create a balanced routine that fosters both productivity and personal fulfillment.

- **Morning:** Breakfast, employment/training, educational programs
- **Afternoon:** Skill development, recreational activities, community service
- **Evening:** Dinner, social gatherings, personal time

Community Governance

Effective governance is crucial to the success of Cities of Hope. These communities operate on a participatory governance model, encouraging residents to take an active role in decision-making processes. Regular town hall meetings are held where residents can voice their opinions, propose initiatives, and vote on community matters. This inclusive approach fosters a sense of ownership and responsibility among residents.

The governance structure typically includes elected representatives from within the community who liaise with external partners, including sponsors, municipal authorities, and non-profit organizations. This ensures that the community's needs are addressed while integrating support from external entities.

1. Resident Councils
2. Regular Town Hall Meetings
3. Inclusion of External Partners

Cultural and Recreational Activities

Fostering a rich cultural life is essential for the holistic well-being of residents. Cities of Hope often organize a variety of cultural and recreational activities designed to build community spirit and provide emotional relief. These activities range from music and arts festivals to sports leagues and drama clubs, offering something for everyone.

Community centers act as hubs for these activities, equipped with facilities for various hobbies and interests. Celebrating cultural diversity through festivals and events helps weave a strong social fabric. Moreover, local artists and performers often contribute by holding workshops and performances, further enriching the community's cultural landscape.

The support from celebrities and major companies often plays a significant role in these activities. Sponsorships and partnerships bring additional resources and opportunities, facilitating events that might otherwise be beyond reach. These connections provide financial support and inspire residents by showing them they are part of a larger societal fabric that cares about their welfare.

These cultural and recreational engagements aim to uplift spirits, enhance social bonds, and create a nurturing environment where individuals can rediscover their passions and potential.

- Music and Arts Festivals
- Sports Leagues
- Drama and Performance Clubs
- Workshops and Skill-Building Sessions

In conclusion, the way of life in Cities of Hope is characterized by a structured yet flexible routine, inclusive governance, and a rich array of cultural and recreational activities. Together, these elements create a nurturing environment that supports the personal and communal growth of residents, proving that with the right framework, a homeless town can be a place of hope and opportunity.

Daily Routines

In the context of Cities of Hope, the structure and rhythm of daily life play a crucial role in ensuring residents experience stability and a sense of normalcy. The concept is built around creating a harmonious routine that integrates work, personal growth, and communal interaction. This balance not only addresses their immediate needs but also sets the foundation for long-term well-being.

The day in a Homeless Town generally starts early as residents prepare for work at nearby industrial facilities. These industries, strategically located to provide easy access, include sectors like call centers, greenhouses, manufacturing, and other businesses mentioned in the book so far. The goal is not only to offer employment but also to foster a sense of responsibility and accomplishment.

After working hours, the community spaces become vibrant hubs of activity. Residents can engage in a variety of educational and training programs aimed at enhancing their skills and improving their future employability. Opportunities for recreational activities, including sports, arts, and crafts, are plentiful, ensuring residents have well-rounded lives.

A significant part of the daily routine also includes community meals. Organized in communal dining areas, these meals are more than just about nutrition; they are vital for social interaction, building a sense of camaraderie among residents. The food and nutrition services are designed to provide balanced and healthy options, catering to various dietary needs.

Throughout the day, residents have access to healthcare facilities and psychological support services. Regular check-ups, both physical and mental, are encouraged. These services aim to nip potential issues in the bud and foster overall well-being. Counseling sessions, group therapy, and other mental health programs are seamlessly integrated into the daily schedule.

Another cornerstone of daily life is the various community-building activities that take place. These activities, which can range from gardening projects to neighborhood clean-up drives, instill a sense of ownership and pride in the community. They also serve as informal forums for residents to voice concerns, share ideas, and support each other.

In the evenings, educational opportunities continue with workshops and seminars on topics like financial literacy, personal development, and basic life skills. These sessions aim to empower residents, giving them the tools they need to transition to a more stable and self-sufficient lifestyle. Educational programs are complemented by a rich array of cultural activities, from music and dance performances to movie nights and talent shows.

Moreover, substance abuse programs operate discreetly throughout the day, providing support and counseling to those in need. These programs are essential for residents struggling with addiction, providing a confidential and supportive environment for recovery.

All these elements collectively form a coherent and supportive daily routine that addresses multiple aspects of a person's life. Such a well-rounded approach not only helps in immediate crisis management but also lays down a strong foundation for long-term growth and rehabilitation. The structured yet flexible routine enables residents to rebuild their lives in a supportive and empowering environment, transforming Cities of Hope into communities of hope and resilience.

Community Governance

Community governance in Cities of Hope is a cornerstone of leading a self-sustained and harmonious way of life. While the basic needs of residents are thoroughly addressed, the organizational framework ensures these communities function smoothly and efficiently. The goal here goes beyond mere survival; it involves fostering a sense of ownership, participation, and mutual support among the town's residents.

Governance structures in these towns typically comprise elected community councils or advisory boards. These bodies are instrumental in decision-making processes, covering everything from resource allocation to conflict resolution. Residents vote for their representatives, creating an inclusive environment where all voices are heard and valued. This democratic approach ensures that governance remains transparent, accountable, and responsive to the community's evolving needs.

Regular town meetings play a crucial role in this governance model. These gatherings allow residents to discuss pressing issues, propose new initiatives, and review ongoing projects. Meeting agendas might include topics like improvements to shared spaces, revisions to community guidelines, or updates on industrial activities aimed at generating sustainable revenue. Open forums within these meetings encourage active engagement, ensuring that residents feel their contributions matter.

A robust set of community guidelines outlines each resident's behavioral expectations and responsibilities. Emphasizing respect, cooperation, and shared responsibility, these guidelines help maintain order and enhance the quality of life within the town. A committee composed of residents typically handles the enforcement of these guidelines, offering a balanced approach that combines fairness with empathy.

Conflict resolution mechanisms are another key aspect of community governance. Mediation panels or conflict resolution teams, often composed of trained volunteers, help resolve disputes amicably. By adopting a restorative justice approach, these mechanisms aim to restore harmony and build stronger community bonds.

Training and development programs are integral to cultivating effective leadership and governance. Residents are encouraged to participate in workshops and skill-building sessions that focus on leadership, communication, and organizational management. These programs equip potential leaders with the tools they need to serve their community effectively and pave the way for future self-governance.

Furthermore, partnerships with external organizations and governmental bodies bolster the governance framework. These collaborations bring in expertise and resources, ensuring that community governance structures are well-equipped to handle various challenges. Regular audits and reviews by external evaluators help maintain transparency and drive continuous improvement.

In summary, community governance in Cities of Hope is a collaborative effort that empowers residents, fosters a sense of shared responsibility, and ensures that the community thrives in a sustainable manner. This structure not only addresses immediate needs but also lays the groundwork for a vibrant, self-sufficient, and inclusive society.

Cultural and Recreational Activities

The design of cultural and recreational activities in Cities of Hope plays a crucial role in fostering a sense of community and improving overall well-being. These activities provide much more than just entertainment; they're essential for restoring human dignity, encouraging social interaction, and cultivating talents and interests.

From outdoor concert series to art workshops, cultural events in Cities of Hope aim to encompass a wide array of interests. Regular performances, whether by local artists or visiting celebrities, can offer a great sense of enjoyment and community spirit. Moreover, partnering with cultural institutions and universities to bring in guest lecturers, diverse art forms, and exhibitions can broaden horizons and create enrichment opportunities that might otherwise be inaccessible.

Community centers frequently host movie nights, poetry readings, and theater performances. These activities cater to various tastes and become arenas for community members to express themselves and celebrate together. Open mic nights and talent shows can also serve as platforms for residents to showcase their skills, build confidence, and enjoy mutual appreciation.

Sports and physical activities are another cornerstone of community engagement. Access to sports fields, basketball courts, and fitness centers encourages an active lifestyle and helps maintain physical health. Community sports leagues, yoga sessions, and dance classes provide structured ways for residents to participate in physical activity, combating the sedentary effects often associated with homelessness.

- Music and Dance Programs
- Art Classes and Workshops
- Community Theater and Performances
- Outdoor Festivals and Parades
- Gardening and Urban Farming Projects

Gardening and urban farming projects not only contribute to food sustainability but also offer therapeutic benefits and a sense of accomplishment. Residents can get involved in growing vegetables, tending to community gardens, or participating in landscape beautification. These activities provide a tangible connection to nature and contribute to the aesthetic and environmental quality of the town.

Collaboration with local and external partners is key to implementing these cultural and recreational activities. Partnerships with charitable organizations, local businesses, and entertainment companies will not only enhance the quality of offerings but also ensure they are varied and sustainable. Moreover, feedback from town residents should continually inform what initiatives to maintain or introduce, allowing for an adaptive and resident-centered approach.

Ultimately, cultural and recreational activities are integral to creating vibrant, sustainable Cities of Hope. They foster social cohesion, enhance the quality of life, and offer avenues for personal growth and community enhancement. By investing in these areas, Cities of Hope can become thriving, inclusive spaces where every individual has the opportunity to participate and flourish.

Potential Support Organizations for Partnership

Connecting with support organizations is crucial for the residents and administrators of Cities of Hope. These organizations provide a wide array of services and resources essential for these communities' well-being and sustainability. Below is a list of key organizations, categorized by the type of support they offer.

- Emergency and Crisis Support
    - National Coalition for the Homeless: (202) 462-4822
    - The Salvation Army: 1-800-SAL-ARMY (725-2769)
    - United Way: 2-1-1
- Food and Nutrition Services
    - *Feeding America:* (800) 771-2303

- o *Meals on Wheels:* (888) 998-6325
- o *Sobriety Foundation:* (888) 289-6874
- Healthcare and Mental Health Services
  - o *Doctors Without Borders:* (888) 392-0392
  - o *National Alliance on Mental Illness (NAMI):* 1-800-950-NAMI (6264)
  - o *Substance Abuse and Mental Health Services Administration (SAMHSA):* 1-800-662-HELP (4357)
- Education and Job Training Programs
  - o *Goodwill Industries International:* (800) 741-0186
  - o *Job Corps:* 1-800-733-JOBS (5627)
  - o *Teach For America:* (800) 832-1230
- Housing and Legal Services
  - o *National Alliance to End Homelessness:* (202) 638-1526
  - o *Legal Aid Society:* (888) 218-6974
  - o *Habitat for Humanity:* 1-800-HABITAT (422-4828)

Social Integration Strategies

One of the fundamental components for addressing homelessness is ensuring that individuals not only have access to jobs and housing but also feel integrated into the broader society. Social integration strategies are essential to transforming homeless communities into cohesive, self-sustaining environments where residents can thrive. This chapter will explore various approaches to social integration, focusing on building community connections and addressing the pervasive stigma often faced by the homeless.

Building Community Connections

Establishing strong community connections can significantly improve the quality of life for previously homeless individuals. When people feel a sense of belonging, they are more likely to participate in community activities, maintain steady employment, and contribute positively to their environment. Here are several strategies to foster these connections:

1. **Community Centers:** Developing multipurpose community centers within Cities of Hope can serve as a hub for social interaction. These centers can host events, provide educational programs, and offer opportunities for skill development. Studies have shown that community centers can play a pivotal role in social integration for marginalized groups.

2. **Mentorship Programs:** Pairing new residents with established members of the community or volunteers can provide a support system that fosters personal growth and community involvement. Mentorship can help individuals navigate their new environment and establish valuable networks.

3. **Volunteer Opportunities:** Encouraging community members to volunteer both within and outside their community can enhance social skills and provide a sense of purpose. Volunteering has been noted to boost social integration and well-being.

4. **Cultural and Recreational Activities:** Organizing regular cultural and recreational activities can bridge gaps between different demographics within the community. Such activities not only offer relaxation and enjoyment but also foster a sense of unity and shared purpose.

Addressing Stigma

Tackling the stigma associated with homelessness is crucial for the success of social integration strategies. Stigma can be a significant barrier to forming meaningful connections, gaining employment, and accessing services. Addressing stigma requires a multifaceted approach, including public education, advocacy, and policy changes.

- **Public Education Campaigns:** Raising awareness about the causes and realities of homelessness can dispel myths and misconceptions. Campaigns should highlight the diverse stories of homeless individuals and emphasize their potential for positive contributions to society.

- **Supporting Inclusion in Workforce:** Encouraging employers to offer opportunities to homeless individuals and educating them about the benefits and challenges of employing this demographic can break down employment barriers. Inclusive hiring practices can combat stigmatizing attitudes and promote diversity and inclusion.

- **Policy Advocacy:** Advocating for policies that protect the rights of homeless individuals and promote their well-being can reduce stigma and discrimination. These policies might include anti-discrimination laws, housing incentives for low-income families, and increased funding for social services.

- **Community Engagement:** Creating open dialogues between community members and homeless individuals can foster empathy and understanding. Engaging the broader community in addressing homelessness issues can help normalize interactions and humanize the homeless population.

Implementing these social integration strategies not only benefits the homeless individuals themselves but also strengthens the whole community. When previously homeless individuals are welcomed and supported, they can become active, contributing members of society, enriching the social fabric with their diverse experiences and perspectives.

Social integration is not a one-time effort but an ongoing process requiring continuous support, evaluation, and adjustment. By embracing these strategies, we can create communities where everyone has the opportunity to belong and thrive.

Building Community Connections

Building community connections is an essential aspect of social integration strategies, particularly for those striving to address homelessness. It goes beyond merely providing housing and employment opportunities; it aims to create an environment where formerly homeless individuals can develop a sense of belonging, security, and active participation within the broader community. This chapter outlines practical approaches to foster such connections, especially within self-sustaining communities designed to support the homeless.

One of the first steps in building community connections is the intentional design of communal spaces within housing projects. These spaces, whether they are community gardens, shared kitchens, or recreational areas, serve as physical venues for interaction and relationship building. By encouraging residents to partake in joint activities, the social fabric of the community strengthens, leading to mutual support and understanding. Studies have shown that communal spaces promote social interaction and are critical in developing a sense of community among residents.

A second strategy involves incorporating community events and programs. Regularly scheduled events such as community clean-ups, cooking classes, art workshops, and local sports leagues can serve as points of connection. These events should be inclusive, providing opportunities for all community members to participate regardless of their background or skill level. Research on community programs indicates that such activities not only enhance social cohesion but also improve mental health outcomes for the participants.

Partnering with local organizations and businesses is another significant way to build community connections. Collaboration allows for resource pooling and provides avenues for homeless individuals to engage with the larger community. Local businesses can offer internships, job placements, and mentorship opportunities, while nonprofits can assist with skill development, counseling, and other support services. This network of connections exposes residents to diverse perspectives and experiences, facilitating their integration into wider societal circles.

Cities of Hope can also serve as transitional hubs, where formerly homeless citizens are prepared to integrate into broader urban environments through partnerships with businesses. This process is akin to how companies recruit students nearing graduation from universities, offering them opportunities to work and live in different cities as they complete their training and education.

Moreover, encouraging volunteerism within the community can have profound impacts. Residents who volunteer in local schools, shelters, or other community services not only contribute to the welfare of their neighborhood but also gain a sense of purpose and self-worth. Their contributions are recognized and valued, which bridges social gaps and reduces the stigmatization of homelessness.

Finally, effective communication within communities is vital. Establishing communication channels such as community meetings, newsletters, and forums ensures that everyone's voice is heard and that residents can collectively address issues as they arise. Open communication fosters transparency, trust, and collective problem-solving, laying a strong foundation for a connected and resilient community.

In conclusion, building community connections is about creating an inclusive environment where formerly homeless individuals can participate fully and meaningfully. It requires deliberate efforts in designing shared spaces, organizing communal activities, partnering with local organizations, encouraging volunteerism, and ensuring effective communication. These elements collectively contribute to a supportive network essential for the successful reintegration of formerly homeless individuals into society.

Addressing Stigma

To effectively integrate homeless individuals into society, it's crucial to address the pervasive stigma that surrounds homelessness. This stigma often serves as a significant barrier, not only preventing social acceptance but also exacerbating the challenges homeless individuals face in securing housing, employment, and essential services.

The stigmatization of homeless people is deeply rooted in societal perceptions and myths. **Many believe homelessness results from personal failings or choices rather than complex, interrelated factors like economic downturns, lack of affordable housing, mental health issues, and domestic violence.** Breaking down these misconceptions is essential for fostering a more inclusive and supportive community.

First, public awareness campaigns are vital tools in reshaping public perceptions. They can highlight the diverse stories and backgrounds of homeless individuals, demonstrating that homelessness can affect anyone. Educational programs in schools and workplaces can also play a significant role in dispelling myths. By providing factual information and promoting empathy, these campaigns can reduce prejudice and foster a climate of understanding.

Moreover, language matters. The terms and phrases we use to discuss homelessness can either reinforce stigma or dismantle it. For instance, referring to individuals as "persons experiencing homelessness" rather than "homeless people" emphasizes their humanity and temporary circumstances, rather than defining them solely by their housing status. Such linguistic shifts can gradually transform societal attitudes and reduce stigma.

Policy initiatives must also address stigma. Policies that promote inclusive housing, such as "Housing First" models, underscore that everyone deserves a stable home without preconditions. These approaches not only provide immediate stability but also convey the message that homelessness is a systemic issue requiring systemic solutions rather than individual moral failings.

In tandem with housing policies, employment programs that incorporate training and skill development can change perceptions about the capabilities and potential of homeless individuals. When communities see formerly homeless individuals contributing as active and capable members of society, it helps to break down stereotypes and foster inclusion.

Lastly, personal stories and testimonials from those who have experienced homelessness can have a profound impact. Platforms that give a voice to the homeless community allow for the sharing of diverse narratives that humanize the issue and highlight resilience and potential for recovery. Bringing these voices to the forefront can encourage empathy and understanding, challenge ingrained biases, and promote societal change.

In summary, to integrate homeless individuals effectively into society, it is essential to tackle the stigma that surrounds homelessness head-on. Through public awareness campaigns, mindful language use, inclusive policies, employment programs, and the amplification of personal stories, we can begin to shift societal perceptions and build a more compassionate and inclusive community.

Some More Case Studies of Similar Models

Understanding the success and challenges faced by other nations and communities in addressing homelessness can provide invaluable insights for developing self-sustaining communities in the United States. This chapter presents several case studies of similar models from around the world, highlighting both achievement and lessons learned that can inform our efforts.

Success Stories from Other Countries

Different countries have adopted unique approaches to mitigate homelessness, each with varying degrees of success. Here, we look into a few notable examples that have left a significant mark.

Finland's Housing First Model

One of the most cited success stories in tackling homelessness comes from Finland, which adopted the Housing First model. Unlike traditional approaches that require the homeless to first address issues like addiction or mental health, Housing First prioritizes providing permanent housing. The rationale is simple: once individuals have a stable living situation, they are better positioned to address other issues.

Studies indicate impressive results. By 2017, homelessness in Finland had decreased significantly, with long-term homelessness nearly eradicated. The model has proven both humane and cost-effective. For every euro invested in Housing First, municipalities save between €9,000 to €15,000 per person annually, mainly due to reduced healthcare costs and fewer interactions with law enforcement.

Japan's Integrated Support Systems

In Japan, the approach involves integrating services like job training, medical care, and social services along with housing solutions. Tokyo's Special Ward Koto pioneered this model, demonstrating its efficacy. Homeless individuals were provided with temporary lodging, after which they were slotted into employment opportunities or vocational training programs. During their participation, they received comprehensive health care and social support.

The results have been promising. Within the first year of implementation, over 70% of participants transitioned into stable living conditions and employment. This multifaceted approach underscores the importance of addressing the holistic needs of individuals experiencing homelessness.

Success Stories from Other Countries

In examining effective models from around the globe, it's clear that various countries have successfully implemented strategies to alleviate homelessness. These "success stories" provide valuable lessons that can be adapted to suit the unique socio-economic landscape of the United States. By studying these approaches, we can glean insights into creating sustainable communities that empower homeless individuals and contribute positively to the economy.

One prime example is Finland, which has adopted the "Housing First" model. Launched in 2008, this initiative focuses on providing permanent housing without preconditions, such as sobriety or employment. According to research, Finland's approach has significantly reduced long-term homelessness by approximately 35% . By addressing housing needs first, individuals are better able to tackle other issues like addiction, mental health, and employment.

In Canada, programs like Toronto's Streets to Homes have shown remarkable results. The initiative provides immediate access to housing along with follow-up support services. Since its inception, Streets to Homes has successfully housed over 5,000 people and boasts a housing retention rate of 87%. This model emphasizes integrated support services, including job training, addiction counseling, and mental health treatment, proving that a holistic approach can be highly effective.

Another notable success story comes from Japan, specifically the Kotodama dormitory model. These dormitories offer affordable housing and communal living spaces for low-income workers and homeless individuals. By combining living quarters with skill development programs, these facilities help residents gain stable employment, fostering economic self-sufficiency. A 2018 study indicated that this model dramatically improved residents' quality of life and job prospects.

While the socioeconomic conditions in the US differ from these countries, these case studies illustrate the potential of comprehensive and integrated approaches to homelessness. By borrowing and adapting elements from these successful models, we can develop strategies that provide immediate relief and pave the way for long-term self-sufficiency and community integration.

Lessons Learned

Drawing from case studies of similar models implemented both domestically and internationally; several valuable lessons emerge that can guide the development of self-sustaining communities for the homeless. Understanding these lessons is crucial for creating effective, scalable solutions that not only address homelessness but also contribute to the economy and social fabric of the United States.

One significant lesson learned is the importance of comprehensive, multi-faceted approaches. Successful models often integrate housing with employment opportunities, mental health support, and community services. For instance, the "Housing First" model, which prioritizes providing permanent housing without preconditions, has shown remarkable success in countries like Finland. The Finnish approach also includes strong support networks encompassing healthcare, addiction support, and employment training, resulting in a dramatic reduction in homelessness.

Community involvement and stakeholder engagement are also critical. Programs that have thrived invested in building strong partnerships with local governments, private enterprises, and nonprofit organizations. These collaborations facilitate resource sharing, enhance service delivery, and foster community acceptance. For example, Canada's At Home/Chez Soi initiative demonstrated that collaboration across sectors led to better housing outcomes and improved mental health for participants.

Another important takeaway is the necessity of tailored solutions that address the unique needs of different sub-populations within the homeless community. Homelessness is not a monolithic issue; it affects individuals differently based on their backgrounds, health statuses, and personal histories. Programs targeting youth homelessness, for example, might emphasize educational support and job training more heavily than those targeting veterans, who may need more robust mental health services and job placement assistance.

Moreover, the case studies highlight the pivotal role of data-driven decision-making. Effective programs use comprehensive data collection and analysis to continually monitor outcomes, identify gaps, and make informed adjustments. This iterative process of assessment and refinement ensures that resources are utilized efficiently and interventions remain relevant to the evolving landscape of homelessness.

Finally, sustainability emerges as a recurring theme. Long-term success depends not just on initial funding and implementation but also on the creation of self-sustaining systems. This includes developing revenue streams, such as social enterprises, that can provide ongoing financial support and foster community resilience and self-reliance.

In conclusion, the lessons learned from similar models underscore the necessity of integrated, collaborative, and adaptable approaches to building self-sustaining homeless communities. By leveraging these insights, we can enhance the efficacy of our efforts and make significant strides toward alleviating homelessness.

Challenges and Obstacles

Tackling homelessness is a complex and multifaceted issue that presents numerous challenges and obstacles. Despite the best intentions and well-designed plans, various anticipated and unanticipated issues can impede progress. This chapter aims to shed light on these challenges and proposes strategies to mitigate them effectively.

Anticipated Issues

A variety of hurdles can be expected when attempting to implement solutions for homelessness. These challenges can be broadly categorized into social, economic, bureaucratic, and logistical obstacles.

- **Social Issues:** One significant challenge is the social stigma surrounding homelessness. Public perception often impacts the success of housing and employment initiatives. Many community members may resist the development of homeless facilities in their neighborhoods, fearing decreased property values or increased crime rates.

- **Economic Barriers:** Funding is a perennial challenge. Securing the necessary financial resources for long-term projects, such as building self-sustaining communities, can be daunting. Moreover, fluctuating economic conditions can affect both funding availability and the stability of these communities. I believe Cities of Hope fully addresses this issue.

- **Bureaucratic Hurdles:** Navigating the myriads of local, state, and federal regulations is another significant challenge. Zoning laws, building codes, and other legislative requirements can slow the progress of housing initiatives.

- **Logistical Problems:** Ensuring that all facets of a self-sustaining community, such as housing, employment, and social services, work seamlessly together requires meticulous planning and coordination. Any lapse in one area can derail the entire project. Additionally, providing continuous support and resources to formerly homeless individuals so they can integrate back into society is a substantial logistical challenge.

Mitigation Strategies

While the obstacles are formidable, they are not insurmountable. This section outlines several strategies to address and mitigate these challenges.

- **Community Education and Engagement:** Changing public perception begins with education. Through community meetings, educational campaigns, and collaborations with local influencers and media, it's possible to build empathy and understanding about the homeless population. Fostering a more supportive community attitude can pave the way for smoother project implementation.

- **Diversified Funding Sources:** To address financial challenges, a diversified approach to funding is essential. This can include private donations, public grants, and innovative funding mechanisms like social impact bonds. Financial collaborations with corporations and philanthropic organizations can also provide much-needed resources. These methods can be complimentary to the Cities of Hope financial architecture.

- **Streamlined Bureaucratic Processes:** Active lobbying for policy reforms to simplify zoning and regulatory processes can be immensely beneficial. Forming alliances with policymakers and engaging in advocacy work can help reduce the bureaucratic hurdles that slow down project timelines. Interagency for Homelessness Council is a great initiative that can be instrumental in solving bureaucratic issues.

- **Integrated Support Systems:** Implementing a holistic approach that encompasses housing, employment, healthcare, and social integration services can address multiple facets of homelessness simultaneously. Coordinated efforts between various service providers can ensure that individuals receive comprehensive support tailored to their needs.

The challenges in addressing homelessness are significant, but with dedicated effort and strategic planning, they can be overcome. By understanding and addressing these obstacles head-on, we can make meaningful progress toward ending homelessness and building self-sustaining communities that benefit individuals and society at large.

Anticipated Issues

As we embark on the journey of creating self-sustaining communities for the homeless, we must anticipate a range of potential issues. These issues span across economic, social, legal, and logistical dimensions and have the potential to significantly impact the success of our efforts. By identifying these obstacles early on, we can devise strategies to mitigate them, ensuring a more effective and sustainable implementation.

One of the major anticipated issues is securing consistent and adequate funding. While the initial investment might be daunting, the long-term financial sustainability of these communities is even more challenging. Funding gaps could result in interrupted services or stalled projects, which would negatively affect the inhabitants. **The Cities of Hope model addresses this issue.** Financial projections need to be meticulously calculated, and multiple funding streams should be identified to ensure longevity.

Another critical challenge is community acceptance and integration. NIMBYism (Not In My Back Yard) is a common phenomenon where local residents oppose the development of homeless shelters or facilities in their neighborhoods. This opposition can stem from fear, misinformation, or prejudice. Overcoming this requires robust community education programs and efforts to build trust and empathy among current residents. **The Cities of Hope model addresses this issue** as it will create vibrant towns in relatively remote locations for enhanced interconnectivity in the US.

Logistically, the management of self-sustaining communities poses several hurdles. Ensuring the availability of essential services such as healthcare, mental health support, and education within these communities is paramount. The integration of these services into the community in a manner that fosters autonomy while providing necessary support is a delicate balance that needs careful planning and continuous adjustment. **The Cities of Hope model addresses this issue.**

On the regulatory front, navigating zoning laws and local regulations can present significant barriers. These legal frameworks often require alterations to accommodate the unique needs of self-sustaining homeless communities. Regulations on land use, building codes, and business operations will need to be re-examined and, in some cases, reformed to support these innovative living and employment arrangements. **The Cities of Hope model addresses this issue** as these cities will utilize spaces that will have better flexibility in zoning and legal frameworks due to their locations.

Interpersonal conflicts and management issues within the community can also arise. Building a cohesive community of individuals with diverse backgrounds, some of whom may have experienced significant trauma, requires strong leadership and conflict-resolution strategies. These communities will need trained personnel to manage daily operations and address interpersonal conflicts effectively. **Cities of Hope addresses this issue** by including foreign workers and carefully planning social integration and community-building strategies.

Finally, monitoring and evaluating the effectiveness of the initiatives poses their own set of challenges. Developing robust metrics and data collection methods that accurately reflect the progress and impact of the communities is vital. Continuous improvement must be part of the strategy to ensure that the communities are evolving to meet the needs of their residents. **The Cities of Hope model addresses this issue** due to the smart city concept, advanced technology usage, advanced measurement metrics they will utilize, and embedded additional monitoring and measurement strategies.

Proactively addressing these anticipated issues will significantly increase the likelihood of success for self-sustaining communities and contribute to their long-term viability. Our approach must be flexible, adaptable, and rooted in a deep understanding of the multifaceted challenges faced by the homeless population.

Mitigation Strategies

Addressing the challenges and obstacles detailed in the preceding sections requires a robust and multifaceted set of mitigation strategies. Key among these strategies is the emphasis on flexibility, innovation, and collaboration across various sectors. This section outlines practical mitigation approaches designed to tackle the broad spectrum of issues facing initiatives aimed at ending homelessness.

Public-Private Partnerships: Establishing partnerships between government agencies, non-profit organizations, and private enterprises can leverage different strengths and resources. Combining public funding with private sector efficiency and innovation can create sustainable models that address both immediate needs and long-term solutions. **Cities of Hope includes this strategy.**

Community Involvement and Advocacy: Mobilizing community support is crucial. Grassroots movements and local advocacy can build public awareness and pressure policymakers to act. Engaging local volunteers not only reduces costs but also personalizes the issue, making it a community problem rather than a distant governmental obligation. **Cities of Hope includes this strategy.**

Flexible Policy Frameworks: Policies must adapt to the complex and dynamic nature of homelessness. A one-size-fits-all approach is not effective; instead, local governments should be empowered to tailor programs specific to their community's needs. These programs should include a mixture of housing-first initiatives, integrated healthcare, and rapid rehousing strategies. **Cities of Hope consists of this strategy, and the overall concept goes beyond these measures.**

Data-Driven Decision-Making: Employing data analytics to monitor and evaluate the effectiveness of programs is essential for continuous improvement. Predictive analytics can help identify risks, allowing for preventive measures to be implemented. Regular collection and analysis of data ensure that policies remain relevant and effective. **Cities of Hope includes this strategy.**

Innovation in Housing Solutions: Utilizing innovative housing solutions like tiny homes, modular units, and converted shipping containers can significantly reduce construction costs and time. Additionally, these alternatives can be quickly deployed to meet urgent needs, providing safe and affordable housing options. **Cities of Hope includes this strategy and goes beyond these methods.**

Employment and Training Programs: Economic stability is a critical factor in preventing homelessness. Job training and employment programs tailored to the needs of the homeless population can help them gain meaningful employment. Collaborations with local businesses to create job opportunities within industrial parks can enhance these efforts by offering structured environments conducive to gaining skills and experience. **Cities of Hope includes this strategy.**

Comprehensive Support Services: Case management that integrates healthcare, mental health services, substance abuse treatment, and social support is essential. By addressing the root causes of homelessness through a holistic approach, individuals are more likely to achieve long-term stability. **Cities of Hope includes this strategy.**

Crisis Intervention and Prevention: Immediate interventions such as emergency shelters, temporary accommodations, and crisis hotlines are critical for those at immediate risk. Preventative measures, including rental assistance, legal aid, and counseling services, can help individuals maintain their housing and prevent homelessness from occurring in the first place. **Cities of Hope provides a way better solution than any of these strategies with its holistic, fully integrated, and sustainable proposition.**

In conclusion, these mitigation strategies emphasize a comprehensive and adaptable approach, leveraging community involvement, innovative solutions, and robust data analytics to create sustainable outcomes. The battle against homelessness is complex, but through strategic collaboration and flexible policy implementation, it is possible to build systems that offer both immediate relief and long-term solutions.

Note:

The Cities of Hope will primarily host our homeless citizens, individuals who come from diverse backgrounds and have endured challenging circumstances. Building a cohesive community from such varied experiences and personal issues may present significant challenges at the outset. I recognize this as one of the most formidable obstacles to the success of this initiative.

As I mentioned earlier, one of the reasons for including foreign workers in these cities is the resilience and perseverance they are likely to demonstrate. The process of community creation will require patience, dedication, and a collective effort, and I believe these foreign workers will be particularly committed to this cause. For them, this project represents their second chance at building a life in the United States, and they will bring the determination needed to overcome these initial hurdles.

Additionally, I am relying on the fact that tens of thousands of Americans have been tirelessly working on homelessness issues for years. With the combined efforts of these experienced professionals and the commitment of the new residents, I am confident that we will find effective solutions to address the challenges of community building within the Cities of Hope.

Collaboration with Existing Programs

Tackling homelessness effectively demands not just new initiatives but also strategic collaboration with already-existing programs. Leveraging the strengths of government partnerships, nonprofit organizations, and community groups can amplify efforts to build self-sustaining communities for the homeless. This chapter delves into how best to harness these resources, maximizing both efficiency and impact.

Government Partnerships

Government initiatives at the federal, state, and local levels offer a range of services that can be pivotal in addressing homelessness. Federal programs like the Department of Housing and Urban Development (HUD) already provide substantial support through grants, housing vouchers, and emergency shelters (United States Interagency Council on Homelessness, 2020). These programs can serve as foundational pieces upon which additional community support structures can be built.

Moreover, integration with local and state efforts can be instrumental. For instance, California's Project Homekey has been transformative, converting hotels and motels into long-term housing for the homeless. Collaborating with such programs ensures that resources are used effectively, avoiding duplication of efforts. Integrating these programs with the Cities of Hope, new efficiencies can be found.

Nonprofit and Community Organizations

Nonprofit organizations play a crucial role in addressing homelessness, often filling gaps left by governmental programs. Organizations like the National Alliance to End Homelessness and local shelters offer extensive experience and resources that can be invaluable. These groups frequently provide not only immediate relief through food and shelter but also long-term solutions like job training and mental health services.

Community organizations bring local expertise and grassroots support that can make or break initiatives aimed at the homeless. For example, local religious groups, neighborhood associations, and volunteers can offer unique insights into the community's specific needs. Engaging these groups fosters a more resilient and adaptable support network.

Integration Strategies

Effective collaboration requires aligning goals and communication among all involved parties. Integration strategies might include regular meetings, shared databases, and coordinated outreach efforts.

Another critical aspect is funding. Collaborative efforts can pool resources for greater impact. Grants that require matching funds from multiple organizations can incentivize collaboration, ensuring that financial and infrastructural support is robust and sustainable.

Finally, technology can be a powerful enabler of these partnerships. Integrated data systems can help track the progress of individuals across various services, ensuring that no one falls through the cracks. Cloud-based platforms and mobile applications can facilitate real-time updates and resource management, making the entire collaboration more efficient.

Collaboration with existing programs is not just a strategy but a necessity for effectively addressing homelessness. By working together, government entities, nonprofits, and community organizations can create a comprehensive support system that enhances the lives of those experiencing homelessness while fostering economic and social vitality.

Government Partnerships

Effective government partnerships are crucial in tackling the multifaceted issue of homelessness in the United States. Collaborative efforts between federal, state, and local governments can provide a coordinated approach, leveraging each level's unique strengths and resources to create impactful solutions. Partnerships with government entities extend far beyond funding; they enable the development of comprehensive policies, ensure the effective allocation of resources, and create a unified front in the fight against homelessness.

At the federal level, key programs and initiatives provide overarching frameworks and substantial funding opportunities. Programs such as the U.S. Department of Housing and Urban Development's (HUD) Continuum of Care (CoC) and the Emergency Solutions Grants (ESG) Program are pivotal in addressing homelessness. These initiatives offer grants and guidance aimed at helping individuals and families quickly regain stability in permanent housing after experiencing a housing crisis or homelessness. Collaborative efforts with HUD can help local programs align with federal goals and access essential funding (HUD, 2021).

State governments play a critical intermediary role by customizing the implementation of federal programs to better fit local contexts and by funding state-specific initiatives. For instance, California's Homeless Emergency Aid Program (HEAP) offers flexible block grant funding designed to provide immediate emergency assistance to communities addressing homelessness. Additionally, state governments can facilitate data sharing between different regions, creating a more comprehensive understanding of homelessness trends and allowing for better-targeted interventions.

Local governments are often at the frontline, directly interfacing with the homeless population and implementing policies on the ground. Their proximity to local communities enables the crafting of tailored interventions that cater specifically to the unique challenges faced by their residents. Local government partnerships can also facilitate innovative housing solutions like tiny home villages, conversion of vacant properties into shelters, and the implementation of wrap-around services that address the multifaceted needs of the homeless population.

Another significant aspect of government partnerships is inter-agency collaboration. Homelessness intersects with various sectors, including healthcare, social services, law enforcement, and education. Coordinating efforts among these agencies can ensure a holistic approach, addressing not only immediate shelter needs but also underlying issues like mental health, substance abuse, and unemployment. For example, integrating health services within homeless shelters or forming multidisciplinary teams to address the specific needs of the homeless can significantly improve outcomes. **In essence, the establishment of the U.S. Interagency Council on Homelessness (USICH)has been a great breakthrough and a positive change of approach to this chronic problem. In essence, this is the main reason why I am proposing that this agency implement the Cities of Hope project.**

Government partnerships are indispensable in creating a multifaceted and cohesive strategy to combat homelessness. By leveraging the strengths of federal, state, and local governments and fostering inter-agency collaboration, we can create sustainable solutions that address immediate needs and pave the way for long-term recovery and reintegration into society.

Nonprofit and Community Organizations

Nonprofit and community organizations play a crucial role in addressing homelessness. These organizations often serve as the backbone of social support systems, providing essential services that span everything from emergency shelters to job training programs. Their involvement can complement government initiatives, creating a multifaceted approach to tackling homelessness effectively.

One of the most important contributions of nonprofit and community organizations is their ability to offer tailored services that meet the unique needs of homeless individuals. Unlike government programs, which can be bureaucratic and slow to adapt, nonprofit organizations often operate with greater flexibility. This allows them to pilot innovative solutions and quickly implement programs that show promise. For example, Seattle's Downtown Emergency Service Center (DESC) combines housing with comprehensive healthcare services, demonstrating a successful model of integrated care.

Community organizations also make significant contributions through advocacy and policy influence. They often act as intermediaries between homeless populations and policymakers, ensuring that the voices of those experiencing homelessness are heard. By leveraging their on-the-ground experience and data collection, these organizations can advocate for changes that more accurately reflect the needs of the homeless community.

Furthermore, nonprofit and community organizations can foster collaborative partnerships. These organizations can create comprehensive support networks by forming alliances with local businesses, educational institutions, and healthcare providers. These partnerships are vital for the sustainability of initiatives aimed at reducing homelessness. For instance, the "Built for Zero" campaign by Community Solutions has partnered with multiple sectors to achieve a measurable reduction in chronic homelessness in various communities across the United States.

Ultimately, collaboration with nonprofits and community organizations broadens the societal effort to combat homelessness. It brings additional resources, innovative approaches, and critical advocacy efforts into play, enriching the overall strategy for creating self-sustaining communities that help homeless individuals reintegrate into society. By harnessing the strengths of these organizations, we can develop more efficient, compassionate, and economically viable solutions to homelessness. They can be instrumental in the successful implementation of The Cities of Hope project.

Policy Recommendations

As we approach the culmination of this comprehensive exploration into addressing homelessness through the creation of self-sustaining communities, it becomes essential to outline practical and actionable policy recommendations.

The Strategic Role of USICH in the Cities of Hope Initiative

The U.S. Interagency Council on Homelessness (USICH) is ideally structured to lead the development and sustainability of the Cities of Hope initiative. By coordinating with 19 federal agencies, USICH can leverage specialized expertise across housing, health, labor, and legal services to address homelessness comprehensively.

Key agencies under USICH's umbrella include:

- **HUD**: Manages housing development and funding, ensuring affordable and sustainable housing solutions.

- **HHS**: Provides essential healthcare, mental health services, and substance abuse treatment.

- **DOL**: Offers job training and employment services to integrate residents economically.

- **VA**: Supports veterans with specialized housing, healthcare, and job opportunities.

- **Department of Commerce:** Promotes economic growth in the United States by fostering innovation, supporting trade, and ensuring fair business practices.

- **USDA**: Assists in developing agricultural practices, enhancing self-sufficiency in rural Cities of Hope.

- **DOJ**: Ensures legal protections and addresses barriers to the success of the initiative.

Additionally, collaboration with the **Department of Commerce** can enhance the economic sustainability of these communities. By partnering with the SBA, state economic development teams, and business associations, the Department of Commerce can help establish industrial hubs, attract corporate investments, and support small businesses, turning the Cities of Hope into vibrant economic centers.

This comprehensive approach, coordinated by USICH, ensures that the Cities of Hope are not only shelters for the homeless but also thriving communities that contribute significantly to the nation's economic and social well-being.

Advocacy Strategies

Advocacy plays a critical role in gaining public and political support for the proposed policies. Below are several strategies to enhance advocacy efforts:

- **Coalition Building:** Form coalitions of stakeholders, including nonprofit organizations, community groups, and business leaders, to create a broad-based support network. This network can collectively lobby for legislative changes and public funding.

- **Public Awareness Campaigns:** Utilize media and social platforms to educate the public on the benefits of self-sustaining homeless communities. Highlight success stories and data to counter common misconceptions about homelessness.

- **Grassroots Mobilization:** Encourage community involvement through town hall meetings, petitions, and volunteer opportunities. Grassroots support can exert significant pressure on lawmakers to act.

Evaluating and Revising Policies

Finally, continuous evaluation and revision of policies are necessary to adapt to changing circumstances and improve effectiveness:

- **Performance Metrics:** Establish clear performance metrics and key performance indicators (KPIs) to assess the impact of policies. These should include metrics for housing stability, employment rates, and health outcomes.

- **Annual Reviews:** Conduct annual reviews of policies and programs, involving stakeholders in the evaluation process. Feedback mechanisms can provide valuable insights into policy adjustments and improvements.

Through these targeted policy recommendations, we can create a robust framework to support self-sustaining communities for the homeless. The collective action of legislators, advocates, and community members can make a significant difference in addressing and potentially eradicating homelessness in the U.S.

The Strategic Role of the U.S. Interagency Council on Homelessness

I firmly believe that the U.S. Interagency Council on Homelessness (USICH) is exceptionally well-structured and equipped to oversee and implement the comprehensive tasks required for the successful development and sustainability of the Cities of Hope initiative. With its extensive reach, access, and coordination capabilities, the USICH is uniquely positioned to harness the strengths of various federal agencies, ensuring that each plays a pivotal role in addressing different facets of homelessness.

The USICH, operating as an independent agency within the federal government, serves as a coordinating body that brings together 19 federal agencies. Each of these agencies possesses specialized expertise and resources that, when combined, can effectively tackle the multifaceted challenges of homelessness. Here's how the key agencies under the USICH umbrella can contribute to the Cities of Hope initiative:

- **Department of Housing and Urban Development (HUD)**: As the primary agency responsible for housing policy, HUD is ideally positioned to manage the housing development and funding aspects of the Cities of Hope. HUD can issue bonds and provide the necessary financial architecture to support the initiative's housing infrastructure, ensuring that affordable and sustainable housing solutions are available.

- **Department of Health and Human Services (HHS)**: HHS can play a critical role in addressing the health and well-being of residents in the Cities of Hope. This includes mental health services, substance abuse treatment, and other healthcare needs that are essential for the stability and integration of formerly homeless individuals into these communities.

- **Department of Labor (DOL)**: The DOL is crucial in providing job training and employment services to residents. By facilitating access to meaningful work opportunities and skill development programs, the DOL can help ensure that residents of the Cities of Hope are equipped to contribute economically and regain their self-sufficiency.

- **Department of Veterans Affairs (VA)**: 33.000 homeless individuals are veterans, and the VA's involvement is vital to providing targeted support services for this group. The VA can offer specialized housing, healthcare, and employment services tailored to the unique needs of veterans within the Cities of Hope.

- **Department of Agriculture (USDA)**: For Cities of Hope located in rural or semi-rural areas, the USDA can provide expertise in developing sustainable agricultural practices and food security programs, which can enhance the self-sufficiency of these communities. USDA can also be instrumental in bringing SMEs to these Cities thanks to its vast database as a result of its funding programs.

- **Department of Justice (DOJ)**: The DOJ's role would include ensuring that the legal rights of homeless individuals are protected throughout the process and that any legal barriers to the success of the Cities of Hope are addressed.

Department of State: The novel visa program proposed within this initiative would be effectively managed by the Department of State. This program would generate substantial fees from applications, which could serve as the equity portion for the overall funding of the Cities of Hope while attracting skilled foreign workers to help stabilize and build these communities. USICH can establish a joint task force with DOS to create efficiency and effectiveness for the overall program.

Leveraging Collaboration Between USICH and the Department of Commerce for the Cities of Hope

While the U.S. Interagency Council on Homelessness (USICH) primarily collaborates with agencies focused on housing, health, and social services, the Department of Commerce's involvement can significantly enhance the economic viability and sustainability of the Cities of Hope. With the Department of Commerce already under the umbrella, the USICH can develop these communities' industrial and business aspects, ensuring they are not only places of refuge but also hubs of economic activity and opportunity.

The Department of Commerce, with its focus on economic development, can play a pivotal role in attracting and fostering business ventures within the Cities of Hope. By working closely with the **Small Business Administration (SBA)**, state economic development teams, **Manufacturing.org**, and various business associations, the Department of Commerce can help create a robust economic framework for these towns.

Key Areas of Collaboration

1. **Business Development and Sponsorship:**

   o The Department of Commerce can facilitate partnerships between the Cities of Hope and major corporations, industry groups, and local businesses. The department can identify project sponsors willing to invest in these communities through outreach and collaboration with state economic development teams and business associations. These sponsors could range from small businesses to large corporations, each contributing to the economic fabric of the town by establishing manufacturing plants, call centers, or service industries.

2. **Small Business Support:**

   o The **SBA** can provide crucial support by offering loans, grants, and technical assistance to small businesses within the Cities of Hope. These businesses, in turn, can create jobs and drive economic growth. The SBA's involvement ensures that local entrepreneurs have the resources and support needed to start and grow their businesses, contributing to the town's economic stability and prosperity.

3. **Industrial and Manufacturing Development:**

   o Partnering with organizations like **Manufacturing.org**, the Department of Commerce can spearhead initiatives to establish industrial hubs within the Cities of Hope. These hubs would focus on key sectors such as textile production, food processing, and renewable energy projects, creating sustainable job opportunities for residents. The department can also facilitate the integration of advanced manufacturing technologies and training programs to ensure that these industries remain competitive and innovative.

4. **State Economic Development Collaboration:**

   o By collaborating with state economic development teams, the Department of Commerce can align the Cities of Hope with broader regional and state economic strategies. This ensures that these towns are not isolated efforts but integrated into the larger economic ecosystem. State agencies can assist in securing state-level incentives, tax breaks, and other financial tools that make the Cities of Hope attractive to investors and businesses.

5. **Revenue-Generating Initiatives:**

   o The collaboration between USICH and the Department of Commerce will be crucial in identifying and developing revenue-generating opportunities within the Cities of Hope. This could include attracting corporate investments, developing public-private partnerships, and exploring innovative business models that ensure long-term economic sustainability. By engaging with business groups and industry associations, the department can help secure corporate commitments to jointly or solely run businesses within these communities, ensuring that they contribute to local and national economies.

By leveraging the Department of Commerce's expertise in business development, industrial growth, and economic strategy, the USICH can ensure that these communities are not only places of refuge but also engines of economic opportunity and innovation. This will help create a sustainable economic foundation for the Cities of Hope, enabling them to contribute significantly to the nation's overall prosperity while addressing the critical issue of homelessness.

Conclusion

In conclusion, the USICH's structure and collaborative mandate make it the ideal body to oversee the Cities of Hope initiative. By aligning federal resources and expertise with the needs of the homeless population, the USICH can ensure that this ambitious project is executed efficiently, sustainably, and with the full backing of the federal government.

Advocacy Strategies

Effective advocacy is essential to transform policy recommendations into concrete actions. The goal is to build strong support for creating self-sustaining communities for the homeless, which can integrate them back into society and, in turn, provide economic benefits to the United States. Below, we outline several advocacy strategies aimed at engaging a broad spectrum of stakeholders, from policymakers and community leaders to the general public.

1. Engaging Policymakers

Advocacy must begin with the policymakers who have the power to enact legislative changes. To persuade these officials, it's essential to present well-researched data, case studies, and evidence of successful implementations. Constituents should be encouraged to communicate with their representatives through letters, emails, and town hall meetings to emphasize public support for homelessness policies. Organizing lobbying days where advocates can meet with legislators face-to-face can also be highly effective.

2. Public Awareness Campaigns

Creating wide-ranging public awareness is critical for building grassroots support. Utilize social media platforms, traditional media outlets, and community events to disseminate information about the benefits of self-sustaining communities. Emotional appeals, paired with factual information, can be powerful in shifting public opinion. Highlighting personal stories from individuals who have successfully exited homelessness can humanize the issue and galvanize public support.

3. Forming Coalitions

Building coalitions with other organizations with similar visions can amplify advocacy efforts. These might include non-profits, advocacy groups, religious organizations, and businesses. A united front can pool resources for larger campaigns and comprehensively support legislative changes. Regular coalition meetings to share strategies and progress can maintain momentum and collaboration.

4. Utilizing Research and Data

Providing robust, empirical evidence strengthens the call for policy change. Commissioning studies that evaluate the economic impacts of homelessness and the benefits of self-sustaining communities can provide a compelling argument for policymakers and the public. Collaborating with academic institutions for ongoing research ensures that advocacy efforts remain grounded in the latest data and trends. Regularly publishing reports and white papers can keep the issue at the forefront of public discourse.

5. Media Engagement

Strategic media engagement can amplify advocacy messages. Press releases, opinion pieces, and interviews with key advocates can keep the narrative active in the media. Training spokespeople to effectively communicate the benefits and necessity of proposed policies ensures consistent and persuasive messaging. Partnering with journalists interested in social issues can lead to in-depth coverage that informs and educates the public.

6. Educational Outreach

Educational initiatives aimed at schools, universities, and community groups can foster a deeper understanding of homelessness and potential solutions. Curriculum modules focusing on social justice, economics, and public policy can inspire the next generation of advocates. Workshops, seminars, and educational materials can equip community members with the knowledge and tools they need to advocate effectively.

7. Legislative Testimonies

Orchestrating testimonies from experts, affected individuals, and advocates during legislative sessions can significantly impact. Personal stories combined with expert testimony provide a compelling narrative that statistics alone cannot convey. Preparing witnesses to deliver clear, impactful testimonies ensures that the message resonates with lawmakers.

Implementing these advocacy strategies requires coordinated efforts and sustained commitment. By employing a multi-faceted approach, stakeholders can push for the legislative changes necessary to develop self-sustaining communities for the homeless, ultimately benefiting both individuals and the broader economy.

Long-term Vision

As we conclude our detailed exploration of homelessness solutions, it's important to turn our focus to long-term goals and sustainable development. Addressing homelessness in the U.S. isn't just about immediate relief; it's about creating lasting, effective change that benefits individuals and society as a whole.

Potential for Expansion

One of the most promising aspects of self-sustaining communities is their scalability. Initially, pilot programs can test the feasibility and refine the strategies involved. As success metrics are met, these communities can be replicated across the country. Ideally, every major metropolitan area would host at least one such community, thereby alleviating local homelessness while also creating a network of shared resources and information.

For example, a city like Los Angeles, which struggles with a high homeless population, could see immense benefits from multiple self-sustaining communities. With careful planning and execution, these communities could house thousands who are currently without stable homes. Similar models can be adapted for smaller cities and even rural areas, each tailored to meet local needs and conditions.

Future Development Plans

The self-sustaining communities aim not just to provide shelter but also to offer a complete ecosystem designed to foster growth and reintegration into society. Key to this vision is a long-term development strategy that focuses on several essential aspects:

- **Continual Improvement:** Technology and methods evolve, and so must our communities. Regular assessments and community feedback will help refine and optimize our approach.

- **Educational Advancement:** Partnerships with educational institutions can offer tailored programs to enhance the skills and qualifications of residents, thereby improving their employability.

- **Healthcare Integration:** Sustainable communities should include comprehensive healthcare services, not just for physical health but also for mental well-being. Telemedicine and mobile clinics could be instrumental in meeting these needs.

- **Environmental Stewardship:** Sustainability isn't limited to social aspects; it extends to environmental goals as well. Incorporating renewable energy sources, recycling programs, and green spaces would be a priority.

Planning for sustainability means thinking beyond the immediate and considering how these communities can evolve 10, 20, or even 50 years from now.

Global Collaboration

Homelessness is not a uniquely American problem; it's a global issue. Long-term vision involves looking beyond national borders to learn from and cooperate with successful initiatives around the world. For instance, Finland's "Housing First" initiative has shown remarkable success in reducing homelessness through similar holistic approaches.

Establishing international partnerships and sharing best practices can provide new insights and innovative solutions. Collaborative research and joint ventures can lead to breakthroughs in addressing homelessness more effectively and efficiently.

Moreover, a global perspective reinforces the notion that combating homelessness is a shared humanitarian responsibility. By building a worldwide network focused on solving this issue, we can pool resources, knowledge, and experiences. Successful implementation of Cities of Hope will provide a leading position to address this issue and this can be further leveraged diplomatically for the benefit of US interests globally.

Policy and Legislative Support

The success of these long-term visions hinges on robust policy and legislative backing. Local, state, and federal governments must be active partners in this journey. Policies that facilitate the creation and maintenance of self-sustaining communities, tax incentives for private sector involvement, and legislative reforms that address root causes of homelessness are essential.

Proactive advocacy is crucial. Policymakers must be consistently engaged and informed about the positive impacts and success stories of these communities. Sustained advocacy efforts can turn pilot projects into widespread policy initiatives with long-lasting effects.

In conclusion, solving homelessness involves more than temporary fixes. It requires a multifaceted, future-oriented approach that integrates housing, employment, healthcare, and education. By envisioning and planning for the long run, we can foster environments where not only are immediate needs met, but where individuals can truly thrive. **I believe The Cities of Hope will accomplish this objective.**

Potential for Expansion

The long-term vision for addressing homelessness through the creation of self-sustaining communities is inherently elastic, designed to adapt and expand as needed. The model's potential for expansion is multifaceted, focusing not only on geographical growth but also on incorporating diverse programs and innovative solutions to meet evolving needs.

First and foremost, geographic expansion can transform localized successes into national movements. By leveraging state and federal partnerships, existing pilot programs demonstrating significant improvements can be scaled up. Urban and rural areas alike can benefit from tailored approaches to developing industrial parks and supportive housing, taking into account local economic and social conditions.

The ability to establish similar communities in various regions across the United States is foundational to this model. **Each new site could serve as a hub for localized economic revitalization, contributing to the larger economic fabric while offering tailored support for homeless populations.** Replicating such models in different socio-economic contexts will be crucial for broader applicability and long-lasting impact.

Beyond geographic considerations, there is substantial room for expanding the range of services and programs within these communities. Health and wellness initiatives can integrate more comprehensive care options, including specialized mental health services, addiction counseling, and chronic disease management. Educational programs can evolve to meet the changing demands of the job market, offering advanced vocational training and college preparatory courses to further improve employability among residents.

Another key area for potential growth is in technology and innovation. Incorporating smart city concepts, such as IoT-based monitoring systems and sustainable energy solutions, can improve the efficiency and effectiveness of community management. These technologies can help optimize resource allocation and provide real-time data to inform adaptive strategies.

Integrating global perspectives through international collaboration can also drive the model's evolution. By studying successful initiatives from other countries, the U.S. can adapt best practices and innovative techniques that have shown promise elsewhere. This cross-pollination of ideas will likely lead to more robust and resilient solutions.

In conclusion, the potential for expansion is not limited to multiplying the number of self-sustaining communities but also enhances the quality and scope of services offered. As these communities grow and evolve, they will serve as dynamic hubs of innovation, continually adapting to meet the needs of their residents while contributing to broader societal and economic goals.

Future Development Plans

As we look toward the future, the development plans for creating self-sustaining homeless communities need to be both visionary and practical. The long-term vision centers around a transformative approach that will ensure these communities not only thrive but also become models of economic and social success. Integrating innovative strategies and leveraging advanced technologies can help us achieve this ambitious blueprint.

One of the cornerstone elements of our future development plans is the concept of "smart" communities. These communities can operate more efficiently and sustainably by incorporating smart city technologies such as IoT (Internet of Things) devices, energy-efficient housing, and sustainable resource management. Deploying smart grids and renewable energy sources will reduce utility costs and environmental impact, freeing up funds that can be reinvested into community services.

Moreover, the concept of modular and scalable infrastructure will be pivotal. Prefabricated, modular housing units expedite the construction process and offer the flexibility to scale up as the community grows. By utilizing recycled and low-cost materials, we can further reduce initial investment costs and make housing more affordable.

Another essential aspect is fostering economic self-sufficiency. By strategically partnering with industries and businesses, we can create job opportunities tailored to the unique skillsets of community residents. Vocational training programs will be essential, equipping residents with the skills they need to engage in meaningful employment. These training centers can be integrated into the community, ensuring residents can access these essential resources easily. (Industrial Parks)

Healthcare and wellness programs will continue to be integral to future development plans. Offering comprehensive medical services, mental health support, and wellness activities will ensure residents maintain a high quality of life. Collaborating with local healthcare providers and integrating telehealth solutions can enhance the accessibility and effectiveness of these services.

In summary, the future development plans for self-sustaining homeless communities are multifaceted and ambitious. Through the integration of smart technologies, scalable infrastructure, economic opportunities, and comprehensive healthcare, we aim to create thriving communities that not only provide for their residents but also contribute positively to the broader economy and society.

Final Thoughts on the Cities of Hope Concept

The Cities of Hope initiative is not just an ambitious project but a transformative vision to address the homelessness crisis in the United States with innovative, practical, and scalable solutions. As we conclude, reflecting on this concept's flexibility, potential challenges, and far-reaching benefits is essential.

1. **Financial Flexibility and Alternative Funding** While designed to generate substantial revenue for the project, the proposed novel visa program is just one of many potential funding avenues. Should it fall short of its targets, the Cities of Hope initiative remains highly attractive to Impact Investing and ESG-focused institutional capital. U.S. investors, particularly those aligned with socially responsible investment strategies, will likely see the equity investment opportunities in these industrial towns as profitable and purpose-driven.

2. **Alternative Employment Strategies** If the employment goals for formerly homeless citizens are not fully realized, the Cities of Hope can be restructured to rely more heavily on U.S. labor. This approach would maintain the project's profitability while ensuring housing and care

solutions are provided for the homeless. The flexibility in labor sourcing ensures that the core objectives of the Cities of Hope are met, even under varying circumstances.

3. **Engagement of Non-Working Residents** For those who are not yet ready for formal employment, simpler, dignified tasks can be designed to integrate them into the community. Activities such as cycling to generate power using simple gadgets (e.g., *web link for power-generating bicycles: https://www.instructables.com/How-to-Build-a-Bicycle-Generator/*), participating in community affairs, and helping run town operations can provide physical and mental benefits. Furthermore, blockchain-based applications could be introduced to create a transparent and rewarding system for their contributions.

4. **Tailored Community Structures** Recognizing the homeless population's diverse mental and health conditions, the Cities of Hope can be organized into different types of communities that cater to specific needs. This tailored approach would enhance community-building efforts by ensuring that each resident is placed in an environment that best supports their rehabilitation and integration into society.

5. **Corporate Participation and Incentives** Major corporations can be incentivized to co-invest in the Cities of Hope alongside HUD funding. In return, they could be offered tax credits, amortized over five years at a favorable coefficient. This would minimize the need for initial government funding. At the same time, revenues generated by the industrial towns could eventually be used to reimburse the U.S. Treasury, echoing the success of the TARP program from the 2008 financial crisis. Such participation would also allow corporations to meet their Corporate Social Responsibility (CSR) goals and regulatory obligations, similar to how U.S. banks invest in SBIC funds.

6. **Scalability and Adaptability** The Cities of Hope are designed to be both scalable and adaptable, capable of evolving to meet new challenges and opportunities. The project's structure allows for modifications in response to emerging needs, ensuring its long-term viability and success. This initiative's economic, social, and humanitarian benefits far outweigh any initial liabilities, making it a robust solution to one of America's most pressing social issues.

The Cities of Hope concept represents a bold, comprehensive approach to ending homelessness in the United States. Its success will hinge on strategic flexibility, robust funding, and the collaborative effort of government, private sector, and community stakeholders. The vision is clear: to transform lives, revitalize communities, and demonstrate that with the right approach, no challenge is insurmountable.

H. Burak Erten

About the Author – H. Burak Erten – www.burakerten.us

H. Burak Erten is a dedicated advocate for sustainable development and social justice. With extensive past experience in real estate development & construction and his continuous conversations with homeless individuals since 2011, Burak has been thinking about coming up with solutions for this grave issue. His financial expertise, reflected in the five books he published in addition to his capital markets experience, has led him to come up with a holistic solution provided in this book summary. This book summary reflects his commitment to innovative solutions that address the root causes of homelessness and foster inclusive, thriving communities.

In addition to his professional achievements, Burak is a Senior Policy Advisor at the COH Foundation (https://www.coalitionofhope.org/), where he contributes his expertise to develop and implement policies that promote comprehensive and sustainable solutions to humanitarian issues. His work at the COH Foundation underscores his commitment to humanitarian efforts and his dedication to improving the lives of those affected by homelessness.

Author's Other Books

Unlocking Capital Resources through Books

01	02	03	04	05
Unlocking Capital: The The Power of Bonds in in Project Finance	**Unlocking Capital: The Insiders Guide to Luxembourg Financial Structures**	**Unlocking Capital: How How to Speak the Language of Wall Street Street**	**Unlocking Capital: How How to Structure Bankable and Bondable Bondable Projects**	**Prosperity Bonds Agency – A Call to Action to G7**
Explore the impact of bonds in project finance.	Gain insights into financial structures in Luxembourg.	Learn the language of Wall Street for effective communication.	Discover strategies for for structuring bankable bankable projects.	Engage in the call to action to G7 by the Prosperity Bonds Agency.

11 / Unlocking Capital Resources: A Journey of Expertise and Innovation

Appendix A: Appendix

This appendix serves as a repository of supplementary information, resources, and tools relevant to the discussion of homelessness and the creation of self-sustaining communities as presented throughout the book. Designed for politicians, academics, professionals, bureaucrats, officials, students, retired individuals, and anyone eager to contribute to the solution, this section aims to provide additional context, support, and direction for further investigation and action.

Additional Resources

- **Government Reports and Statistics:** Utilize databases such as the U.S. Department of Housing and Urban Development (HUD) for comprehensive reports and up-to-date statistics on homelessness.

- **Academic Journals:** Journals such as "Housing Policy Debate" and "Urban Affairs Review" offer peer-reviewed articles on various aspects of homelessness, policy responses, and innovative solutions.

- **Nonprofit Organizations:** Organizations such as the National Alliance to End Homelessness (NAEH) and the Coalition for the Homeless provide valuable resources, fact sheets, and case studies.

- **Books and Publications:** Titles like "Homelessness in America" by Jim Baumohl and "The Homeless" by Christopher Jencks provide in-depth analyses and historical context.

- **Online Platforms:** Websites like the National Coalition for the Homeless and Homeless Hub serve as knowledge hubs offering research articles, policy briefs, and multimedia resources.

These resources support the book's main content by offering diverse perspectives and detailed information that can aid in the development and implementation of effective strategies for combating homelessness in the United States.

Additional Resources

The following section provides a curated list of resources that readers can utilize to deepen their understanding of homelessness and the various strategies proposed to address it in this book.

1. **Government and Policy Documentation:**

   - *United States Interagency Council on Homelessness (USICH):* Visit the USICH website for comprehensive federal strategies to prevent and end homelessness. [USICH]

- o *Department of Housing and Urban Development (HUD):* Access HUD's Homeless Assistance Programs, including the Continuum of Care (CoC) Program and Emergency Solutions Grants (ESG). [HUD]

2. **Academic Research and Publications:**

- o *National Alliance to End Homelessness:* This nonprofit organization offers a range of research papers and policy analyses on homelessness. [National Alliance to End Homelessness]

- o *Journal of Social Distress and the Homeless:* A peer-reviewed journal that explores the issues surrounding homelessness and social distress. Subscribe for detailed studies and reviews. [Kim, S., & Garcia, R. (2020). Homelessness and mental health. *Journal of Social Distress and the Homeless*, 29(3), 215-231]

3. **Community and Nonprofit Organizations:**

- o *National Coalition for the Homeless:* A well-known organization focused on advocacy and awareness. Their resources include reports, newsletters, and volunteer opportunities. [National Coalition for the Homeless]

- o *Shelter (UK):* While primarily based in the UK, Shelter's insights on housing issues can be valuable for comparative studies. [Shelter]

4. **Data and Statistics:**

- o *Homeless Management Information Systems (HMIS):* HMIS is a local information technology system used to collect client-level data on the provision of housing and services to homeless individuals and families and persons at risk of homelessness. [HMIS]

- o *Annual Homeless Assessment Report (AHAR):* Published by HUD, this report provides nationwide estimates of homelessness. [HUD, 2022]

These resources offer a solid foundation for further exploration and understanding of the multifaceted issue of homelessness. Utilizing these tools can aid policymakers, academics, and concerned citizens in developing informed, effective solutions.

Glossary of Terms

This glossary provides definitions and explanations for key terms and concepts discussed throughout the book. It is intended to help readers better understand the issues and solutions related to homelessness in the United States.

Affordable Housing

Housing that is deemed affordable to those with a median household income or below, as defined by the country or region in which they reside.

Chronic Homelessness

A term used to describe individuals or families who have experienced homelessness repeatedly over an extended period, often due to disabling conditions like mental health issues or substance abuse disorders (National Alliance to End Homelessness, 2021).

Continuum of Care (CoC)

A regional or local planning body that coordinates housing and services funding for homeless families and individuals. CoCs are crucial in addressing homelessness at the community level.

Domestic Violence

A form of abuse involving physical, emotional, or psychological harm by a partner or family member. Domestic violence is a significant factor contributing to homelessness, especially among women and children.

Emergency Shelter

Short-term accommodation providing immediate relief for individuals and families experiencing homelessness. These shelters often offer additional services such as meals, counseling, and medical care.

Homelessness

The condition of lacking stable, safe, and adequate housing. This can include living on the streets, in shelters, or in temporary accommodations like motels or friends' couches.

Industrial Parks

Planned areas developed to accommodate businesses and promote economic growth. In this context, they are explored as potential sites for offering employment opportunities to the homeless population.

Low-Income Housing Tax Credit (LIHTC)

A federal program that incentivizes the investment in affordable housing projects for low-income individuals through tax credits.

Mental Health Services

A range of services designed to support individuals experiencing mental health issues, including counseling, therapy, medication management, and crisis intervention. These services are vital for many individuals experiencing homelessness.

Permanent Supportive Housing (PSH)

A housing intervention that combines affordable housing assistance with voluntary support services to address the needs of chronically homeless people. PSH is intended to help individuals live more stable and independent lives (HUD, 2020).

Point-in-Time (PIT) Count

An annual count of sheltered and unsheltered homeless persons on a single night in January, mandated by the U.S. Department of Housing and Urban Development (HUD). The PIT Count provides critical data on homelessness trends and demographics.

Rapid Rehousing

An intervention aimed at quickly connecting individuals and families to permanent housing through financial assistance and support services. Rapid Rehousing is designed to reduce the amount of time people spend being homeless.

Section 8

A federal program that provides housing vouchers or rental assistance to low-income individuals and families, enabling them to afford housing in the private market.

Transitional Housing

A temporary residence that offers supportive services to help individuals and families transition from homelessness to permanent housing. This type of housing typically includes a limited duration of stay and supportive services like case management.

Veterans Affairs Supportive Housing (VASH)

A program that combines Housing Choice Voucher (HCV) rental assistance for homeless veterans with case management and clinical services provided by the Department of Veterans Affairs (VA).